Introduction to
Library Services

LIBRARY SCIENCE TEXT SERIES

Audiovisual Technology Primer. By Albert J. Casciero and Raymond G. Roney.

The Collection Program in High Schools: Concepts, Practices, and Information Sources. By Phyllis J. Van Orden.

The Collection Program in Schools: Concepts, Practices, and Information Sources. By Phyllis J. Van Orden.

Developing Library and Information Center Collections. 2d ed. By G. Edward Evans.

Foundations and Issues in Library and Information Science. By Bruce A. Shuman.

The Humanities: A Selective Guide to Information Sources. 3d ed. By Ron Blazek and Elizabeth Aversa.

Immroth's Guide to the Library of Congress Classification. 3d ed. By Lois Mai Chan.

Information Sources in Science and Technology. By C. D. Hurt.

Introduction to Cataloging and Classification. By Bohdan S. Wynar. 8th edition by Arlene G. Taylor.

Introduction to Library Automation. By James Rice.

Introduction to Library Public Services. 5th ed. By G. Edward Evans, Anthony J. Amodeo, and Thomas L. Carter.

Introduction to Library Science: Basic Elements of Library Service. By Jesse H. Shera.

Introduction to Library Services. By Barbara E. Chernik.

Introduction to Technical Services for Library Technicians. 5th ed. By Marty Bloomberg and G. Edward Evans.

Introduction to United States Government Information Sources. 4th ed. By Joe Morehead and Mary Fetzer.

The Library in Society. By A. Robert Rogers and Kathryn McChesney.

Library Instruction for Librarians. 2d rev. ed. By Anne F. Roberts and Susan G. Blandy.

Library Management. 3d ed. By Robert D. Stueart and Barbara B. Moran.

Micrographics. 2d ed. By William Saffady.

Online Reference and Information Retrieval. 2d ed. By Roger C. Palmer.

Problems in Library Management. By A. J. Anderson.

Reference and Information Services: An Introduction. Richard E. Bopp and Linda C. Smith, General Editors.

The School Librarian as Educator. 2d ed. By Lillian Biermann Wehmeyer.

The School Library Media Center. 4th ed. By Emanuel T. Prostano and Joyce S. Prostano.

The Social Sciences: A Cross-Disciplinary Guide to Selected Sources. Nancy L. Herron, General Editor.

INTRODUCTION TO
LIBRARY SERVICES

BARBARA E. CHERNIK

1992
LIBRARIES UNLIMITED, INC.
Englewood, Colorado

This book is dedicated
with deep affection
to my family,
my colleagues,
and the teachers and students
who welcomed the earlier edition

LIBRARIES UNLIMITED, INC.
P.O. Box 6633
Englewood, CO 80155-6633
1-800-237-6124

Library of Congress Cataloging-in-Publication Data

Chernik, Barbara E., 1938-
    Introduction to library services / Barbara E. Chernik.
    xi, 230 p. 17x25 cm. -- (Library science text series)
    "Replaces and largely updates its earlier edition, Introduction to
library services for library technicians"--Pref.
    Includes bibliographical references and index.
    ISBN 0-87287-931-3 (cloth) -- ISBN 1-56308-053-2 (paper)
    1. Library science. 2. Library technicians. 3. Libraries.
I. Chernik, Barbara E., 1938-   . Introduction to library services for
library technicians. II. Title. III. Series.
Z665.C538   1992
020--dc20   92-5486
                                                              CIP

CONTENTS

LIST OF FIGURES

FIGURE

FIGURE

PREFACE

Introduction to Library Services provides an introduction to libraries and library services for persons who would like to understand more about libraries and their materials and services. Designed for the uninitiated, this book presents library terminology and concepts in terms that the layperson can easily understand. It discusses the basic concepts that govern libraries, explaining why communities have so many libraries and why and how these libraries differ from one another. It describes the principles and philosophies that libraries follow as they establish their policies and procedures. Finally, the book discusses the personnel, materials, and services that make up today's modern American library.

Introduction to Library Services replaces and substantially updates its earlier edition, *Introduction to Library Services for Library Technicians*. Although this new edition is still designed as a textbook for library media technology courses, its broadened scope can make it equally useful for library science courses or in-service library training programs. This new edition includes an updated historical overview of libraries and their objectives as well as an updated and broadened chapter on library/media/information personnel. The chapter on library resources has been substantially revised to include automated and computer-based resources and telecommunications services. Other library automation areas are included throughout the text in their appropriate places. Chapters on library organization and the four major types of libraries — public, school, academic, and special — present updated developments and trends in library standards, programs, and services in each type of library. Library networks, including national automated systems such as Online Computer Library Center (OCLC), are now presented in their own chapter, as are recent developments in library facilities and furnishings. The chapter on auxiliary library services has been expanded to include electronic and automated services. The final chapters on developing good library service and entering the library world have not only been completely revised, but they have also been broadened to relate to any person working in a library.

Throughout this text, the major focus and purpose is to introduce the reader to the exciting and dynamic world of libraries and library services. From discussions of library goals and objectives, to the identification of personality traits needed by staff members, to the review of innovations in library materials and services, the book emphasizes the need for each person connected with a library to understand and contribute to that library's goals and objectives. The author sincerely hopes that all readers will personally adopt the philosophy of good library service that is presented here.

CHAPTER 1

THE DEVELOPMENT
OF LIBRARIES

WHAT IS A LIBRARY?

Libraries are probably as old as writing itself, which began in 3500 to 3000 B.C. Yet, if the question "What is a library?" were asked of a group of people on the street, the answers would probably be as varied as the people themselves. Many people would probably define a library simply as a building with a lot of books. Other persons might go one step further and describe those books — ones read for pleasure, others for study — and some might even comment that the books are organized in a certain manner. However, probably very few persons would think of the library as a "collection of information organized for use," the definition libraries prefer.

Even to librarians, however, this definition is not quite adequate. It does not include the fundamental function of a library: the acquisition, preservation, and dissemination of materials and information in all their forms to help educate, enrich, entertain, and inform. To some librarians, this means that the library is part of society's educational and informational system. To them, a library helps educate citizens and exerts a cultural influence on society. To other librarians, this means that the library should make all information and graphic materials available and should not be an arbiter of culture. Finally, for some librarians, the library should be a free institution, open to all and serving the needs of every age and every group.

This difference of opinion about what a library really is results from the many different kinds of libraries that have been developed to serve the needs of particular groups of people or segments of our society. For example, school libraries have been developed to provide materials that support the school curriculum. College and university libraries, or *academic libraries*, not only support the curriculum, but they also provide and preserve information and resources for projects ranging from term papers to original research. Other libraries may be devoted to supporting research in companies or industries. These latter libraries are often called *special libraries* because they serve the needs of special groups of people.

The type of library that is probably most familiar to the majority of American readers, however, is the public library. Yet, even this institution has developed many different forms to satisfy a variety of needs or purposes. Public libraries are used for leisure reading, answering questions, fulfilling class assignments, self-improvement, enjoyment, and learning in general. These various public needs, or library objectives, have been identified as educational, informational, cultural or aesthetic appreciation, recreational, and research objectives. These basic objectives, combined with the additional needs of social responsibility and the preservation of ideas, have guided the development of libraries throughout history.

NEEDS AND CONDITIONS OF LIBRARY DEVELOPMENT

The variety of libraries—public, school, academic, and special—did not spring up full-blown overnight. Instead libraries have developed over the thousands of years since writing began to meet certain needs and conditions of the societies in which they existed.[1] Though societies throughout history have developed differently, their information needs have remained surprisingly similar. Societies need to preserve governmental and other archival documents for future generations. They also need to support general education as well as religious and moral instruction. Educated and cultured people need literature and information for self-education and self-improvement; they may also have a general interest in scholarly research and in the exploration of new fields of knowledge. In addition, many cultured people have shown an aesthetic need for collecting and possessing books just for the beauty and pleasure they give. These societal needs have influenced the growth of libraries, and libraries in turn have influenced the growth of the societies in which they have prospered. However, because not all societies developed strong libraries, it is important to look at the conditions that foster library growth.

Libraries tend to prosper when a combination of certain social, political, and economic conditions exist in a society. Libraries develop during stable social climates when there are periods of relative peace and tranquility that enable individuals to pursue leisure activities. They also prosper wherever a literate population emphasizes the arts and culture, self-improvement, and intellectual creativity. Societies with large urban areas usually stimulate scientific discovery and technological advancement which encourage the use and growth of libraries. When society's institutions—its schools and government—need to educate and inform the citizenry, libraries also become important. Finally, economic prosperity and a surplus of wealth are needed to provide the financial support for library growth. This economic support is a very important factor in library development; without it the other conditions of society may not provide enough support for library development.

When all of these conditions combine favorably in a society, a flourishing culture and flourishing libraries develop that can influence the course of history.

DEVELOPMENT OF WESTERN LIBRARIES

Although different types of libraries have developed to meet similar needs, the form and function of each library has been largely determined by the society it has served. The most striking difference between these societies is in the formats of their written materials. Records were first made on clay tablets, then on rolls of papyrus or parchment, and finally on materials fastened together in a format similar to that of our present book. Despite these differences, libraries could not have flourished unless the raw materials were easily and cheaply available and a book trade was well established.

Writing and the history of Western libraries began around 3000 B.C. in an area around the Tigris and Euphrates Rivers (modern Iraq) called the *Fertile Crescent*.[2] (See figure 1.1, page 4, for historical library sites.) Between 3000 and 650 B.C., this area saw the development of three civilizations: Sumer, Babylonia, and Assyria. The Sumerian and Babylonian civilizations developed libraries of clay tablets which consisted of archives or government and tax records. By contrast, the Assyrians established large, well-organized libraries that covered many subject areas. Unfortunately, Roman conquerors later destroyed these libraries.

All the conditions necessary for library development were present in Greece around 600 B.C. A literate population enjoyed peace and tranquility and the economic ability existed to pursue intellectual creativity and scientific inquiry. Little concrete evidence of Greek libraries has remained thanks to the Roman invaders, but historians assume that libraries had to exist to support the achievements of the Greek civilization. For example, it is known that the Athens public library stored original copies of Greek plays for persons to read or copy. The major Greek libraries, however, were the private libraries of Greek citizens. Plato had a large library, and Aristotle collected one of the largest libraries in Greece, which has been called the greatest library of the ancient world. These private libraries supported self-education rather than just providing aesthetic pleasure for their owners. When the Roman generals invaded Greece in 86 B.C., they captured these magnificent libraries and took them back to Rome as trophies. In Rome, private libraries had become status symbols rather than libraries for the edification of their owners.

Greek libraries were not the only libraries conquerors destroyed. The Egyptian library at Alexandria eventually met a similar fate. This great library was founded in 290 B.C. by descendants of Alexander the Great and became one of the most important libraries of its time. Its collection was enormous; 700,000 papyrus rolls covered every subject and contained almost all of the literature of the ancient world. All ships and travelers who came to Egypt had to surrender any manuscripts they possessed. These were copied, the originals placed in the library, and the copies returned to the original owners. Alexandria's library was rivaled only by the great library at Pergamum. In fact, such a great rivalry between the two developed that Alexandria refused to export the papyrus reeds needed to make writing material. In defense, Pergamum developed the process of curing lamb and kid hides to make parchment for their rolls. The Pergamum library supposedly was brought to Cleopatra by Mark Antony in 43 B.C. However, the Alexandria library itself was slowly dismantled, beginning in 47 B.C. with the siege of Julius Caesar and ending with its complete destruction by the Muslims in A.D. 642.

Parts of the Alexandria library were probably added to the private libraries of the Roman conquerors. However, the conditions in Roman civilization were also very favorable for the development of all kinds of libraries. A.D. 96 to 180 was a time of peace, prosperity, and order, which allowed public libraries to prosper. The demand for books stimulated a book trade, and the *codex* or book form replaced papyrus and parchment rolls. In addition to private and public

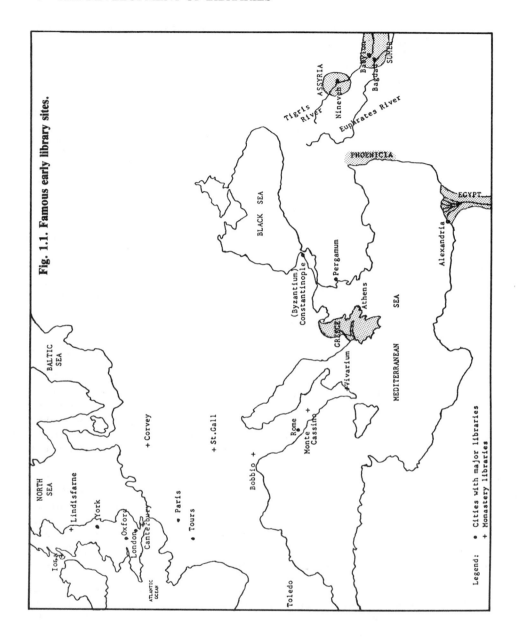

Fig. 1.1. Famous early library sites.

libraries, early Christian libraries were developed which set the pattern for later monastic libraries. Roman libraries were themselves threatened and destroyed by the time Rome fell in the fifth century.

The fall of Rome would have been disastrous for the history of libraries if the Roman Emperor Constantine had not moved his capital to Byzantium, or Constantinople as he renamed it, in A.D. 325. Many Roman libraries were moved to this new capital, and the remains of Aristotle's library also found a new home in this growing civilization. The Byzantine empire flourished from the seventh to the eleventh century, and it preserved the works of both the Greek and the Roman cultures. This became important because the conditions in Europe during these centuries were so chaotic that library development practically came to a standstill there for many centuries.

The sixth to the tenth centuries in Europe became known as the *Dark Ages* because Europe had been invaded by peoples who were interested neither in culture nor in writings. Also, the social, political, and economic conditions necessary for a society to flourish were not present. This was generally a time when the most dominant need for libraries was to preserve ideas for future generations. During these centuries, writings and ideas were preserved in monasteries and their libraries because the clergy formed the only literate class. These havens of learning began to loan their copies of Greek and Latin manuscripts back and forth and to make catalogs of their collections. When the political and social climates began to change in the twelfth through the fourteenth centuries, these libraries were ready to provide a basis for learning.

In contrast to the decline of libraries in Europe during these centuries, the libraries in the Middle East were flourishing. In addition to the Byzantine culture, the Muslims established an Islamic empire centered in Baghdad from 750 to 1050. This society emphasized literacy and encouraged the establishment of schools. Learning was encouraged, and medical and scientific advancements were made. Paper was used as a writing material, and books were highly prized. The power and influence of the Islamic culture stretched from Persia (modern Iran) around Northern Africa to Spain. In fact, many manuscripts were taken to Spain where they were translated into Latin and passed into the universities of Europe. In the eleventh, twelfth, and thirteenth centuries, this Muslim culture was finally destroyed from without by the Crusades and the Mongols and from within by civil wars and religious dissension. The Christian crusaders conquered parts of both Byzantium and Islam and brought back many of the library treasures that had been preserved by these Middle-Eastern libraries. Aristotle's library was even returned. A brisk trade developed in classical manuscripts which contained ideas that encouraged the beginning of the Renaissance.

Europe during the thirteenth, fourteenth, and fifteenth centuries began to stabilize. Societies became more secure, and economic trade between countries developed. Persons other than clerics began to read and to feel a need for learning. New ideas were generated based on the classical writings returned from the East. Students who had traveled around following their teachers from city to city began to settle down and establish universities. This Renaissance, or rebirth of learning, and a renewed interest in the humanities and arts flourished from the fourteenth through the sixteenth centuries. Conditions were favorable for the development of libraries. There was enough wealth to begin large libraries such as the Vatican Library, the Sorbonne Library at the University of Paris, and state and royal libraries. In fact, many of Europe's great libraries were founded during this time.[3]

In the 1400s, the development of printing coincided with a strong growth in nationalism. This meant that books could be written in the vernacular or local language and that many copies could be made available. The Reformation also encouraged the growth of national religions which needed religious materials for everyone to read. These needs helped encourage the spread of literacy and the production of new literature.

From 1500 to 1800 there was a spread of literacy and libraries throughout Western Europe. Town libraries sprang up in Germany, and circulating or lending libraries provided popular reading. Great Britain founded municipal libraries in the 1600s, and when the British Parliament passed the first Public Libraries Act in 1850, there were already 800 small libraries in Britain. University libraries began to expand during this time. At first, universities had relied upon book stores to supply students with copies of the needed texts. However, as the universities grew, libraries soon developed because there were not enough books for the students to use. Private donations such as that of Thomas Bodley to Oxford University provided the basis for the development of great university collections as well as the expansion of national libraries. The British Museum was based on the donation of private collections, and the Bibliotheque Nationale in Paris was based on royal libraries confiscated in the French Revolution. National and state libraries became depositories for the written products of a country. At the end of the 1800s, the library had been firmly established as an institution that satisfied the needs of Western-European societies.

DEVELOPMENT OF AMERICAN LIBRARIES

The development of American libraries paralleled the growth of European libraries from 1500 to 1800.[4] During this period, not only were private library collections developed, but many also became the basis for great university libraries. One private library, that of Thomas Jefferson, even became the basis for the United States' national library, the Library of Congress. The first important American libraries were private collections gathered by colonial leaders such as Thomas Jefferson and William Byrd, both of Virginia, and Governor John Winthrop, Jr. of Connecticut. The subject content of these collections ranged from theology to law, farming, and science, and the volumes were shared with friends and neighbors. These libraries were important because, early in the history of the United States, it was recognized that ideas and education were needed if new colonies and a new nation were to survive.

To satisfy these needs, colleges and universities were quickly established in the new colonies. John Harvard gave his collection of 300 books to help the founding of Harvard University in 1638, and a group of ministers gave some of their own books to found the Yale University library. However, among the early colleges there was a protective attitude toward these library collections, and as in Europe, students' access to them was limited. As late as the 1850s, some libraries were only open one or two hours a week. To enrich themselves in spite of this attitude, students formed library societies and developed their own libraries. These were later incorporated into the college libraries when educators realized that students needed easier access to the library's great store of knowledge. In fact, this need for information eventually caused universities and colleges to develop some of the best and largest library collections in the world.

The early colonists believed in the freedom of ideas, the freedom of religion, and the right of people to pursue knowledge. Many brought books with them from Europe and shared them among their friends. In 1731, Benjamin Franklin and some of his friends started the first subscription library in Philadelphia. This library was the forerunner of the many subscription or social libraries that developed in the United States before 1850. These voluntary association libraries were supported by dues used to buy books everyone could use. The subscription libraries fulfilled people's needs for self-improvement and self-education: self-improvement so they could become more cultured and perhaps move upward in society, and self-education so they could get better vocational training. There were subscription libraries for the general public, merchant's apprentice libraries for those learning trades, mercantile libraries for clerks in the new businesses, and libraries for the factory and labor towns. Often these libraries were begun by persons who wanted to improve young people and keep them out of trouble during their leisure hours in the teeming mill towns and urban centers. These social libraries were the true forerunners of the American public library.

In 1800, the Library of Congress was founded to give Congress members access to the information they needed. When the Capitol building was built, space was made available for a library to serve the needs of legislators. This library was destroyed when the British burned the Capitol in the War of 1812.[5] To replace the library's collection, Congress purchased Thomas Jefferson's private collection of 6,700 volumes for $25,000. Because Jefferson's collection covered a wide subject range, this purchase changed the course of the library's development. Instead of remaining a small library to serve legislators' needs, the Library of Congress began to develop into the great national library it has become today.

The first American public libraries were begun in 1803 in Salisbury, Connecticut, and in 1833 in Peterborough, New Hampshire. However, it was not until the Boston Public Library was begun in the 1850s that the publicly supported library we know today became a part of the American scene. This is probably because the conditions necessary for developing strong libraries came together at that time. Public library development follows public education, and by the middle of the nineteenth century formal systems of education had been accepted as important to the American way of life. Many people recognized that learning should continue after formal education. The development of the American lyceum and chautauqua public education movements provided public programs and concerts that enhanced education, encouraged continuing education by adults, and helped awaken an interest in the arts, literature, and sciences.

Social, economic, and cultural conditions were all favorable to library development in the latter half of the 1800s. Urban areas were growing, a dynamic nation needed trained persons to work in new occupations, and a democratic country needed an informed citizenry. Most importantly, a surplus of wealth was available to establish and support libraries. The Boston Public Library and the New York Public Library were begun by donations from wealthy businessmen and philanthropists. All over the country, libraries in colleges and towns were begun and named after alumni or citizens who took great pride in establishing libraries. The steel magnate, Andrew Carnegie, gave over $40 million to public libraries throughout the United States. The only stipulation made by most of these donors was that local communities had to agree to provide continued support for the libraries through public taxation. Beginning with the last quarter of the nineteenth century, public libraries became an important educational and social agency in communities all over the United States.

The century of library development from 1876 to 1976 began with several important library events. In 1876, the American Library Association (ALA) was founded, and the magazine *Library Journal* began publication. Both of these helped promote the dissemination of information about library services. In that same year, Melvil Dewey published his classification system that was designed for all libraries to organize their collections. Several years later, Dewey opened the first library school at Columbia University for training professional librarians. Thus, professional staffs, associations, and publications were combined with the right social, political, and economic conditions to encourage the development of strong American libraries.

In addition to the tremendous growth and expansion of academic and public libraries, the twentieth century also brought the establishment of libraries in the public schools.[6] Growth of school libraries has depended upon the educational philosophy of the school systems of which they were a part. Although school libraries had begun in the 1800s, it was not until the educational philosophy of study and inquiry became prevalent in the 1900s that school libraries became important. This change in philosophy encouraged high schools to develop libraries that supported students' inquiries into classroom subjects and that would meet their needs for college preparation. Because this latter incentive was a negligible one for elementary and junior high schools, and because the spirit of inquiry there was less pronounced, library development at these levels was also less widespread. Although libraries in elementary and junior high schools did develop in large metropolitan areas, they were often few and far between in rural areas. In fact, the country's need for libraries in elementary and junior high schools was not fully recognized until the Soviet Union launched the first space satellite, *Sputnik*, in 1957.

This event shattered the myth that the United States was the world leader in science and mathematics. It emphasized a need for teaching science, mathematics, and modern foreign languages at all levels and thrust the United States into a technological and scientific race for national supremacy. Because most educational institutions were unprepared for this, the federal government stepped in and provided federal monies to help schools, colleges, and libraries prepare people to acquire technological skills and retraining. In 1958, the National Defense Education Act was passed to provide monies for school resources and was followed by such acts as the Library Services and Construction Act, the Elementary and Secondary Education Act, and the Higher Education Act. A new technological science, information science, was also founded and integrated into the library's information resources as libraries tried to meet the technological needs of their society.

These technological needs also brought into being the fourth major type of library, the special library. These libraries were primarily developed in the twentieth century to satisfy needs for research and access to information. They are found in businesses, industries, organizations, institutions, and government agencies. Special library collections may be in-depth subject collections, extensive collections of specific types of materials (e.g., maps or music), or collections of an organization's historical records and documents. However, it is not the content of their collections that sets special libraries apart but their emphasis on providing information for the members of their parent institutions or organizations. Whether special libraries are large or small, they generally serve the same objective: to provide the needed information to the patron as quickly as possible. For this reason, these libraries have filled the important need for specialized knowledge that a technical society has and that other libraries cannot afford to meet.

In fact, this need to provide access to the enlarged universe of information needed by a technical society has influenced the direction of American library and information services in the last third of this century. Library leaders have begun to look to the national arena for support in setting a national library policy. They hope to ensure that the informational needs of all Americans are being met. The U.S. National Commission on Libraries and Information Science (NCLIS) was established in the 1960s to investigate the nation's library and information services and determine whether national policies and national programs should be established. After a decade of study, NCLIS identified a number of major problems facing U.S. libraries in the 1970s.[7] Primarily, their growth had been fragmented and uneven, and the libraries in well-financed areas had developed better services than those in poorer sections of the country. Library collections in colleges and schools were too small to meet the demands of the post-Sputnik society, and funding was inadequate at every level. The tremendous growth in the twentieth century in the amount of materials being produced and information being made available made it impossible for every library to purchase all the information it needed. Special libraries only served the needs of a limited clientele, and their information was not accessible enough to others who could use it. Finally, there was a critical need to address the problems of those people who were without basic library service.

NCLIS recommended a national program to attempt to solve these problems and ensure basic minimums of library and information services for all the American people. This program was based on the principle that "information is a national resource," and as such it is as important as natural resources. Among other things, the program encouraged the strengthening of existing library systems and the development of a national information network. It also recognized that the problems NCLIS identified could best be remedied by providing leadership and funds on a national or federal level.

As part of this national leadership, another commission, the National Commission on Excellence in Education, published its report, *A Nation at Risk*, in 1983. This report concluded that the United States had let its formal educational system deteriorate to such a dangerous degree that it had become a nation at risk. To help the country address this problem, librarians responded with a statement, *Alliance for Excellence*.[8] This statement recognized the need to create a learning society and identified the important role libraries should have in helping people gain information and skills to function successfully in such a society. Additional impetus for this learning society came from the new and improved technologies that required an ability to read. This need for a literate work force encouraged society to look at how it could better educate its children. It also forced society to look at its need to reeducate and retrain those adults who had gone through the educational system without becoming literate.

These ambitious national programs, however, were stymied when the surplus of wealth needed to finance dynamic library services dried up during the 1970s and early 1980s. Even a federally funded White House Conference on Library and Information Services in 1979 was not able to stem this tide. Many libraries found that they were not able to expand their library services to use new technologies and provide access to increased information. Instead, they had to curtail their programs and activities to keep from operating in the red. In this curtailment process, libraries began to identify the needs of the people they served to determine which needs could best be met locally and which could be better met through cooperative efforts on a regional or national basis. Libraries joined together in library systems and cooperative networks to share costs and access to their resources. In particular, cooperative automation programs and projects were developed on local, regional, and national levels to provide information access even for the smallest rural library.

Further impetus and support for these cooperative activities came from a resurgence in the American economy in the late 1980s. Once again, state and federal monies were made available to support library and information services. Grants for library construction, cooperative technological advancements, literacy projects, humanities programs, and other developments helped libraries contribute to the learning society. However, such financial support did not come without extensive lobbying at all levels by library supporters. One result of such lobbying was the convening of a second White House Conference on Library and Information Services in 1991. To ensure that this conference would truly address national library and information concerns, over 20 organizations joined together in adopting a national statement on these concerns. As a result, the conference's goal was to develop recommendations for further improvements in library and information services to increase productivity, expand literacy, and strengthen democracy. Library supporters had finally learned that if libraries were ever to become permanent centers for learning and culture, they must not be subject to the whim of financial winds. They must instead convince society that strong library and information centers were needed to satisfy those important societal needs that no other agency could fulfill.

SUMMARY

Throughout history, the development of strong libraries has depended upon the social, political, and cultural climates of the societies to which they have belonged. Strong libraries have always flourished in strong societies with stable cultural and economic climates. The earliest libraries were developed in the Greek and Roman societies, although the development of libraries as we know them today had their beginnings in the European Renaissance. Since the 1600s, European and American libraries have followed similar paths as they have developed to meet the educational, informational, cultural, recreational, and research needs of society.

In meeting these societal needs, every library has attempted to fulfill the fundamental function of a library to acquire, preserve, and make available information in all its forms. However, because no one library can meet all of these needs or provide all of the world's information, many different libraries have developed. These libraries are usually distinguished from each other by the objectives they fulfill and the clientele they serve. Libraries that serve the same major objectives are said to belong to the same type of library and are generally identified as either a public, school, academic, or special library. Each of these types of library provides different materials, programs, and services to meet one special segment of a society's population. However, because all libraries share the same fundamental function, they all work together to ensure that the informational needs of all American people are being met.

REVIEW QUESTIONS

1. Use the definitions librarians prefer to define a library.

2. Identify the major needs or conditions that encouraged the development of the following libraries: Renaissance libraries, college and university libraries, subscription or social libraries, school libraries, special libraries.

3. Identify the major needs and conditions that encouraged American library development in the twentieth century.

4. Briefly state your own concept of library service based on your definition of a library and the major objectives a library should fulfill.

5. Choose a local library and identify the needs or conditions that encouraged this library's establishment.

NOTES

[1] Jean Key Gates, *Introduction to Librarianship* (New York: McGraw-Hill, 1968), 89-94; Elmer D. Johnson, *History of Libraries in the Western World*, 3d ed. (Metuchen, NJ: Scarecrow, 1976), 4-5.

[2] For more information on the history of libraries, consult the "Selected Readings" at the end of this chapter.

[3] Anthony Hobson, *Great Libraries* (New York: Putnam, 1970). This is a beautifully illustrated book that describes these libraries.

[4] For more information on the development of American libraries, consult the "Selected Readings" at the end of this chapter.

[5] In 1978, the Oxford University Press paid the Library of Congress with contemporary five-pound and one-pound notes and with fourteen rare antique shillings (about $13). This served as repayment for the three Oxford University Press books that were burned.

[6] For further discussion of this development, see chapters 5 through 8.

[7] U.S. National Commission on Libraries and Information Science, *Toward a National Program for Library and Information Services: Goals for Action* (Washington, DC: GPO, 1975), 23-24.

[8]*Alliance for Excellence: Librarians Respond to "A Nation at Risk."* (Washington, DC: U.S. Department of Education, 1984).

SELECTED READINGS

Alliance for Excellence: Librarians Respond to "A Nation at Risk." Washington, DC: U.S. Department of Education, 1984.

Armour, Richard. *The Happy Bookers: A Playful History of Librarians and Their World from the Stone Age to the Distant Future.* New York: McGraw-Hill, 1976.

Dickson, Paul. *Library in America: A Celebration in Words and Pictures.* New York: Facts on File, 1986.

Estabrook, Leigh. *Libraries in Post-Industrial Society.* Phoenix, AZ: Oryx Press, 1977.

Hobson, Anthony. *Great Libraries.* New York: Putnam, 1970.

Jackson, Sidney L. *Libraries and Librarianship in the West: A Brief History.* New York: McGraw-Hill, 1974.

Johnson, Elmer D. *Communication: An Introduction to the History of Writing, Printing, Books, and Libraries.* 3d ed. Metuchen, NJ: Scarecrow, 1976.

_____. *History of Libraries in the Western World.* 3d ed. Revised by Elmer D. Johnson and Michael H. Harris. Metuchen, NJ: Scarecrow, 1976.

Kent, A., and H. Lancour, eds. *Encyclopedia of Library and Information Science.* New York: Dekker, 1968-

Knight, Douglas M., and E. Shepley Nourse, eds. *Libraries at Large: Tradition, Innovation and the National Interest.* New York: Bowker, 1969.

Porter, Alan. *The Great Libraries of America: A Pictorial History.* Palm Springs, CA: Monitor, 1983.

Shera, Jesse. *Foundations of the Public Library: The Origins of the Public Library Movement in New England, 1624-1855.* Hamden, CT: Shoe String, 1965.

U.S. National Commission on Excellence in Education. *A Nation at Risk.* Washington, DC: GPO, 1983.

U.S. National Commission on Libraries and Information Science. *Toward a National Program for Library and Information Services: Goals for Action.* Washington, DC: GPO, 1975.

CHAPTER 2

LIBRARY AND MEDIA PERSONNEL

To operate today's complicated libraries, many different types of library personnel are needed, ranging from head librarians or library directors to librarians, library assistants, technicians, clerks, aides, pages, and even bookkeepers and custodians. Each category requires specific knowledge and experience and is defined by specific duties that separate it from the next position in a classification system. For example, librarians require a broad general education background and a foundation in the theory of library science to direct and organize a library. Library media technicians require some general education and library knowledge to help librarians run the internal operations of the library. These personnel are supported by library clerks, aides, and pages who have more limited library knowledge and who perform specific library operations. Together, they have the knowledge and skills necessary to provide library services.

PERSONAL CHARACTERISTICS

In addition to a general education and knowledge of how a library works, other characteristics are important for library employees. These are personal characteristics and qualities that center on an individual's inner interests and motives and indicate his or her potential success as a library employee. Recent personality profile studies, such as the Myers-Briggs Personality Profile, can help in this identification process. These studies have identified common characteristics for personality types and discussed their relationship to a person's vocational choices.

It would probably be difficult to use one or two traits to describe all the attributes of library staff members. However, a number of personal characteristics and qualities have been identified as necessary for most library workers. Although each staff member is not expected to possess all of these qualities, they may serve as useful guidelines for encouraging library employees to develop such qualities. Contrary to myth, persons in libraries do not have to love books or have a love of reading, and they certainly do not spend their working days reading books. Instead, the two most basic characteristics persons working in libraries need are an interest in working with people and a concern for the accuracy of details. Very few library or media jobs are free from a need for these two characteristics.[1]

Practically all library staff members are involved with bringing people and these informational materials together. If they do not like being with people or helping people, library staff members will not be successful in fulfilling this library function. The library maxim, "the right information for the right person at the right time," cannot be adhered to if staff members cannot "tune in" to a person's needs. Part of this "tuning in" involves attending to details. Because a library law seems to be that the requested item has either just been checked in or checked out to someone else, the staff member must be interested enough to remember such details. Much of the work in libraries is similar to detective work in that staff members must often fit the pieces of a puzzle together to solve a problem or answer a difficult question. They must locate details, analyze them, and make decisions based on their findings. It is the interest with which library staff members approach these decisions that forms a common bond among them.

Other important characteristics of good library personnel are the ability to exercise judgment and the ability to be flexible. Good judgment is the characteristic many employers most often seek, and yet it is often the hardest to develop. A staff member's judgment should be based on realistically applying library rules and procedures so that the spirit of a library's policies and objectives is carried out. It should also involve flexibility that will help the employee experiment or adapt when changes seem appropriate or necessary. Finally, good judgment includes the ability to admit one's limitations and, if necessary, to turn a question or problem over to someone who is better able to handle it because of training or experience. Staff members who exercise these abilities are those who help defy and destroy the negative stereotypes and myths surrounding the library profession.

Too often library staff members are portrayed in the media as tight-lipped, stern-voiced martinets who are only concerned with maintaining silence and restricting access to their collections. Such stereotypes can be destroyed if library staff members will not set themselves up to be "the custodians" of knowledge, rules, and library behavior. Instead, they should know that persons approach information and learning in different ways because of differences in their personality types and that this is acceptable in a library situation. They should also exhibit the same personal characteristics with library patrons and other staff members that they would show in any other interpersonal situation. These characteristics include a pleasant and courteous manner, tact, imagination, intelligence, an open mind, consideration, a good memory, an ability to communicate well, and a good sense of humor. Although this list reads more like a job description for "Superperson," there are personnel who have fulfilled these descriptions and, by their examples, have made many friends for the library profession. Through their friendliness and their awareness of the latest trends in dress, culture, and ideas, they have helped establish a positive image of modern library staff.

LEVELS OF PERSONNEL

Today's libraries have generally outgrown the type of library operation in which one person could perform all duties, from checking out and shelving materials to selecting, ordering, and classifying them. Rather, in all but the smallest library, several employees usually have distinct job functions with varying levels of responsibility. These levels of responsibility were first identified in 1933 by Pierce Butler of the University of Chicago Library School. He defined three levels of library classification: professional library worker, technical library worker, and clerical library worker. He used the word *professional* to describe the librarian because a *profession* is defined as a vocation with a service orientation that is based on highly specialized knowledge that comes from extensive education. Butler stated:

> A professional library worker must possess a scientific, generalized knowledge which will enable him to discover the complex library needs of a mixed community. His primary concern is with the social effect of the institution. A technical library worker must have been vocationally trained to control the apparatus of the library for an effective realization of its prescribed purpose. His concern is internal institutional efficiency. The clerical worker needs operative skill for performing a particular process. His concern is with the operation performed at his desk.[2]

Although Butler identified these three mutually exclusive levels of library responsibility, they were not generally adopted until the 1970s. Until that time, most libraries had two levels of personnel: professional librarian and nonprofessional personnel. The professional librarian usually had a bachelor's degree in a subject field and a master's degree in library science (MLS). This MLS was usually received from a university program accredited by the ALA. The school librarian would often have a bachelor's degree in education with a minor of 18 to 24 hours in library science. The only education usually required for nonprofessional personnel was a high school diploma. However, these clerical employees might have several years of college or even a bachelor's or master's degree in another subject area. The shortage of librarians brought on by the growth of all libraries after *Sputnik* in 1957 caused many head librarians or library directors to reexamine these personnel categories to make maximum use of the librarians available.

This reexamination led the ALA to adopt a *Library Education and Personnel Utilization* statement in 1970. This statement identified the titles, basic requirements, and nature of responsibility for four categories of library personnel at both the professional and supportive library positions. (See appendix A.) For the first time, the library world had officially recognized that different levels of library knowledge and skills existed for the professional librarian and the untrained nonprofessional. This policy statement also recognized that other professionals, such as media and information specialists, had equal professional status with the librarian who had traditional library training. This factor became important as school libraries and school audiovisual centers upgraded their staffs to require master's degrees in library, media, or educational technology and merged their facilities into school library media centers.

The different personnel categories identified by the *Personnel Utilization* statement were based on the principle that the skills, aptitudes, and knowledge needed by each level of library worker can be distinguished from the other in several important areas. At the top level, the professional librarian or specialist first needs the breadth and depth of knowledge that can be gained from extensive education. Then, the professional needs to exercise creative, interpretive, evaluative, and analytical abilities to develop library service programs. Finally, the professional needs to apply the philosophy, principles, and theories of library services to develop, assess, and adapt these programs in response to a community's changing needs.[3]

For the professional librarian to develop these knowledges, abilities, and library principles and theories, an MLS is required for the entry-level professional position. Advanced professional positions may require further education beyond the master's degree, such as a sixth-year specialist degree in advanced library or information science. (This specialist degree should not be confused with the position of library media specialist.) Other positions may require a doctorate in library science or an additional degree in a related field. For example, librarians in law libraries may also need a law degree, and library administrators may need a doctorate or a master's degree in administration. School librarians in the past only needed a bachelor's degree with a minor in library science. However, since the 1980s, most school library media specialists have needed a master's degree in library, media, or educational technology, as well as education courses to certify them as teachers.

The *Personnel Utilization* statement also identified three levels of supportive positions to assist these professional librarians and specialists. This identification was important because it was the first time the library world had acknowledged that there were persons working in libraries who were interested in library careers at a level other than the professional librarian level. The career levels for these supportive staff members were labeled as *subprofessional*, *paraprofessional*, and *nonprofessional* and recognized that persons who work in libraries as technicians and clerks not only fulfill important functions in the library but also tend to stay in these positions for many years.

As identified in the statement, the library associate at the subprofessional level requires the judgment and subject knowledge usually represented by a bachelor's degree. The associate is also considered a preprofessional position for those persons taking library school courses while they hold this position.[4] However, although many libraries do provide classifications for personnel with bachelor's degrees, the title of library associate has not been widely used. Instead, the basic duties and responsibilities of this classification may be assigned to the top paraprofessional position, such as a library assistant IV or library technician IV.

The library technical assistant is a paraprofessional position. It requires specific library or technical skills that come from experience or from specialized formal training such as that provided in a two-year, college-level program. Such programs provide the specialized knowledge that separates a technical assistant from an advanced clerk. They also provide training that many librarians prefer employees in this category to have. This training includes the general education and library media knowledge recommended in the ALA *Criteria for Programs to Prepare Library Technical Assistants*. Library technical assistants are primarily concerned with performing and supervising procedures within the policies of the institution in which they work.[5] They are expected to exercise some judgment as they analyze library information and situations and compare them to predetermined guidelines and policies.

In contrast, the clerk or nonprofessional worker does not require formal academic training because the needed skills are based upon general clerical and secretarial proficiencies. Any need for familiarity with basic library terminology and routines needed to adapt clerical skills to the library's environment is best learned on the job.[6] The employee at this level does not exercise judgment or evaluative abilities and is only concerned with specific job duties. The library clerk is more concerned with *how* to do something than with *why* it is done.

In addition to the levels identified in the *Personnel Utilization* statement, libraries also staff other positions that require minimal library knowledge and skills. Library pages and student employees usually work part time a few hours at a time to shelve library materials and keep them in order. These employees may also assist library clerks in other duties such as inventory or serial control. In the administrative area, library secretaries, bookkeepers, and custodians perform duties for the library world that are similar to their counterparts in the school or business worlds. In addition to paid employees, some libraries have active volunteer programs to assist the library staff. In libraries with such volunteer programs, the volunteers' duties should supplement and support library staff services rather than replace them.

The ALA *Personnel Utilization* statement attempted to establish personnel categories so that a library position in one library could be easily equated to a library position in another library. However, there has not been much progress in this area. Although many libraries welcomed the establishment of separate levels of library personnel as a recognition of current library staffing patterns, there were problems with the names of the levels. Some library staff objected to the negative connotation of the terms *preprofessional*, *subprofessional*, and *nonprofessional*. They considered themselves to be just as professional in the performance of their duties as the "professional librarians." In recognition of this movement, some libraries began to use the term *support staff* instead.

Many also felt the educational requirements that distinguished the library associate from the library/media technical assistant were too narrowly defined to receive wide acceptance. For example, many library technicians had advanced to such positions through on-the-job training rather than through formal education programs. A review of state standards and job want ads showed that by 1990 the favored job title for this level of employee was technician rather than library associate or library/media technical assistant. A sample representation of the titles some libraries use to indicate positions at the professional, technical, and clerical levels is in figure 2.1, page 18.

Fig. 2.1. Identification of library personnel categories. (A representative sample of position titles used to identify personnel performing library/media/information responsibilities within an organization.)

LEVEL	TITLE	ENTRY-LEVEL EDUCATION
PROFESSIONAL	Librarian Specialist Media Specialist Information Specialist Bibliographer Research Specialist Senior Librarian Senior Specialist School Library Media Specialist Instructor Assistant Professor	Master's degree

TECHNICAL	Library Associate
	Assistant Librarian
	Library Technician
	Library Technical
	    Assistant
	Library/Media Tech-
	    nical Assistant
	Library Media
	    Technician
	Library Assistant II-IV
	Library Technician,
	    GS 4-7
		Bachelor's degree
		Associate degree
		Post-secondary training
		On-the-job training

CLERICAL	Library Clerk
	Library Media Clerk
	Media Clerk
	Library Assistant I
	Library Aide GS 1-3
	Media Aide
	School Library Media
	    Aide
	Page
	Shelver
		High school diploma
		Some high school
		    education

PERSONNEL RESPONSIBILITIES

Although the ALA *Personnel Utilization* statement was not implemented on a national basis, it did provide an incentive for librarians to reevaluate their staffing patterns. Faced with a projected shortage of librarians by the 1970s, library organizations began to study the various job tasks and responsibilities of library personnel. Job evaluations or task analyses were undertaken in the 1970s for school libraries by the School Library Manpower Project. Public libraries were analyzed by the Illinois Library Task Analysis Project. Special libraries were analyzed by the Alberta Government Libraries' Council Job Specifications Committee. In the 1980s, studies were conducted by groups such as King Research Company to identify the library and information competencies needed by librarians and other staff members to perform their duties.

Many of these analyses were based on the premise that

> analysis of the nature of the work precedes the determination of both the kinds of personnel needed and the kinds of educational preparation they should have. Analysis on a task-by-task basis of the work performed reveals more closely the nature of the work itself in terms of its demands for skills, aptitudes, and knowledge on the part of the worker.[7]

The results of these analyses showed that many tasks and responsibilities that had been performed by professionals could be performed by trained technical support personnel. In addition, the introduction of technology to many library operations also contributed to a reexamination of library staff duties and responsibilities. In response, librarians were encouraged to reexamine the staff's duties and responsibilities at their own libraries to determine if these duties were being performed at the most appropriate staff level and position.

In this reexamination, librarians generally considered the professional and nonprofessional nature of the duties librarians performed. For example, when the position of circulation librarian was reevaluated, it was usually determined that most of the circulation supervisor's responsibilities required technical rather than professional expertise. Libraries found they could transfer the professional responsibilities of this position to the public services librarian and appoint technicians to supervise circulation operations. (Differences among these levels may be more clearly observed by comparing the example duties and the choice of verbs used for each level in figure 2.2, page 20.) Similarly, when the acquisitions librarian position was reevaluated, it was found that the professional duties (primarily selection) could be separated from this position. An acquisitions technician could then handle the job just as well as, and more economically than, a librarian could.

Based on these reevaluations, many libraries began to revise their staffs to reflect a new ratio of librarians to support staff members. Many libraries changed their staffing ratio from "1 professional : 1-2 support staff employees" to "1 professional : 2-4 support staff employees." By 1990, the ratio generally advocated in library literature was "1 professional : 2 support staff employees."[8] These support staff members usually included both technical and clerical personnel. In some library standards, the recommended ratio had become "1 professional : 1 technical : 1 clerical." Thus, the personnel classification levels first identified by Butler in 1933 had finally become the accepted norm by 1990.

Fig. 2.2. Examples of personnel duties from task analyses. (Reprinted by permission from *Personnel Utilization in Libraries: A Systems Approach.* Prepared for the Illinois Library Task Analysis Project by Myrl Ricking and Robert E. Booth [Chicago: ALA, 1974].)

2 COLLECTION ORGANIZATION SUBSYSTEM

P Professional	T Technical	C Clerical
1 Develops and expands classification systems	1 Performs descriptive cataloging of materials for which LC cards or MARC tapes are not available	1 Types cards or inputs data for catalogs, shelf list, and other files from copy provided
2 Establishes, and directs maintenance of, cataloging records	2 Catalogs fiction	2 Reproduces cards in quantity by a variety of processes: tape, photocopy, multigraph, mimeograph
3 Supervises contributions to union catalogs and bibliographic centers and participates in cooperative cataloging arrangements	3 Performs simple classification of materials identified in standard tools	3 Arranges catalog cards in sets, following established procedures

5 CIRCULATION SUBSYSTEM

P Professional	T Technical	C Clerical
		a Registration Module
1 Establishes circulation system for all types of materials	1 Supervises established circulation and registration procedures	1 Explains the library's registration policies and procedures 1.1 Gives applicants any printed information available about the library's services, collections, and procedures
2 Receives and responds to sensitive complaints and inquiries	2 Responds to user complaints, presented in person, by mail, or telephone 2.1 Checks out reasons for problem described 2.2 Interprets policies 2.3 Explains regulations 2.4 Corrects any errors in action or procedure on the part of the library 2.5 Refers to professional staff problems on which assistance is needed	2 Checks to see if applicants have had cards previously

Librarian and
Media/Information Specialist

The terms *librarian* and *specialist* are usually reserved for those positions that are filled by someone with a master's degree whose entry-level professional responsibilities and duties require the knowledge and abilities this degree provides. Primarily, librarians analyze the needs of a community, company, or school so they can identify goals and objectives to meet these needs. This means that librarians and school library media specialists are often away from the library attending meetings with city or company officials, citizens, and faculty members to find out what these people want the library to provide for them. Librarians also are constantly reading current literature to keep abreast of new developments in the field. Once they have gathered this background information, librarians use it to direct the library staff in developing library policies and operations to satisfy these community needs.

In the development of these policies and operations, librarians are responsible for administering and supervising the total operations of a library or a library unit. Such responsibilities include staff selection, training, and evaluation, as well as financial planning and budgeting. Librarians also establish and administer collection development policies such as evaluating, selecting, and weeding the library's collections. Technical services librarians may direct the library's cataloging operations, including the original cataloging of complex or foreign-language materials. Public services librarians provide reference and readers' advisor assistance to library patrons of all ages. These reference librarians may also compile bibliographies and indexes as well as conduct online computer database searches. In some libraries, librarians may be subject specialists providing research assistance for professionals in other fields such as law, medicine, or business. In other libraries, they may plan and present adult and youth programs as well as provide outreach services to the aged, the disadvantaged, or the adult learner. Librarians may conduct classes in the use of libraries and develop individualized courses to help patrons use the library by themselves.

In some libraries, professional specialists with master's degrees in areas other than library science may also perform duties at the professional level. Specialists with an educational technology background may design graphics or audiovisual materials that teachers can use. Other specialists with professional backgrounds in areas such as computer systems analysis, television production, public relations, personnel, or accounting have become important members of the library's professional team. However, for these positions to be classified at the professional level, their duties should require evaluative and analytical abilities similar to those librarians need.

Library Technician

Since 1970, many libraries have established some position at the paraprofessional or midmanagement level to support the professional librarian staff. The title for this technical position may vary from library technician to library media technical assistant to library assistant. However, where this technician fits in a library's organizational structure, and not the job title, is important.

Before 1970, a technical classification level for technicians did not exist. Instead, these duties were performed by beginning professionals, library assistants with college degrees, or clerks with years of experience, or they were not performed at all. Although college graduates or experienced clerks may have performed some of these duties, they often did not have the library knowledge needed to perform them well. For this reason, beginning professional librarians often performed many of these quasi- or semiprofessional duties. Beginning librarians were assigned to supervise circulation routines, revise catalog card or shelf-list card filing, and catalog simple original materials or materials using prepared copy. In some libraries, senior librarians performed these duties because it was easier than training someone else to do them. In other libraries, librarians did so because they were afraid that persons who were not professionally trained would fail to recognize the limits of their knowledge and would overstep their job responsibilities. However, these latter fears have proven to be groundless.

What encouraged librarians to adopt this technical-level position and revise their personnel categories to include it? One major factor was organizational. Library administrators learned that they could take advantage of the task analyses to reorganize their personnel structures. This reorganizational capability was also affected by a second major factor: economics. Libraries found they could hire less-expensive personnel to perform these restructured jobs. Faced with a shortage of professional librarians, libraries began to support two-year library technology programs. Once library administrators realized that trained technicians were available to perform tasks that had previously been done by beginning librarians, they understood that it was more cost effective for technicians to do them.

A third factor was the establishment of local, state, and federal civil service personnel categories such as the U.S. government's Library Technician 1411 series (1966). Although the U.S. Office of Personnel Management had tried since 1980 to revise this series (and the Librarian series), both series were instrumental in establishing criteria for library positions. In particular, they established different levels of responsibility, difficulty of assignments, and personal contacts for library aide and library technician positions that did not need professional training. A fourth factor was the recognition that vocationally trained paraprofessionals had been accepted as valuable team members in other professions such as law and medicine.

The final and most important factor in the acceptance of library technicians has been the impact of automation and technology upon the library world. As technology and the use of automation in libraries has become more commonplace and sophisticated, librarians have recognized that newer automated systems have eliminated the need for professional decisions in many routine library operations. With this knowledge, librarians have been glad to leave supervision of such automated library systems to library technicians and the operation of such systems to library clerks. They have also been glad to turn general supervision of all the library's internal operations over to the library technicians and clerks.

In the supervision of these library operations, personnel at this technical level follow established procedures developed by librarians. The authority for a technician's responsibilities is based upon reference to staff policy manuals and adherence to established library policies. The technician usually deals with a wide variety of situations that frequently may involve public and personnel contacts. Because errors in judgment at this level may injure staff and public relations, independent actions and decisions by the technician are generally subject to review.[9] Although this level of staff member can perform the tasks of the library clerk, technicians usually train and supervise clerks rather than perform these duties themselves.

It is in this latter area of supervising clerical and other technical personnel that technicians have come into their own. This phenomenon occurred for several important reasons. First, the library technical assistant programs begun in the 1970s trained technicians in supervisory techniques. This training contrasted with professional library science courses that did not necessarily provide librarians with similar supervisory training. Second, librarians such as catalogers, children's librarians, and reference librarians might work years in a library before they were in positions that required them to supervise other personnel. Third, economics and other considerations encouraged library systems to put technicians in charge of bookmobiles, branches, or small libraries. In these positions, they were required to train and supervise library personnel and to introduce them to the concepts of library service.

Technicians are often responsible for a service unit in a library or library media center. In small libraries, a technician may supervise the operations of an entire library that is part of a library system. In larger libraries, technicians may be in charge of separate units such as a bookmobile or small branch or special subject areas such as art, music, or serials. For example, a technician may supervise a service unit such as the circulation department and direct its procedures, train and supervise its staff, and handle problems with the public. Technicians may be in charge of reserve or government document collections or work as interlibrary loan technicians. In public services, they may serve as information desk assistants, reference technicians, or bibliographic assistants providing preliminary bibliographic searching. Some technicians may not only assist patrons in using resources and equipment, but they may also provide instruction in their use. Technicians in children's libraries often help provide programming and displays. In technical services, technicians have not only been put in charge of acquisitions, but they have also been put in charge of binding, serials, and materials processing. In the cataloging area, the increased availability of prepared cataloging information has made it possible for well-trained technicians to catalog items that formerly required original cataloging by professional librarians.

Many library technicians also use specialized computer skills in performing their responsibilities. Technicians use computers for word processing, film booking, magazine check-in and routing, interlibrary loan searching, and many other duties. Often technicians are in charge of in-house computer operations that may operate a library's automated systems. Technicians may also supervise any computer labs, including maintaining the computer equipment and training patrons and staff to use this equipment. As library media technicians, they may maintain and repair audiovisual equipment, or they may be responsible for equipment inventories and the evaluation and selection of audiovisual equipment. Library media technicians may plan and prepare displays as well as design and prepare audiovisual materials. They can maintain videotape collections and help produce in-house video programs. Library media technicians with more specialized training can also work as photographic assistants, graphics assistants, or TV technicians or as assistants in other specialized media areas. However, in all of these areas, the technician will still adhere to adopted library policies and exercise judgment within the library's established guidelines.

Library Clerk

With the advent of the technician level of library employee, the duties at the clerical level have become more library and department specific. The duties of a library clerk are primarily simple tasks of a clerical or secretarial nature related to some library function or activity. These tasks tend to be repetitious in nature and are usually performed under close supervision by strictly following guidelines established by the supervisor.[10] Typical examples of clerical duties would be checking materials in and out, sending overdue notices, entering computer data, filing catalog cards, checking in new magazines, processing materials, ordering rental films, and preparing transparencies. Because library clerks often remain in their positions for a number of years, some libraries have been able to take advantage of this stability to establish several levels of library clerk from beginning to advanced clerk. In such cases, the more advanced clerks may take on more involved clerical duties such as complex computer data entry, word processing, or serial records maintenance. In other cases, beginning library clerks may take on the duties of the traditional library page such as shelving materials, shelf reading, and retrieving materials from closed library stacks.

However, no matter how senior a library clerk may be, an important distinction between the advanced clerk and technician still remains. Advanced clerical employees may become very experienced in performing particular library tasks. However, this experience may not provide them with enough knowledge or ability to examine or evaluate a task to determine if it should be changed or eliminated. Without further education or training, even an experienced library clerk may not be able to see the relationship between a particular task and the overall objectives of an activity or service. For this reason, whenever questions or problems arise in performing these duties, any library clerk should check with the supervisor to help answer the question or determine the solution. A library clerk or page at any level does not have the authority to say no to a patron or leave a patron dissatisfied. Instead, clerks must recognize the limits of their authority and call upon others more qualified by education or experience to handle unusual situations.

SUMMARY

Today's libraries need many different types of library personnel, from librarians to technicians, clerks, and pages, if they are to provide effective library service. These library employees share common personal traits or characteristics that enable them to work with people and provide "the right information to the right patron at the right time." Library positions are generally divided into three personnel classification levels—professional, technical, and clerical—that differ according to education, duties, responsibilities, and level of supervision. Professional employees are librarians or specialists whose master's-level library education has prepared them to establish and direct library services to meet a community's needs. Technical employees are technicians or library media technical assistants whose library education has trained them to supervise the internal operations of a library and perform complicated technical library operations. Clerical employees are clerks and pages who are trained on the job to perform specific library operations. All three of these types of employees are needed to perform library procedures and provide library services if a library is to meet its goals and objectives.

REVIEW QUESTIONS

1. List the major personal qualities every library staff member should possess.

2. Describe the major differences that distinguish professional, technical, and clerical positions.

3. Identify the major categories of personnel by job title, education, and level of classification in the form of a career ladder similar to that in appendix A.

4. Define the position of librarian and identify the most important abilities needed by this level of employee.

5. Define the position of library technician and identify the technician's relationship to librarians and library clerks.

6. Discuss four factors that contributed to the development of the technical classification level in library staffing.

7. Define the position of library clerk, including the types of duties the clerk would perform and how the person would be supervised.

8. Compare the personnel categories and organizational charts of two local libraries representing any type of library.

NOTES

[1]Over the past 30 years, I have noticed other interesting personality traits that seem to be common among librarians. The first of these traits is a love of eating, and in particular, a love of desserts! (It is difficult to know whether librarians are drawn to this profession because of this love, or whether it is bred into them in library school.) In any case, library meetings and staff rooms usually have goodies on hand for everyone to enjoy. A second common trait among librarians seems to be a preference for drinking tea over coffee, and at least 85-90 percent who do drink coffee drink it black. A final observation is that an unusually high proportion of librarians have domestic cats in their homes, and many of them have more than one cat. Although the author cannot guarantee the validity of these observations, they can generally be counted on to provide a common interest whenever librarians meet!

[2]Pierce Butler, *Introduction to Library Science* (Chicago: University of Chicago Press, 1933), 111-12.

[3]ALA, "Report of the Interdivisional Ad Hoc Committee of LAD and LED on Subprofessional or Technician Class of Library Employees," rev. by Dorothy Deininger, chairperson (Chicago: ALA, 1967), 2.

[4]American Library Association, Office for Library Education, *Library Education and Personnel Utilization* (Chicago: ALA, 1970), 5.

[5]ALA, *Library Education*, 4.

[6]ALA, *Library Education*, 4.

[7]Myrl Ricking and Robert E. Booth, *Personnel Utilization in Libraries: A Systems Approach*. Prepared for the Illinois Library Task Analysis Project (Chicago: ALA, 1974), 1.

[8]Margaret Myers, "Staffing Patterns," in *Personnel Administration in Libraries*, 2d ed., ed. Sheila Creth and Frederick Duda (New York: Neal-Schuman, 1989), 41-42.

[9]ALA, "Report of Interdivisional Committee," 8.

[10]ALA, "Report of Interdivisional Committee," 5.

SELECTED READINGS

American Library Association, Office for Library Education. *Library Education and Personnel Utilization*. Chicago: ALA, 1970.

American Library Association. "Report of the Interdivisional Ad Hoc Committee of LAD and LED on Subprofessional or Technician Class of Library Employees." Revised by Dorothy Deininger, chairperson. Chicago: ALA, 1967.

Creth, Sheila. *Personnel Management in Libraries*. 2d ed. Edited by Sheila Creth and Frederick Duda. New York: Neal-Schuman, 1989.

Keirsey, David. *Please Understand Me: Character and Temperament Types*. 4th ed. Del Mar, CA: Prometheus Nemesis, 1989.

Kroeger, Otto, and Janet M. Thuesen. *Type Talk: The Sixteen Personality Types That Determine How We Live, Love and Work*. New York: Delacorte, 1988.

Library Mosaics: The Magazine for Support Staff 1- (September/October 1989-). Culver City, CA: Library Mosaics.

Ricking, Myrl, and Robert E. Booth. *Personnel Utilization in Libraries: A Systems Approach.* Prepared for the Illinois Library Task Analysis Project. Chicago: ALA, 1974.

"Special Reports: The Image of the Librarian." In *Bowker Annual Library and Book Trade Almanac.* 35th ed., 72-105. New York: Bowker, 1990.

Taylor, Richard. *Job Descriptions for Library Support Personnel.* Edited by Richard Taylor and Raymond G. Roney. Cleveland, OH: Council on Library/Media Technicians, 1985.

White, Herbert S. *Library Personnel Management.* White Plains, NY: Knowledge Industry Publications, 1985.

CHAPTER 3

LIBRARY RESOURCES

The fundamental purpose of a library is to acquire, preserve, and make available information in all its varied forms. This purpose requires today's libraries to include a variety of resources and in-depth information that would have been unheard of only a few decades ago. By expanding their collections beyond the traditional print materials to include graphic, audiovisual, and computer resources, libraries now preserve and present information in all its many forms. In addition to books, magazines, newspapers, and pamphlets, library patrons have access to such other media as records, films, audio- and videotapes and discs, compact discs (CDs), art prints, games, toys, and computers. Many libraries also provide access to computer-based information available from online database services, CD-ROM (Compact Disc Read Only Memory) databases, and other libraries and sources accessible through telecommunications links. These various media have been included in libraries because their unique characteristics enable patrons to use the media according to their own abilities, interests, or needs. They have also been included because much of the information in our largely visual and verbal society may only be recorded in these specific forms.

Yet, for many reasons, libraries must choose from among the variety and quantity of media and resources available. Because more than 55,000 books, 120,000 magazines and newspapers, 3,900 databases, and thousands of video- and audiotapes are published or produced each year, no library can afford to buy everything written, printed, or produced. Even if they could afford to do so, very few libraries would want to. To serve its patrons effectively, each library must judiciously select those resources that will help fulfill its stated objectives. Thus, the collections and resources from library to library will usually differ by types of media as well as by subject content.

PRINT RESOURCES

Print media including books, magazines, and pamphlets are probably the resource formats most familiar to library users. Although the decline of print and the rise of a "paperless society" have been widely predicted over the last several decades; economic conditions and human preferences have combined to ensure that books and magazines will probably remain major media formats in libraries in the coming decades. One reason is that print media have proven to be an economical form for providing permanent, nonchanging information such as literary works, children's picture books, and permanent records of research reports. Another reason is that books and magazines are portable enough to be taken anywhere anytime without the need for equipment to use them. Many library users prefer this capability to "curl up with a good book" rather than reading the same information on a computer screen. In addition, users often prefer to transfer information from a computer or telecommunications-based media into print form so they can make notes or review passages more easily at a later time.

However, this preference for using print media may be hampered by unfortunate preservation problems that have occurred with much of the print materials available since the early 1900s. Twentieth-century changes in publishing processes and the cloth content of paper have caused an alarming deterioration rate among these print materials. It is estimated that 70 percent of the books printed in this century will be unusable by the year 2000. To counteract this destruction, libraries have established deacidification programs to protect print materials. They have also developed programs to transfer threatened materials to more durable or computer-accessible form. Thus, the user's preference for using print media may be offset by the need to preserve this print media for future generations.

Books

A *book* has been defined as a collection of more than 48 pages that has a distinctive title and is fastened together in a binding. It may be called a *volume* in libraries or a *tome* in literature. A book may also be called a *monograph* if it is a complete narrative or treatise on a particular subject written in detail but limited in scope. Monographs that are related to each other may belong to *sets* or *series*. Copies of a book that are printed from the same type set-up or from the same printing plates are said to belong to the same *edition*. If the content of the book is changed and the type is changed, a new edition of a book is printed. Sometimes the same book content may be published or printed in several different bindings or on different paper and be advertised as different editions. Some publishers print a book in a hardcover binding as well as in a paper binding. Other books may be printed in two hardcover editions. The first is a *trade edition* intended for sale in bookstores and written for the general reader. The other is a *textbook edition*, which includes additional information (usually study guides and questions) of interest to students and teachers. Some books are even published in a *library binding* which is sturdier than the hard cover of the normal trade edition. *Paperback* books used to be published either for the mass market or as "quality paperbacks." However, rising publishing costs have produced many books in paperback that would have been published in hard cover in earlier years. With all of these various editions available, librarians usually prefer to purchase particular editions of a book. For example, some public libraries may not buy textbooks and children's libraries often prefer to buy books in library binding editions. Each library's policy is usually based on its budget and the use its collection receives.

Parts of a Book: Physical

Each part of the physical book itself usually has a technical term to describe it. The binding of the book is called the *casing* or the *cover*, and the back edge with the lettering for the name or title of the book is called the *spine*. The lining papers on the inside of the covers are called *end papers* and may often bear decorative illustrations. The insides of the book are called the *contents* or *text* of the work. The weight and quality of the paper on which the contents are printed may vary greatly from book to book. Older books often have the illustrations printed on one weight of paper and the words printed on a lighter paper. The illustrations themselves often represent various printing techniques and have technical names such as *line*, *half-tone*, or *color*. Selecting the cover, paper, page design, and typefaces to be used in a book is the special art of publishing. The designer or editor in charge of this may be listed at the front of the book, or a statement describing this may be included at the end of the book. This type of editor, however, should not be confused with an editor who contributed to the intellectual content of the book.

The contents of the book are made up of sheets of paper or *leaves*, which are printed on both sides or *pages*. These pages are referred to as the *recto*, or the page on the right side of an open book, and the *verso*, the page on the other or reverse side of the same leaf. The text of a book is first printed on large sheets of paper which are then folded and cut to make pages in a book. Sometimes the pages may not be completely cut through in a particular copy of a book so they must be cut to read the book. Each folded sheet of paper is called a *signature*, and these signatures are often numbered or lettered so the printer knows in which order to gather them for the book. The number of times a printed sheet of paper is folded will determine the size of the finished book. If the signature is made by folding the paper once to make two leaves or four pages, it is called a *folio*. Readers may have heard of Shakespeare's folios, which were named after the printing size rather than the content. A signature folded twice makes four leaves and eight pages and is called a *quarto*. Signatures folded three times contain eight leaves or sixteen pages and are called *octavos*. The octavo, or 16-page signature, and the 32-page signature are the most commonly found book sizes. In fact, the definition adopted by the United Nations in 1964 designates that a book is made of more than 48 pages, or more than three signatures of 16 pages. Large-sized or *oversized* books may be indicated in some libraries by adding the letters Q (for quarto) or FOL (for folio) to the location number of a book so readers will know the books are shelved in separate areas of the library.

Parts of a Book: Bibliographic

Librarians refer to the description of the contents of a book as *bibliographic description*. A bibliographic description identifies the title, personal or corporate author, publishing information, and the distinctive characteristics of a book. The *title* or name of a work is the distinctive phrase or words used to identify the work. It may be expanded or further explained by a phrase called a *subtitle*, which is often in smaller print than the words of the title or separated from it by punctuation such as a colon or a semicolon. Although the title may be printed on the first page of a book called a *half-title*, the next page of a book usually includes the title, subtitle, any statement of responsibility, and publishing information. It is called the *title page* and is used by libraries to provide the information recorded in library catalogs. (See figure 3.1, page 32.)

The title is usually followed by a *statement of responsibility*. This statement may be the "author" of a work, that is, the person or persons responsible for the intellectual content of the book. It may be an organization, such as the ALA, which has issued the work. Any persons who have contributed significantly to the book are also usually mentioned on the title page. Persons such as editors, translators, illustrators, and writers of introductions may also be listed. (E.g., in figure 3.1 Bohdan S. Wynar is the original author and Arlene G. Taylor is the editor of the 1992 eighth edition.) The last information on the title page usually consists of the publishing information. This information includes the major cities in which the publishing company is located and the name of the publishing company. It may also include the publication date of the book. These three items may be referred to collectively as the *imprint*. An edition statement may also be printed on the title page to indicate that a book is an edition other than the first.

The verso of the title page lists important bibliographic information for libraries, including the publishing and copyright history of the book. A *copyright*, indicated by the symbol © followed by the year, is a legal right to exclusive ownership given by a government to a person or organization for a particular period of time. When the content of a work is changed, it is considered to be a new edition. Each different edition of a work will have a separate copyright date. Thus, "Copyright © 1992, 1985, 1980, 1976, 1972, 1971, 1967, 1966, 1964" in figure 3.1 would indicate that nine editions of the work have been published and copyrighted.

The publisher might also indicate the number of times a book has been reprinted from the same plates or type, such as "Seventh Printing." However, librarians are more interested in the copyright date than the printing or publishing date because the copyright date indicates how current the information is. For example, a book listed as the "Seventh printing, 1991" may have a copyright date of 1971. In addition to the publishing date, other information about the publishing history might also be given here, such as any former titles or any other editions that have been published. In figure 3.1, for example, a new copyright holder, Arlene G. Taylor, was added to the 1992 edition.

Several items of principal interest to librarians are often printed on this verso page. The Library of Congress Catalog Number (e.g., 91-24851) is used by libraries to locate Library of Congress cataloging. An ISBN (International Standard Book Number) is also included on books published after 1972 and is used by libraries and publishers for ordering books. An ISBN (e.g., 0-87287-811-2 [cloth] and 0-87287-967-4 [paper] in figure 3.1) is a distinctive number identifying each particular edition of a title by a publisher. Many American books also include Library of Congress Cataloging-in-Publication (CIP) data that libraries may use to catalog their books. Librarians are also concerned with describing the unique physical characteristics of the book. These characteristics include the number of pages (e.g., xvii and 633), whether or not the book is illustrated (e.g., none in this example), and the size of the book (e.g., 17x25 cm.). All of this information is recorded on the library catalog record.

The title page or its verso may also indicate that a book belongs to a *series*. A series (e.g., Library science text series in figure 3.1) is the collective title given to a group of separate books or volumes related to one another by subject or purpose

Fig. 3.1. Book title page and verso. (Reprinted by permission.)

LIBRARIES UNLIMITED, INC.
P.O. Box 6633
Englewood, CO 80155-6633

Library of Congress Cataloging-in-Publication Data

Taylor, Arlene G., 1941-
  Introduction to cataloging and classification / Bohdan S. Wynar.
- 8th ed. / by Arlene G. Taylor.
  xvii, 633p. 17x25 cm. -- (Library science text series)
  Includes bibliographical references and index.
  ISBN 0-87287-811-2 (cloth) -- ISBN 0-87287-967-4 (paper)
  1. Cataloging. 2. Classification--Books. 3. Anglo-American cataloguing rules. I. Wynar, Bohdan S. Introduction to cataloging and classification. II. Title. III. Series.
Z693.W94 1991
025.3--dc20   91-24851
                                                                  CIP

BOHDAN S. WYNAR

INTRODUCTION TO CATALOGING AND CLASSIFICATION

eighth edition

ARLENE G. TAYLOR

1992
LIBRARIES UNLIMITED, INC.
Englewood, Colorado

and is the last item included in the bibliographic description. Series may also be published in a uniform format with similar bindings and may be numbered in succession. Each book in the series is a complete monograph and should not be confused with a serial (see below). The publisher determines what books will be published in a series; the series title is then usually included on the half-title page, title page, or cover of the book. A list of the books in a series may also be printed in each book of the series.

The introductory materials, or front matter, following the title includes the table of contents and may include a *preface* or the author's statement of the purpose for writing the book. A *table of contents* is a listing of the chapters or sections of the book in the order in which they appear in the text. Other materials may include an acknowledgments page and an introduction. The introductory material that follows the title page and precedes the first page of the actual text may be numbered in small roman numerals at the bottom of the pages. This numbering distinguishes the pages of introductory material from the major content of the book. Literary works often have introductory sections that can run 40 to 50 pages. The front matter is followed by the body of the text that is numbered in arabic numbers. The text may be followed by *appendixes* (or appendices), which are supplementary material. Common appendixes include *glossaries* (definitions of the terms used in a book), *bibliographies* (lists of resources on the subjects discussed in the book), and an *index*. An index is an alphabetical listing of the subjects or items in the book and the page numbers on which they will be found.

Serials

The term *serial* refers to publications issued in parts at regular intervals for an indefinite period of time. When a person first hears the term *serial*, a TV program or story "to be continued" may come to mind, but in the library world, *serial* is used as a generic term. It includes magazines or periodicals (these are synonymous terms), journals, newspapers, annuals, and any publication meant to be published on a continuing basis. The major types of serials are important in libraries because they provide current information on many subjects. Magazines and newspapers contain current or topical information that may not appear in book form for several years, if at all. They also contain short-term information that is of interest this week or month but which may not be needed next year. For this reason, libraries will have varying policies concerning the serials they will buy and retain in their collections. For example, some serials may be kept forever while others might be thrown out at the end of the year. Or some serials might be kept in print format while others might be kept in microform or accessed through computerized databases (see page 46).

The most common serial is a *magazine* or *periodical*, as it is referred to in most libraries. In fact, a definition of a periodical and a serial are the same (although not all serials are periodicals). A periodical is issued in parts, which means that it is published or issued at regular intervals, and each issue or part is meant to be read as it is published. Periodicals contain articles written on general subjects by several contributors and are usually written for the layperson. If the periodical contains in-depth articles on subjects of interest to scholars or subject specialists, it may be called a *journal*, such as *Library Journal* and *The Journal of*

Economics. Journals are often published by institutions, associations, or learned societies and may also contain current news and reports of their activities and work in a particular field.

Periodicals may be issued at regular intervals—weekly, monthly, quarterly, semiweekly, biweekly, bimonthly, etc. Each issue is usually dated or numbered (or both) and one complete year of a periodical's issues is called a *volume*. Often the pages of each volume are numbered consecutively so that a January issue might start on page 1 and a December issue start on page 1098. Almost every periodical begins publication with a volume 1. However, because the first issue of a periodical may have been published at any time of the year, its volume may begin in January, February, June, or October. Periodicals issued on a quarterly basis may be identified by month (January, April, July, and October) or by season (winter, spring, summer, and fall). Some periodicals may not publish issues in the summer months so that a monthly periodical may appear to have gaps in its issues.

As if this variety were not confusing enough, periodicals often change their names or publication frequencies without any warning to subscribers. Sometimes publishers will spin off new publications from established magazines, such as *People* magazine from *Time* and *Weekly Record* from *Publishers Weekly*. Some periodicals that ceased publication may be revived as new publications, such as *The Saturday Evening Post*. This magazine was originally published as a weekly, stopped publication, was revived as a quarterly, and in 1990 was published nine times a year. This variety in serial publication requires libraries to devote many staff hours to make sure that each issue of every serial has been received.

Newspapers are serials that report current events and discuss topics of current public interest. They are most often published daily, but some newspapers are published weekly or even less frequently. Newspapers are excellent sources of local information. Libraries will usually subscribe to national, state, and local newspapers to provide well-rounded coverage of current events.

Indexes are special kinds of serials that provide access to the information found in many of these periodicals and newspapers. Indexes usually provide author, title, and/or subject access to the articles found in specific periodicals during a specific period of time. They may cover general periodicals, as the *Readers' Guide to Periodical Literature* does, or they may cover specific subjects, as the *Applied Science and Technology Index* does. Indexes also may cover newspapers rather than periodicals. *Abstracting services* are similar to indexes, but they also provide brief summaries of the articles or information they index. These services usually cover international publications in specialized subject areas as *Chemical Abstracts* and *Biological Abstracts* do. The characteristics of these indexing and abstracting services have made them so well-suited for adaptation from print form to computer-based form that they may cease to exist in print form by the end of the century.

Government Documents

Government documents are not a separate form of print media, but they are often treated separately in libraries. A *government document* is a generic term for any publication issued or published at the expense of a governmental agency. Thus, there are local, state, federal, and international government documents.

Government documents can include all types of media, including books, pamphlets, serials, maps, tapes, and databases, and they are often concerned with many subject areas, not just government or politics. The terms *government document* and *government document collection* are most often used in the United States to refer to U.S. federal documents. Most federal documents are printed by the official government printer, the U.S. Government Printing Office (GPO), and many of them are distributed by the administrator or the Superintendent of Documents (SuDOC) or by the federally funded National Technical Information Service (NTIS). Some libraries receive these documents free as part of a national depository collection program. They house these documents in separate collections arranged according to a SuDOC classification system based upon the issuing agency. Libraries like to include government documents from all levels of government in their collections because they are generally objective and reliable sources of information. They also provide current information in useful subject areas at very reasonable prices.

Other Print Resources

Other important kinds of print media can be found in libraries. The pamphlet file or vertical file contains much timely information that has not been published in book form. Most of the information is contained in *pamphlets*, which are usually paper-covered publications of 48 or fewer pages (one to three signatures). Pamphlets provide fleeting information that fills a library's temporary need. Libraries include them in their collections because they provide information that is often not available in any other form. Also, they are often available either free or very inexpensively. Some typical pamphlets are company annual reports, tourist and travel brochures, and bulletins from companies and government agencies. Some agencies even publish series of pamphlets on particular subjects of interest to them. However, libraries must evaluate pamphlets to be sure that the bias of the issuing agency or company has not influenced the pamphlet's content. Libraries must also consider the publishing or copyright date of the material and remove pamphlets that have become outdated or have been superseded.

Among other forms of print materials are technical reports. These may be particularly important in special or academic library collections because they report the progress and current status of scientific research and development. In fact, information published in technical reports may never be published in other print form. Some libraries also develop large clipping files of articles relating to local topics or to specific subject areas. Articles usually are clipped from periodicals or newspapers, arranged by subject in envelopes, and kept in the pamphlet files. They are used extensively in newspaper and historical collection libraries.

MICROFORM RESOURCES

Microform is a generic term used to designate materials that contain micro or small images of printed or graphic material. The most common microforms are produced either on rolls or sheets of film. Rolls of 35mm or 70mm film are called *microfilm*. They contain micro-photo images of pages that have been reduced up to one-twentieth their original size. Many magazines and newspapers are filmed on microfilm because one microfilm roll can usually contain one year's issues of a monthly magazine or six months' issues of a weekly magazine such as *Time* or *Newsweek*. Libraries often purchase microfilm to replace their paper copies because they not only conserve library space, but also prevent theft of magazine issues. Microfilm users view the microfilm on readers that project magnified images onto a small screen equal to or larger than their original size. Reader-printers can print the screen image onto a piece of 8½- × 11-inch paper. Although libraries may purchase either negative or positive microfilm, many libraries prefer negative film because the screen image of white letters on black will print out as black letters on white.

Another common microform is *microfiche*, which was named after the French word for file card. Microfiche are sheets of 3- × 5-inch or 4- × 6-inch film, each containing from 60 to 100 images or pages of material. They usually contain the complete text of a report, a pamphlet, or a single issue of a periodical. Microfiche require their own reader or reader-printer equipment or attachments. They were originally very popular in libraries such as special libraries which needed to store large numbers of technical reports or which needed quick access to individual copies of magazines. However, the fact that they could be easily misfiled or misplaced often hindered their usefulness. In addition, the chemicals used in all microforms sometimes released gases that interacted with their storage boxes and cabinets and ended up damaging the microforms themselves. To resolve these problems, libraries often turned to newer media such as videodiscs and CD-ROM products (see page 47) that eliminated these concerns.

GRAPHIC RESOURCES

In addition to print media, libraries have found that various forms of graphic or visual media are needed to support their collections of printed resources and to fulfill their objectives. Pictures, graphs, maps, dioramas, and sculptures are a few of the items included in libraries to support their education and research objectives as well as their cultural or aesthetic appreciation objective. In choosing these materials, the library staff should be sure that the information is authentic and that the graphic reproductions are of excellent quality. Also, because these materials may come in varying sizes and shapes, they are usually given special handling and may be kept in special shelving facilities.

Two-dimensional graphic representations may include such forms as paintings, drawings, charts, diagrams, graphs, photographs, and posters. They are used by persons such as artists, historians, sociologists, and theater arts people as well as by teachers and students. Drawings and photographs are particularly useful because one picture can be used by several people for very different purposes. For example, a picture of Pilgrims at Thanksgiving can be used for a social studies class as well as for costume designs. These materials are often mounted and included in *picture files* or *pamphlet files*. Some libraries may provide pictures solely because they fulfill their aesthetic appreciation objective. These libraries may provide art print reproductions that patrons may borrow to hang on the walls of their homes.

Another two-dimensional graphic form found in libraries is maps. These are flat representations of the earth, the sky, or a celestial body. Library collections usually include physical maps showing governmental boundaries of states and countries. They may also include thematic or special purpose maps that depict population, vegetation, or historical developments. Detailed maps of the moon and the universe are also published.

Maps are very important in geographic and geological libraries as well as in highway, engineering, historical, and other library collections. They may be kept in a library's pamphlet file, or if a library has many maps, they may be kept as a separate collection in special map cases. Two important items on a map will determine its uses. The scale, or legend, indicates how many miles are represented by one inch of the map. If the scale is not printed on the map, it must be determined and added. Second, the copyright date will indicate how current the information on the map really is. Maps can be obtained from many different sources. Gasoline companies and state governments provide some of the best maps available for individual states or countries. The U.S. Geological Survey, a federal government agency, publishes excellent maps including individual quadrangle maps. These quadrangle maps have divided every mile of the United States into 15- to 17-square-mile areas. They are so detailed that they even show individual houses in rural areas. This detail, currency, and variety makes maps important in library collections.

Three-dimensional or spherical maps are called *globes*. As with maps, globes may be physical, political, or topical; they may also represent the earth's surface or the surface of another celestial body. Many globes may be *relief* globes, which means that the physical features such as mountains are raised on the surface of the globe. The copyright date of a globe is just as important as it is for a map. Too many times, libraries buy a globe and keep it forever, forgetting that political boundaries and even the names of nations have often changed.

Libraries may also include many other types of three-dimensional objects. *Models* and *mock-ups* such as those of a volcano or Shakespeare's Globe Theater may be included. *Dioramas* are three-dimensional scenes that use figures and a background to create an illusion of reality. They may represent such scenes as early American Indian life, prehistoric life, or historical battles. *Displays* and *exhibits* may feature special subjects such as literary authors and their works.

Realia, or real objects, have become very important in some libraries. Sculpture itself is included in many library collections. Both original sculpture (perhaps from a local artist) and low-cost reproductions are often checked out to patrons for use in their homes or to teachers to supplement a class unit. Some library collections may include items such as coins, stamps, or fabric samples. Others might include specimens or live exhibits of insects and animals. Glass slides of laboratory specimens or tissue cultures may be important in scientific and medical collections. In recent years, libraries have also added educational and developmental realia such as games, puzzles, and toys. Games such as Scrabble® and Monopoly® can be used as educational tools by children to help them learn to think, spell, and count. Puzzles and toys can help children develop their gross and fine-motor skills. Sometimes graphic media may be combined with print and audio or visual media to form instructional packages which include realia, books or pamphlets, pictures, and videotapes. If these packages include two or more different media, they may be called *kits*.

Library collections may also include objects such as travel smoke detectors, telephones, microscopes, or calculators that patrons can use in many different ways. Libraries may even provide pets that children may check out and take home for several days or weeks. (Usually pet-care instructions and literature are also included.) Some public libraries have provided garden and home-care tools in areas where no rental businesses are available. Finally, the most common realia of all has become audiovisual equipment such as projectors, cameras, recorders, players, typewriters, computers, and printers. This equipment enables patrons to use the various kinds of audiovisual resource materials available.

AUDIOVISUAL RESOURCES

The term *audiovisual* (AV) has been used by libraries to identify audio and visual materials that need to be played on some type of equipment for them to be heard or seen. The types of audiovisual media included in libraries have changed over the years as technology has changed. By the 1970s, library collections included such audio or visual media as records, tapes, films, and filmstrips. As the quality and accessibility of these formats was surpassed by technology, however, many libraries replaced them with more available and commercially successful media such as videotapes and CDs (audio compact discs). As future media such as high-resolution or quality digital audiotapes (DAT), videodiscs, and interactive video or interactive CDs become more popular and accessible in the 1990s, they will probably also be added to many library collections.

Whenever a library adds any audiovisual material or resource to its collection, it must consider the one important characteristic that distinguishes this type of media from print or graphic media. This major characteristic requires that an audiovisual material be used on a machine or piece of equipment. Moreover, each variation of audiovisual material usually must be used on its own distinctive piece of equipment. For example, when both Beta and VHS videotapes were available, a library needed both Beta videotape players and VHS videotape players. (For this reason, by the late 1980s many libraries had limited their collections to the more popular VHS videotapes.) Libraries must carefully evaluate each new media format to be sure they can provide the necessary supporting equipment before adding any such format to their collections.

When adding each media form to a library's collection, it is also important to correctly identify each media item to distinguish it from the same title in other media formats. It is not uncommon for a library to have a book, audiotape, CD, and videotape of the same work, such as *Hamlet*. Cataloging rules have been established that distinguish among these various formats by providing a descriptor or *general material designation*. This designation follows the title on a cataloging record and is a term that describes the broad class of media to which an item belongs (e.g., microform or videorecording). The physical description of the item will usually indicate its characteristics so that the correct type of equipment can be selected.

Audio Resources

Several of the first audiovisual media found in libraries were records and audiotapes. Records were phonorecordings of music, poetry, and drama on plastic discs that were identified by their playback speeds of 33⅓, 78, 45, or 16 RPM (revolutions per minute). Their audio quality or "definition" was far superior to audiotapes that were sound recordings on magnetic tape. Audiotapes originally needed bulky tape recorders to wind the tape from one reel onto another. However, improvements in technology enabled the tapes to be wound on smaller reels and encased in plastic cases or *cassettes* that could be inserted into very small and portable tape recorders. These audiocassettes were often pre-recorded in various time lengths from 15 to 120 minutes per tape. They were welcomed by libraries because they were not only easy for patrons to use, but they were also less easy to erase or damage than either reel-to-reel tapes or records. Libraries also appreciated the great variety of audiocassette tapes from recorded music of all types to dramatic readings (Books on Tape) of plays, novels, and poems. Library patrons particularly appreciated listening to Books on Tape while they were performing other activities such as commuting or jogging. Because many library patrons also preferred the convenience of audiocassette tapes over the superior audio quality of records, libraries in the 1980s often provided both formats.

The problem of audio quality of cassette tapes was resolved when audio CDs or *compact discs* were introduced in 1983. These CDs used optical technology generated by a laser to record data on a plastic disc about 4.75 inches in diameter. This data was stored in tracks on the CD in a coded form which was retrieved when the CD was inserted into a CD player. The CD player shined a laser beam onto the disc to "read" or decode the encoded data. The original CDs were only used to record audio or sound, and one individual CD could hold up to 75 minutes of recorded sound. CDs have gained great popularity since their introduction in 1983 because their reproductive quality is so much better than that of records or audiocassettes. Their encoding capability eliminates background noises or distortions, and the long life of the laser in a CD player cannot wear out or scratch the CD itself. This encoding capability also enables CDs to be accessed easily by computer technology. By 1985, CD-ROM products (see page 47) had expanded the capabilities of this medium.

Film Resources

Other common types of audiovisual materials included in library collections are slides and films. Slides are made from pieces of film or transparent material encased in 2- × 2-inch cardboard envelopes. These envelopes slide into a tray or cartridge on a projector for projection onto a screen. They are used by themselves or with accompanying audiotapes or CDs and have been important in art, architecture, history, and social science collections. In the past, slides were such an important medium in some libraries that they were sometimes stored in separate library collections where individual slides were cataloged and filed in large slide cabinets. Smaller libraries and media centers generally cataloged slides together in sets and stored them in ready-to-use projector trays. However, libraries found problems with these slide collections. Slides became more fragile as they aged, and libraries needed better access to them. Libraries began to use newer technological developments in the early 1990s to transfer slides to more permanent and accessible media such as videodiscs (see page 41).

By the 1990s, motion picture films had also been replaced in libraries by videotapes and videodiscs. Motion picture films of many different sizes and shapes had previously been found in many public, academic, and school libraries. They were identified according to the width of the film in millimeters (e.g., 35mm, 16mm, or 8mm), whether they were sound or silent, and whether they were color or black and white. Films expanded a library's collection by providing feature-length films, educational films, "short subjects" on popular subjects, and children's stories. Their advantage was that they could be projected on large screens for large audiences to view at one time. However, video technology soon outstripped film technology and large-screen video projection equipment improved in quality. Libraries found it cheaper and easier to purchase and store video media instead of film media.

Filmstrips were rolled strips of 35mm film that contained 40 to 65 frames or images. They were very popular in libraries before video technology was available. Public libraries found that children enjoyed using filmstrip/audiocassette kits of popular children's picture books. School media centers appreciated the filmstrip's ability to present visual images of short topics. However, as with motion pictures, video technology's ability to combine interactive still images and text and accompany them with sound brought about the decline in library collections of filmstrips and other film media such as 8mm filmloops.

Video Resources

Various forms of video media were available in the 1970s. However, it was not until the 1980s when they were standardized and their costs were reduced that they were commonly included in library collections. The almost universally accepted standard for a nonstudio videotape is a ½-inch videotape magnetically recorded in a VHS format and encased in a plastic "cassette" or box. To view these videotapes, a user inserts the videotape into a VCR (videocassette recorder) attached to a television screen by a cable. VCRs and videotapes have become very popular because of their reasonable cost and because any company's VHS tape can be used on equipment meeting this VHS standard. (This contrasts with the earlier Beta videotapes which could only be used on Sony Corporation equipment.) Videotapes also are popular because they can be either rented or purchased as prerecorded feature films, children's films, musical performances, self-improvement and educational tapes, etc. In addition, blank tapes can be used to record television programs for viewing at a later time. They can also be used in *camcorders* or videotape cameras to record home videotapes. All of these capabilities have made the videotape medium so popular that VCRs could be found in almost 75 percent of U.S. homes by the 1990s.

Other contributing factors to the videotape's popularity are its accessibility, variety, and economical cost for renting or purchasing. Not only are videotapes available in video rental outlets (a marketing phenomenon of the 1980s), but libraries also loan or rent videotapes to help meet the consumer demand. Libraries have found that circulation of their audiovisual materials can sometimes be 15 percent of their total circulation and that the cost per circulation of a videotape can be less than the cost per circulation for other media. Libraries have also found that patrons appreciate the videotape's capability to present integrated video and audio programs of motion picture features and specialized information such as home repairs, cooking classes, travelogs, and dramatic presentations. This capacity not only supplements a library's print collections in these areas, but it also allows library patrons to access such information without regard to its format.

Videodiscs or *laserdiscs* also allow patrons to access information in a new and different way. This second major form of video media was introduced in the late 1980s. By the year 2000, videodiscs may have a revolutionary impact on library collections similar to that of CDs. Videodiscs are similar to audio CDs and may become the most common form of this optical technology. Videodiscs use laser beams to record visual and audio data on separate tracks on a plastic disc from 3 to 14 inches in diameter. They are played back on a disc reader hooked up by cable to a television or computer screen. The disc reader shines a laser onto the disc and the image is projected onto the screen. A videodisc can store up to 54,000 pictures or images as well as text or data and audio accompaniment. Videodiscs are considered to be superior to videotapes in the areas of image, sound quality, and durability. Although videodiscs were originally expected to be the replacement medium for 35mm and 16mm films because of these characteristics, they had not reached mass appeal in the early 1990s because of their cost, complexity, performance limitations, and large size. Instead, their usefulness and success as a viable medium probably will come from their random-access retrieval capability. This characteristic enables computers to access information stored on the various tracks of a laser disc. The laser disc can then be combined with computers and compact discs in "interactive video" or interactive computer technology.

COMPUTER RESOURCES

Library resources and services have been transformed in the last quarter of the twentieth century by technological developments in the electronic and telecommunications fields. These technological developments have enabled libraries to develop automated library systems and services and to expand their resources beyond the wildest imagination of librarians in the 1950s and 1960s. Libraries of all sizes and types have been transformed by advancements that only seemed feasible for large libraries a decade ago. This has been due to the phenomenal growth and development in the computer and electronic fields that has made it possible to process information at an extremely high speed for an affordable price. Libraries have quickly recognized that "the driving force of this technology was its power to generate types of information which heretofore had been unthinkable, store information in small spaces, retrieve and manipulate it with dazzling speed, and transmit it to a distant location within seconds."[1]

Librarians have used these computer capabilities to automate almost every library operation to provide better accuracy, access, and service for their patrons. By 1990, the typical single-function automated circulation or cataloging system of the 1970s had developed into an integrated circulation, cataloging, reference, acquisitions, serials control, and management system. In addition, telecommunication advancements had enabled libraries to join together in cooperative networks to share the cost of developing and operating these automated systems.

Thus, the challenge of automation in libraries for the 1990s is not changing to new technologies but incorporating them into a mosaic of old and new.

Computer Technology

To understand the advantages the computer has brought to library operations, it is important to understand how the computer works. Although many people often talk about the computer as if it were a human being capable of thinking on its own, a computer is only a machine, although a very complex and sophisticated one. It is made up of electronic components that operate on the principle of an electronic impulse's being either "on" or "off" as an electric light is either on or off. Computer technology has developed this simple principle to such an advanced state that millions of electronic impulses called *bits* and *bytes* can be manipulated to represent characters or numbers and letters (as in Morse code) at an unbelievable speed. The computer can also take in and store instructions so that, by switching its electronic impulses on or off, it can move, compare, and relate characters; make simple yes-no decisions; and add characters. Although the computer cannot actually think, it can be programmed to follow complicated logical processes (sometimes called artificial intelligence or expert systems) that are similar to human thought processes.

When a person is first introduced into the world of computers, the language spoken by the "computer people" can seem to be a foreign language. Terms such as *online*, *database*, *floppy disk*, and *modem* can be confusing. The majority of computer terms refer to the machine known as the computer. Actually, the computer is seldom one machine but requires a group of machines or *hardware* to perform integrated functions or computer operations. The three basic elements of a computer are (1) the memory device, sometimes called a CPU (central processing unit); (2) an input device, such as a typewriter keyboard, *mouse*, or a laser light wand or pen; and (3) an output device called a *terminal* or *monitor* that looks like a TV screen. (See figure 3.2.) Information stored in the computer's memory and accessible to users is called the *database*, and instructions to the computer are called the *software* or *programs*.

The original computers consisted of many pieces of large equipment that could fill an entire room. These *mainframe* computers were housed in specially air conditioned rooms and required automation staffs to operate them. Their large capacity enabled them to support many operations at one time and connect many users directly to the computer (online). However, their high costs often forced libraries to join together in networks to be able to afford access to them. Because of their cost, mainframe computers in libraries were largely superseded when "minicomputers" were introduced in 1971. These minicomputers were based on the development of silicon-chip technology that placed all the essential elements of a mainframe computer CPU onto a single tiny square of silicon the size of a fingertip. This capability reduced the computer to a single piece of equipment (about the size of two to three filing cabinets) that could support multiple users and operations without needing special rooms or staff. Further developments of this silicon technology resulted in the development in the 1980s of *microcomputers* or desktop-size *personal computers* (PCs). Although these microcomputers could only be used by one person at a time, their ability to

perform many different functions and their significantly lower costs contributed to their rapid inclusion in libraries.

An important characteristic of the microcomputer was its ability to store instructions or software programs and data on computer disks. These disks were usually 3½-inch square hard plastic disks or 5¼-inch square "floppy" disks encased in plastic jackets. Each disk could hold 50,000 (50K) characters or letters. These disks were inserted into computer *drives* that scanned the data on the disk and transferred it to the computer's internal drive or desktop memory unit. As technology advanced, users began to need greater storage capacity than could be stored on one disk. Soon, floppy computer disks were supplemented by large storage capacity external *hard drives* (Winchesters), which could hold up to 300 million characters (300 megabytes).

In the early days of automation, software instruction programs had to be written by individual *programmers* or *systems analysts* who were specially trained to develop or "write" encoded instruction programs that would interact with the computer. These instruction programs had to be meticulously written. If they were confusing or provided incorrect characters, the electronic components in the computer could not process the instruction or compare the characters correctly. This need for accuracy contributed to the development of a new computer discipline known variously as *data processing*, *automated data processing* (ADP), or *electronic data processing* (EDP). This discipline was soon joined by the development of a new information science as computers and computer technology became more sophisticated and complex.

As these sophisticated microcomputers became readily available on the general market, several characteristics contributed to their popularity and acceptance by the general public. The first characteristic was the introduction of reasonably priced but very powerful microcomputer hardware in the 1980s. Customers were willing to buy these affordable personal computers so they could become computer literate. The second characteristic was the growth in commercial software programs that could be easily installed and used on a computer by anyone with minimal computer training.

These newer software programs included instructions or *documentation* written in everyday language that the layperson could understand. Many of these commercially prepared software programs also used the computer capabilities called *Boolean searching* or *hypertext capabilities*. These capabilities allowed a user to combine or exclude a variety of terms to limit or expand a search of the database. Once software programs were loaded into the computer, they could be accessed by typing in a command or an entry such as an author, title, subject, keyword, etc. Programs also could be accessed by selecting a choice from a *menu* or list of choices or paths of action. If these commercially developed software programs had on-screen instructions that included clear directions and avoided "computerese," they were considered to be "user friendly."

A third important characteristic of these computers was that they could be connected to other computers or other types of equipment. Thus, microcomputers could be attached to many "peripherals" such as television sets, printers, compact disc and videodisc players, and telephone lines to enhance their capabilities. This characteristic enabled a user not only to access databases in other computers, but it also contributed to the development of additional technologies such as CD-ROM (see page 47). Librarians in the 1980s and 1990s were quick to take advantage of these computer capabilities to develop automated library operations and systems they had only dreamed of in the 1960s.

Automated Library Systems

With the rapid advancements in computer technology that have taken place about every five to seven years, it is often impossible for the layperson to comprehend the computer's capacity for storing information and the speed with which a computer can process this information. Laypersons can, however, recognize that these capabilities can be used to perform calculations, routines, and procedures that would be arduous or even impossible to perform in any other way. Librarians have long recognized that these capabilities are ideally suited for manipulating library characters and records. They have found that computers can effectively use the standardized information on a bibliographic record to add information to individual item records, make deletions, and manipulate them in a variety of ways. In fact, the principal characteristics of computers in library data processing have been their high speed in information processing, flexibility of processing, absolute accuracy, and the compatibility of different forms of output from the same computer record.

In spite of this, the computer's first contribution to library operations may not have been the actual automating of library processes but the introduction of "systems thinking" into libraries. Librarians in the 1970s and 1980s were forced to look at each operation in terms of the basic objective it was to fulfill. Once this was determined, librarians were able to work with computer systems analysts to develop the best process to achieve this objective. This rethinking process enabled librarians to refine their operations and eliminate unnecessary procedures and steps. It also helped librarians recognize that they had procedures in common with other libraries that could be automated on a cooperative basis. This realization freed librarians from reinventing the wheel by developing their own systems. It allowed them to look for and purchase packaged or *turnkey* (ready for use) automated library systems.

Advances in computer technology also enabled librarians in the 1990s to view library automation differently than librarians had in prior years. For the first time, automated technology was available at a reasonable price so that libraries of all sizes could fully use the computer's capability to design and install integrated library systems. These systems were based upon a database of computerized records for every item in the library. If a library wanted to purchase an item, it could enter an initial bibliographic record for that item (e.g., author, title, edition, ISBN) into the computer. The computer could compare this record with the records already in the database and generate an order to a vendor if the library did not already own the item. When the item was received, the library could catalog it and add this information to the item record already in the database.

This database could then be used as a library's online public access catalog (OPAC). It could also be used as the basis for the library's circulation system because the location and status of every item in the library would be indicated on each record in the database. When an item was charged out to a borrower, that person's identification number and the date due information would be added to this record. A library could query the computer records to determine where an item was and when it was due back in the library if it were checked out. Libraries can also use this database information to place holds or reserves on items. When items are returned, the computer can identify those that should be held for other patrons. In addition, the computer can be programmed to generate notices such as reserve notices, recall notices, overdue notices, and bills.

Computer systems also include borrower information such as that maintained by parent institutions such as universities or corporations. By combining their borrower records with the bibliographic database, libraries can identify any materials a borrower has checked. They can also determine whether a borrower has any overdue materials or other library obligations. This combination of bibliographic and borrower information can also be used to generate statistics unavailable from manual systems. The computer's ability to store information enables libraries to retrieve statistics that answer questions such as, "How many times has an item circulated in a certain time period?," "Which classification categories are most used?," and "What type of borrower uses particular types of library materials?" Libraries can use these statistics not only to help them develop their collections but also to develop management and financial programs to enable them to better administer their libraries.

Online Databases

No overview of computer resources would be complete without describing the bibliographic and subject databases that are accessible to libraries "online" via telecommunication connections. Libraries access these databases by paying subscription fees to the database producers and telephone charges for the online connect time. The first of these databases were bibliographic cataloging databases developed cooperatively by member libraries in such states as Ohio (OCLC Online Computer Library Center) and Washington (WLN). These databases enabled libraries to locate cataloging information, add their own local information to them, and receive individualized catalog records for their libraries' files.

The second databases were subject databases developed by commercial and governmental agencies. These databases enabled libraries to search large bodies of literature in almost every subject area in a very short span of time. Most of these subject databases were developed as by-products of commercial or governmental indexing and abstracting services that had converted their bibliographic records to machine-readable form. Familiar services such as *Education Index* and *Chemical Abstracts*, as well as many others, could be purchased in either print or machine-readable form. However, it was not the form or format of the databases that interested libraries, but the rapid access these databases provided to the information contained in them.

Online subject databases provide information in practically every subject area: scientific, technical, medical, social sciences, or humanities. These databases offer comprehensive subject access to information contained in such materials as magazines, governmental and technical reports, doctoral dissertations, newspapers, books, and even footnote citations in other articles. The information they provide may range from a short bibliographic entry, to an entry with subject headings or descriptors, to an entry that includes a detailed abstract or summary, to a full-text article. Some databases even enable libraries to request copies of a desired text from another source using telefacsimile transmissions or document delivery. These databases have become so popular in providing access to information that by 1990 almost 4,000 international databases were available through 600 online services.

Because of the variety of databases offered by so many different companies, libraries usually gain access to them by purchasing computer time from commercial information processing centers. Two of the first major information processing centers were the National Library of Medicine (NLM) and Lockheed Corporation. NLM's MEDLINE was a single-subject database for comprehensive medical information. Lockheed's DIALOG combined many scientific and technical databases into one database for easier access by libraries. These centers and others, such as Systems Dynamic Corporation (SDC) and Bibliographic Retrieval Services (BRS), provide access to over 125 databases including more than 25 social science-related subjects, 60 to 70 life-science databases, and even databases for AV materials.

The variety and scope of these databases can be seen in the tremendous growth in agricultural and biological databases. A few examples from the field of agriculture include AGRICOLA and AGRIBUSINESS from the U.S. Department of Agriculture as well as databases for "Foods Adlibra" (raw foods into groceries), "Coffeeline," "Aquatic Sciences and Fisheries Abstracts" (ASFA), "Selected Water Resources Abstracts," and "Agrochemicals Handbook."

However, libraries found there could be a drawback to using such a large variety of databases because each database usually had its own distinct software operating instructions. Purchasing computer time from information centers to access these databases could also be rather costly. Libraries often joined networks to share the communications costs or take advantage of network discounts. In addition, further technological developments in optical disc technology by the end of the 1980s had provided enough cost differential so that many databases were made available on CD-ROM.

CD-ROM Technology

CD-ROM (**C**ompact **D**isc **R**ead **O**nly **M**emory) combined the audio CD's capacity for storing large amounts of information in very small spaces with the computer's capacity to rapidly access such information. To take advantage of these capabilities, manufacturers modified audio CD players and connected them to computers so that a computer could operate the CD player. (See figure 3.3.) This new CD-ROM player used CD-ROM discs that could store up to 260,000 pages of text or 75 minutes of music or video. In computer terms, this represented about 660 megabytes of information that would otherwise need a floppy disk 800 feet across to store the same data.[2] Sometimes access was needed to larger databases stored on multiple CD-ROM discs. Such access was provided by linking or

Fig. 3.3. CD-ROM equipment. (Reprinted with permission of Information Access.)

"daisy-chaining" several players by cable to each other and the computer. Although the speed for accessing this CD-ROM data was not as rapid as if it were online, it was much faster than manual or microform access.

Librarians were quick to take advantage of this new medium format when Library Corporation introduced Bibliofile, the first bibliographic CD-ROM database, in 1985. This system stored Library of Congress (LC) or MARC (MAchine Readable Cataloging) records (see page 132) on four CD-ROM discs. These discs could be easily updated and used by librarians to locate cataloging data for their own materials. Librarians liked having so much information accessible in such small spaces in a permanent form that could not be accidentally erased. The capabilities of CD-ROM were quickly enhanced by the rapid development of national standards for manufacturing CD-ROM software and hardware. Contrary to problems that occurred in the videotape industry, the CD-ROM industry's acceptance of these national standards contributed to the rapid expansion of CD-ROM products in libraries. This acceptance was so universal that by 1989 over 300 CD-ROM titles were available in many subjects and fields.

The explosion of CD-ROM products in libraries has come from a multitude of publishers and sources. Many CD-ROM titles, such as *Books in Print Plus* (Bowker), *Wilsonline*, or *EBSCO Serials Directory*, are by-products from the publishers' online databases. Some titles have been published as CD-ROM versions or editions of other products, such as the *American Heritage Dictionary*, *Federal Register*, or *AV Online*. Thus, librarians might have to choose which version to purchase, or they might be required by CD-ROM licensing agreements to maintain the original version to receive the CD-ROM version. Many new CD-ROM titles and products have been developed, particularly in the fields of government and business, that would not have been possible without the capability of CD-ROM technology. The growth of CD-ROM indexes has been particularly welcomed by librarians because the CD-ROM ability to interfile current data with earlier data on an updated disc reduces the need for multiple searches of back-issue indexes. This updating capability has also been used by libraries to develop and update their own CD-ROM catalogs for use either as a public library catalog, a backup to an online catalog, or as a network database.

Libraries were quick to take advantage of these CD-ROM capabilities. Although the cost of CD-ROM products could be 50-100 percent more than the corresponding print version, their ease of accessibility and indexing was far superior to print products. The cost-per-use of CD-ROM searching was more than the cost of an online search, but these CD-ROM costs would decrease with use of the system rather than increase as online costs would do. Sometimes librarians might combine the best features of both of these methods and use a CD-ROM system first to locate a citation and then use an online full-text database to retrieve the actual article. A library might also use CD-ROM for older or retrospective searches and online databases for current information searches. However, some people have predicted that online database bibliographies may be replaced entirely by optical disc technology by the end of the 1990s. As CD-ROMs have become more popular and useful, libraries have purchased licenses allowing for multiple users on the system or the reproduction of multiple copies for just a few dollars per copy. This enables libraries to distribute copies of CD-ROM products throughout an organization or to hook them up to local area network (LAN) systems (see page 50).

Although CD-ROM promises to be the mass storage medium of choice, librarians need to consider future developments in CD-ROM and optical storage technologies as they make their selections. Advances in CD-ROM technology that could provide up to 1,000 times more data on a single disc were already on the horizon in the early 1990s. By the end of the 1990s, other advancements in technology, such as erasable CD-ROMs and CD-WORMs (Write Once Read Many), will probably be commonly available. This technology allows the user to erase or add data. However, once the disc is full, the data becomes permanent and cannot be altered. Multimedia CD-ROMs, such as compact disc interactive (CD-I) or digital video interactive (DVI), should also be available in the late 1990s. This medium combines the interactive capability of the computer with the realistic audio and video of TV. It combines text, numbers, graphics, pictures, and audio into one full-motion or stop-action format that the user can either view as an observer or interact with as a player.

TELECOMMUNICATIONS LINKS

Computer technology was not the only technological development that affected libraries in the last quarter of the century. Advances in the telecommunications fields enabled libraries to use a variety of telecommunications systems. They could use these systems to interconnect all of their computer equipment within the library as well as provide a sophisticated level of access to information outside the library. The earliest of these telecommunications systems transmitted information as electric signals over telephone and telegraph wires or coaxial cables. These telephone wires were sometimes connected to library equipment such as telex machines, telefacsimile (FAX) machines, and computers via *modems*, or electronic connecting devices, used to request interlibrary loans, search databases, and send or receive telefacsimiles or copies of documents.

The next major telecommunications advancement was the introduction of *fiber optics*, which were hair-thin glass filaments that used light rather than wire to transmit signals. Fiber optics enabled librarians to transmit more information at a much faster transmission rate than was possible over regular wires. The increase in transmission or *baud* rates from 300 and 1200 baud to 4800 and 9600 was particularly welcomed. The higher or faster rates enabled libraries to send or receive more information in shorter time periods. Similarly, advancements in other telecommunications methods, such as satellite, microwave, and cellular radio transmissions, have enabled libraries to take advantage of telecommunications transmissions that travel through the air rather than through wires or filaments. This capability has allowed libraries to develop individualized regional and national networks that extend over long distances and do not depend upon telephone or communication lines.

All of these telecommunications advancements have given rise to new uses of the computer as a library resource. Computers have been hooked up by a modem to a telephone line to access another computer via phone line. This capability is called *dial access* if users from one computer can dial a phone number to access and use another computer. However, such users also need to know the proper protocols and access codes or "passwords" to interact with the called computer. Sometimes this dial access capability has been combined with the computer's tremendous storage capacity to allow a user at one computer to input data, such as a search request, to a computer. The computer encodes the data and transmits it via phone line at a high rate of speed to another computer. The receiving computer rapidly receives the encoded data, locates the needed information, and transmits it back at a high rate of speed. The first computer then "downloads" or stores the data for later decoding and "offline" use after the phone is disconnected.

These telecommunications capabilities have contributed to the rise of "electronic mail" and "electronic bulletin boards" that enable users to dial up or access other computers to receive or leave messages and share information. Librarians also appreciate the telecommunications capabilities that contributed to the development of sophisticated FAX equipment by the late 1980s. This capability enables users to insert a piece of paper into a FAX machine attached to a telephone line. The FAX machine encodes the data on the paper into electrical form and transmits it over telephone lines to another FAX machine that decodes the data and prints out a copy. The overwhelming acceptance of FAX machines in libraries by the 1990s was fueled by the increased speed of transmissions (average of one page in 20 seconds) and the standardization of equipment. This standardization ensured that brands from different manufacturers would be compatible and transmit to each other. Librarians not only took advantage of these FAX capabilities by adding FAX equipment to their resources, but they also adapted computers and terminals to provide this function.

Local Area Networks

As libraries added more and more computers, printers, CD-ROMs, and FAX equipment, they began to take advantage of telecommunications advances to link all of this equipment together in local area networks (LAN). LANs use coaxial cables installed in a loop or other configuration throughout a building in the walls or ceiling. They enable libraries to link together such equipment as computers, terminals, printers, disk drives, modems, and FAX machines. Access to this equipment is controlled by a master "control" or "server" computer. This server operates as a "traffic cop" to direct the flow of data from one computer or device to another. (See figure 3.4A.) The LAN enables a user at one LAN station to access a variety of resources such as the library's circulation system, a cataloging utility such as OCLC, and commercial databases and CD-ROM products.

A LAN also provides online links from one person's computer or workstation to another. Library staff at one workstation or computer can access or enter data into a computer that can be accessed by or sent to any other workstation on the network. This data can be read, reviewed, or revised by anyone at another workstation who has the proper password authorization. Thus, staff members can share any reports and documents, update statistical and fund accounting information, and receive electronic mail without leaving their offices. Libraries find that such communication capabilities enable their staffs to share resources, cooperatively write and edit documents, eliminate repetitive tasks, and reduce the need for multiple copies of draft paper documents.

Fig. 3.4. Interconnected computer networks. (Reprinted by permission from *NETWORK-ING: Choosing a LAN Path to Interconnection* by Marlyn Kemper [Metuchen, N.J.: Scarecrow Press, Inc., 1987]. Copyright 1987 by Marlyn Kemper.)

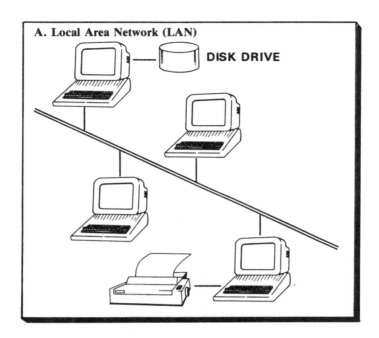

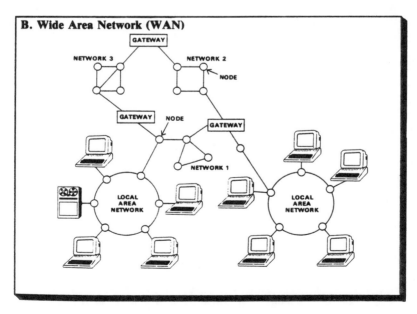

Wide Area Networks and Gateways

The success of LANs, combined with continuing developments in telecommunications, enabled libraries to develop wide area networks (WANs) using microwave, radio, satellite, or even leased PBX telephone communications. Just as LANs provide a communications network for a single building or institution, WANs provide similar capabilities for a region or area that can include several cities. WANs take advantage of high-speed transmission technology to link together computers, terminals, printers, CD-ROMs, and FAX machines at many sites into cooperative library resource networks. These networks enable libraries to develop bibliographic databases, share expensive resources, and develop other cooperative programs.

However, there is often one major difficulty for users who try to access information on the WANs and LANs. In order to use the available information, users often must learn separate software operating system instructions and access points for each resource they want to use. This difficulty may disappear in the 1990s with the acceptance of international standards for ISDN (Integrated Services Digital Networks). These standards would provide "transparent transmissions" by converting the various operating systems for all resources accessible on a network into one operating system.

These transmissions would be passed through a *gateway* or computer service that could connect a computer user to a multitude of online computer services. (See figure 3.4B, page 51.) By the early 1990s, 61 gateways were available through companies such as AT&T. These gateways enabled anyone with a computer and telephone access to connect to any online system. "Telecommunications was no longer simply a means of connecting terminals and computers, it had become an information delivery system that made information in many forms and formats available quickly, easily and economically."[3] Before the end of the century, it should be possible from a single workstation to locate information on any subject (regardless of its medium) in local, regional, or national databases, obtain bibliographic citations or full-text articles, order print documents, use electronic mail, and watch high-definition interactive video presentations.

LIBRARY CATALOGS

The advances in technology over the years have had a tremendous impact on the form of the library catalog or index to all of a library's holdings. The earliest of such catalogs were library indexes in book form. As libraries added more and more materials to their collections, they began to replace these book catalogs with card catalogs. Card catalogs contained 3- × 5-inch cards on which information about each item in the library was recorded. In the early 1900s, the Library of Congress ensured the adoption of the card catalog as the standard U.S. library catalog by reproducing its cataloging information on cards that were sold very inexpensively. In the 1960s, the Library of Congress ushered in another era of library cataloging with its introduction of MARC that could be used by a computer. Libraries were quick to take advantage of this technology to develop a variety of computer-based catalogs. However, no matter how much the format of a library's catalog might change, its purpose and general characteristics remain the same.

Library catalogs usually provide a record of the cataloged materials contained in a library's collection. If these catalogs contain records for materials in more than one library or collection, they are called *union catalogs*. The record for each item in a catalog is called a *cataloging record* and includes a bibliographic description of each item, a location or call number based on its major subject content, and subject headings representing the subject content of the work. Each cataloging record is usually entered in the catalog under three separate types of headings—those for author, title, and subject. Thus, a patron may look for an item by its title, by the name of the persons who wrote or edited it, or by a subject heading.

The basic information for the cataloging record is taken by the cataloger from the item itself although librarians may add other pertinent notes that describe the work to the patron. For example, cataloging information for media items is generally taken from any accompanying written material such as a producer's catalog or from an examination of the work itself. Librarians have attempted to provide all the information on a cataloging record that they think patrons may wish to know about a work. This is particularly important in libraries that do not allow their patrons to browse or for media items that cannot be easily examined.

When librarians first started including audiovisual materials in their collections and recording them in their catalogs, these materials were often cataloged and processed differently from books. Sometimes media catalog cards were designated by color-coded bands at the top of each card, or the catalog cards for media materials might be kept in a separate catalog. The call number for each item usually was a combination media code and accession number, and the materials were stored in cabinets or in special shelving areas. As librarians came to accept that the information contained in an item was more important than its format, they began to catalog audiovisual materials like books and assign call numbers based on their subject content.

There are two major types of library catalogs in any library. One type of catalog is called the *shelf list* and includes a record of all the cataloged items in a particular library arranged in the order in which the items appear on the shelf. The shelf list is most often kept in the staff area and restricted to library staff use. Although the shelf-list information may also be accessible through an online cataloging system, librarians have often retained the shelf list in catalog card format as a security measure or backup to a computer system. The second type of library catalog is called the *public catalog* or *public access catalog* and is the most visible catalog because it is meant to be used by the public as well as by the staff. If the public catalog is a card catalog, it can provide access to items in a library's collection by author, title, and subject. If the catalog is a computer-based catalog, it can provide additional access points by key word, call number, etc., as well as indicate whether the item is on a shelf in the library or checked out. (See figure 3.5, page 54.) And, if the catalog is a union catalog, it can also identify items which are available in other libraries.

This computer capability for providing expanded access to a library's collection contributed to the development of several major types of computer-based catalogs in the 1980s. The first of these catalogs was the computer output microform or COM catalog, which provided computer-generated information on microfilm or microfiche. As computer technology advanced and the costs for computer equipment were reduced, Online Public Access Catalogs or OPACs

Fig. 3.5. Screen for OPAC (online public access catalog). (Reprinted with permission of Innovative Interfaces, Inc.)

began to replace both COM and card catalogs in libraries. These OPAC catalogs enable the patron to interact with the computer and develop search strategies that were not possible with the earlier catalogs. As OPACs have become more "user-friendly," patrons have accepted the challenge of becoming computer literate to take advantage of them.

The development of CD-ROM technology has provided another advancement in computer catalogs. CD-ROM catalogs combine the computer's capability for accessing information with the cost advantages of CD-ROM. Libraries can usually have their whole database on one CD-ROM disc that can be replaced with updated discs on a regular basis. Smaller libraries like the low cost, accessibility, and ease of use of the CD-ROM catalog by the uninstructed. Larger libraries often use them as backup catalogs for the occasions when their OPAC catalogs might "go down" or not be available because of computer or online connection problems.

COMMUNITY RESOURCES

In addition to providing access to information and materials in their collections, libraries also fulfill a unique function in the communities they serve. Many libraries also provide information about, and access to, the local natural, industrial, and social resources available in their communities or parent institutions. Libraries can provide information about the unique natural features of a geographic region as well as information about its historical development. Many libraries maintain local history collections that originally included only print materials but now may also include oral history and videotape collections. Author collections may highlight local authors, and pamphlet clipping files often contain information about famous personages related to the area. Local business and industry collections may include annual business and financial statements. Job applicants and researchers often use these collections to locate product information or the names of company officials.

Many libraries provide organization files that give the purposes, officers, and directory-type information for community organizations. Community information files not only provide social service, legal, and government information, but they also may be used by library staffs to help patrons interact with these agencies. Cultural calendars of events in the region may be published by the library and distributed in the community. Cable television programs or stations may be operated by libraries, and library meeting rooms are often used for community groups, services, and activities. Thus, libraries have taken the major function of a library one step further by "acquiring, preserving, and making available information in *all* of its forms."

SUMMARY

The fundamental purpose of a library—to acquire, preserve, and make available information in all its varied forms—has not changed over the years. However, the resources that a library will acquire to fulfill this purpose have changed dramatically. In addition to providing materials or resources such as books, serials, and pamphlets in traditional print format, libraries have often provided duplicate titles in microform or computer-based formats. As more items have been published or produced in other media formats, libraries have added these graphic, audio, film, video, and computer materials to their print collections. Libraries have also cataloged these newer materials and added them to their bibliographic catalogs and databases. The many advancements in computer and telecommunications technologies have enabled libraries to provide automated library systems including integrated circulation, cataloging, acquisition, and interlibrary loan systems. These advancements have enabled almost any library to have access to computer-based resources such as online databases and CD-ROM products. With these and locally developed community resources, libraries in the 1990s can provide their patrons with access to almost any title in any medium that is available from any source.

REVIEW QUESTIONS

1. Identify the major types of print resources found in libraries today and give two to three examples of each.

2. Identify the major types of audio, visual, and electronic resources found in libraries today and give two to three examples of each.

3. Describe the major bibliographic elements of a cataloging record for both books and audiovisual media.

4. Identify the major characteristics of the microcomputer that make it so useful in a library environment.

5. Describe the major differences between the shelf list and the public catalog.

6. Identify two to three examples of community resources that can be found in a library.

NOTES

[1]Jan Kennedy-Olsen, "Management of Trends in Agriculture Libraries," *Library Trends* 38, no. 3 (Winter 1990): 352.

[2]Norman Desmarais, *The Librarian's CD-ROM Handbook* (Westport, CT: Meckler, 1989), xix.

[3]Larry L. Learn, *Telecommunications for Information Specialists* (Dublin, OH: OCLC, 1989), 2.

SELECTED READINGS

Computers in Libraries, 1989: 4th Annual Conference and Exhibition, March 14-16, 1989. Conference proceedings. Nancy Melin Nelson, chair. Westport, CT: Meckler, 1989.

Desmarais, Norman. *The Librarian's CD-ROM Handbook*. Westport, CT: Meckler, 1989.

Kemper, Marlyn. *NETWORKING: Choosing a LAN Path to Interconnection*. Metuchen, NJ: Scarecrow, 1987.

Learn, Larry L. *Telecommunications for Information Specialists*. Dublin, OH: OCLC, 1989.

Paskoff, Beth M., ed. "Contemporary Technology in Libraries." *Library Trends* 37, no. 3 (Winter 1989): 265-384.

Rosenberg, Kenyon C. *Dictionary of Library and Educational Technology*. 3d enl. ed. Englewood, CO: Libraries Unlimited, 1989.

Saffady, William. *Introduction to Automation for Librarians*. 2d ed. Chicago: ALA, 1989.

Schultz, James C. *Developing and Maintaining Video Collections in Libraries*. Santa Barbara, CA: ABC-CLIO, 1989.

Sherman, Chris, ed. *The CD-ROM Handbook*. New York: McGraw-Hill, 1988.

Soper, Mary Ellen. *The Librarian's Thesaurus: A Concise Guide to Library and Information Terms*. Edited by Mary Ellen Soper, Larry N. Osborne, and Douglas L. Zweizig. Chicago: ALA, 1990.

Tracy, Joan I. *Library Automation for Library Technicians: An Introduction*. Metuchen, NJ: Scarecrow, 1986.

CHAPTER 4

LIBRARY ORGANIZATION

By 1990, more than 30,000 libraries had developed in the United States to provide the same basic library function. All of these libraries were similar in that they developed materials collections, made them accessible, and provided information, programs, and services to meet a specific constituency's needs. Their differences came from serving different types of people. For example, libraries that served the same type of patron, such as college students, tended to develop similar objectives, collections, programs, and services. All libraries are divided into four major types: public, school, academic, and special.

Although there are differences in the way each type of library carries out its basic library function, all libraries have developed certain principles, procedures, and activities in common. In such areas as governing authority, administration, finances, and internal organizational patterns, libraries are very similar regardless of their objectives or type.

Among the more common similarities are organizational patterns or structures. These organizational structures should be based upon each library's individual objectives, functions, and activities. Too many times, the library organizational structure has grown by leaps and bounds as the staff increased from one person to two, and then from two people to four or more. At other times, the organizational structure has developed as a direct result of the personalities and preferences of the people on the staff. For example, rather than developing a single school media center to serve a school's objectives, some schools maintained separate library and audiovisual departments because the librarian or audiovisual specialist did not like working with different materials or equipment. Libraries should not base their organization on such accidents; they should base them instead upon well-thought-out objectives. In addition, a library's organizational structure should be based upon sound administrative principles.

One of the most important administrative principles requires that one person be made responsible and held accountable for leading and directing the library's operations. Although the person in this position may be called librarian, media specialist, information scientist, head librarian, library director, or library administrator, the title is not as important as the fact that responsibility for directing the library is vested in one person. It is this one library administrator who is responsible to a governing authority for guiding the formulation of library objectives and establishing policies and programs to carry them out. A library administrator also engages in activities common to all administrators, such as preparing a budget, supervising buildings and equipment, developing personnel classification and salary schedules, hiring, firing, and supervising personnel, and engaging in public relations.

In carrying out these functions, a library administrator should follow good administrative management practices and principles. Although the head librarian or library director is responsible to a governing authority for the library, he or she should delegate as many responsibilities as possible to subordinates. The number of employees reporting directly to the library director should be small. This allows members of the organization to have easy access to an immediate supervisor who will in turn present their views to a higher supervisor. The organizational structure should be clearly charted and identified so that the relationships among all departments can easily be seen. However, this organizational structure is not permanent and may be altered in response to changing factors. New library building programs or technologies might necessitate a library's reevaluating its structure. Changes in institutional organization or financial support could eliminate positions and force a library to reorganize. When such changes do occur, a library should design the best structure for its new needs rather than persist in using an outdated one.

VARIETY AND CHANGE

Generally, libraries have been very flexible in designing their organizational structures and patterns to suit their purposes. Libraries were originally organized into many departments based upon the specific duties and activities performed by the personnel in each of these categories. (See figure 4.1.) However, as library staffs grew to include more and more people, it became poor administrative policy for the many department heads to report directly to the library director. To address this problem, libraries began using job and cost analyses to reexamine their libraries by activity, function, and program to determine the best organizational patterns for their individual libraries. They also began to revise their departmental structures to reduce the number of administrative levels and streamline the management process. For example, departments whose activities were related, such as ordering, cataloging, and processing, were often organized into a larger department such as technical services.

Fig. 4.1. Public library organization chart.

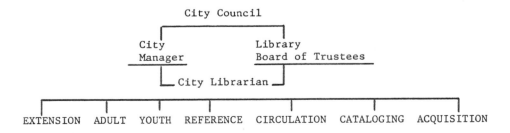

As consolidation into larger departments became more commonplace, more and more libraries began to divide their administration into two major divisions: public services and technical services. (See figure 4.2.) The original distinction between these two major divisions was based on the contact the staff had with the library's patrons. Public services included staff who interacted with the public, and technical services included staff who worked "behind the scenes" making the collection available for the public.

Fig. 4.2. Public library organization chart.

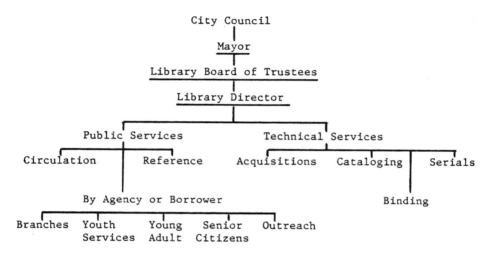

The major function of public services is to provide the best possible service to the user. This department usually combines such formerly separate functions as circulation (the loan and return of materials), reference (helping the patron find specific information), and readers' advisory (helping the patron find "good books to read"). It may also include service to special clientele such as children, young adults, and senior citizens. The director of outreach programs and an extension department (which directs branches or bookmobiles) may also be included in this public services department. Another major purpose of public services is the selection and development of library collections to meet these users' needs.

The original distinction between public services and technical services began to change with the advent of technology. The major function of technical services expanded as automated circulation/cataloging systems made it more practical to include supervision of these areas in technical services rather than in public services. These changes also made it easier for technical services to work with public services on the development of library collections. However, even with these changes, the major purpose of technical services has remained making the collection available for the user. This means that the department is primarily concerned with purchasing and organizing materials after they have been selected. Technical services usually combines the formerly separate functions of acquisitions or ordering, cataloging or organizing the materials, processing materials for use, the receipt and maintenance of serials, and binding books and serials. It is also concerned with the conservation of materials and may supervise their repair or preservation. Technical services also shares a responsibility with public services for developing library policies and procedures to enable "the right patron to receive the right information at the right time."

Although public and technical services have become the two most common departments in today's libraries, several other patterns of organization are also important. Libraries may divide their organization into departments based upon several different categories. Public and technical service departments are excellent examples of departments organized by function. However, libraries may also be organized according to territory or location, clientele or patron, subject matter, or form of resources. Many libraries have departments such as branches or bookmobiles that are based on location or territory. Academic and school libraries may have both territory and subject departments, such as branch science and history libraries or science and English resource centers. (See figures 4.3 and 4.4, page 62.)

Sometimes the administration of these libraries may even be shared with the subject departments. (See figure 4.4.) Public libraries also sometimes divide their main collections and staffs into subject departments such as the fine arts or business departments. Some libraries have departments based on the form of the resources, such as film departments, map departments, serials departments, or government document departments. Special libraries may have library services based upon the use or patron. For example, a hospital may have a medical library for its medical staff and a separate library for its patients. Finally, many libraries have found that basing their organizational structure upon a combination of these categories can provide them with an organization that best meets their needs.

Library organizational structures have also changed over the years to reflect changes in the theories and principles of administrative management. The library director who used to make all major decisions alone is now often joined by a team of management-level department heads who help direct and shape the library's operations. These department heads in turn rely upon their staffs for providing input into the decision-making process. This process has become more complicated as libraries have increased in size and activity. In fact, decisions made in one department can have such a far-reaching effect in other areas that many libraries have adopted group-directed problem-solving techniques. These group-directed efforts may be called task forces, ad hoc committees, interdepartmental committees, or quality circles, but they have all arisen to provide a team approach to solving library-wide problems.

Another type of management practice is evident in the development of several parallel supervisory channels. Many libraries have designated some of their department heads and supervisors as "line" administrators who have direct responsibility for the personnel, operations, and materials under them. In addition, these libraries may also have "staff" administrators who provide subject expertise or specialized knowledge and serve in an advisory capacity. These "staff" personnel do not have any authority over the actual library operations of a department but do provide facts and information that line supervisors can use to make decisions. (See figure 4.4.) Typical staff supervisors in libraries would be

Fig. 4.3. School library media center organization chart.

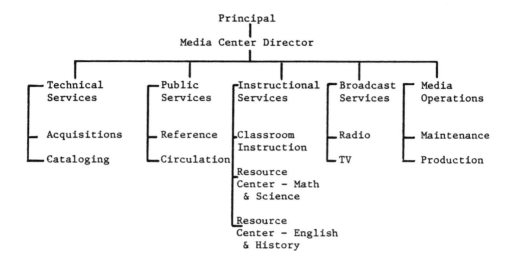

Fig. 4.4. Academic library organization chart.

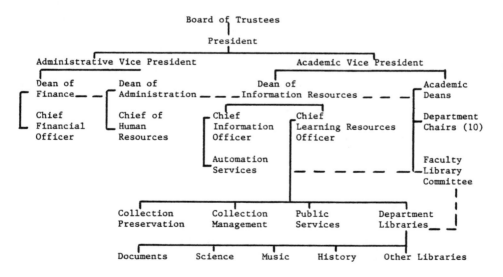

LEGEND: Solid lines indicate line supervision
         Broken lines indicate advisory capacity

personnel officers, automation specialists, and district-level school library media supervisors, while line supervisors would be circulation supervisors, public service librarians, and principals.

These line and staff supervisors are in all of the major types of libraries. Public libraries often have "line" branch librarians who supervise branch operations as well as coordinators of children or young adult services who supervise or coordinate such services for the entire library system. Special libraries may rely on subject specialists within the organization for advice in specific subject areas. (See figure 4.5.)

Fig. 4.5. Special library information center organization chart.

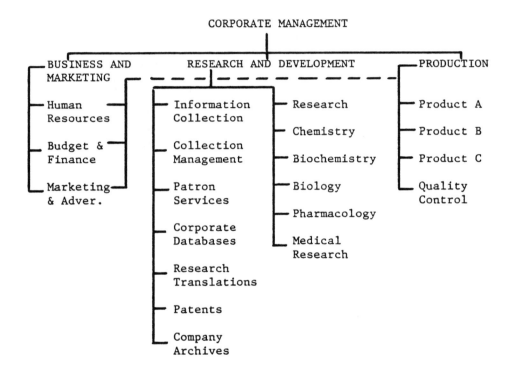

In school library media centers, the line supervisor of a school library media specialist is the principal of the school to whom the librarian reports for the running of the library. If a school system employs a district-level school library media supervisor, this person serves in the capacity of a staff position. This staff supervisor may provide assistance, support services, and advice to the school library media specialist and the principal. (See figure 4.6, page 64.) Usually, the school library media supervisor would also advise on the hiring of library personnel, but the principal, as line supervisor, might be responsible for hiring and firing personnel in the individual library. Academic libraries often have faculty library committees that serve in this "staff" capacity. (See figure 4.4.) Such a committee can be very helpful to the library staff by serving as an advisory board on library policies and collection development and as a communications link between the faculty and the library. However, sometimes faculty library committees overstep this "staff" function and try to assume the "line" function. When this happens, the authority and autonomy of the academic library are seriously threatened.

Fig. 4.6. School library media center organization chart.

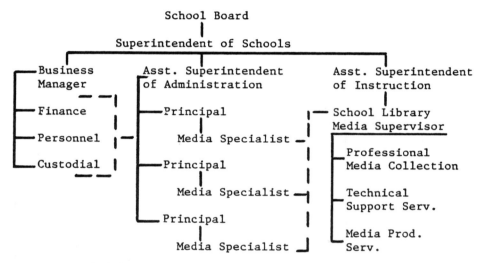

LEGEND: Solid lines indicate line supervision
Broken lines indicate advisor capacity

GOVERNING AUTHORITY

In addition to having their own administrations and organizations, libraries are also usually responsible to the administration of other institutions or to elected governmental bodies. Sometimes a library may be an entity in itself, such as the Linda Hall Library or a public library district, but even then this independent library is governed by a board of trustees or directors. This governing authority is legally responsible to the public or the stockholders for the efficient fiscal and administrative operation of the library. The governing authority usually approves the financial budget and appoints the members of the administrative authority (e.g., city manager, school superintendent, or board of library trustees) who will hire the library director and staff. Most often, the library is a department of a local government, school district, or academic institution and fits into the structure of this governing body for administration, finances, and personnel selection. (See figure 4.7.)

Fig. 4.7. Types of libraries.

LIBRARY	PURPOSES OR OBJECTIVES	CLIENTELE	FINANCIAL SUPPORT	GOVERNING AUTHORITY
PUBLIC: Local County Multicounty	Recreation Information Self-education Culture Social responsibility	Free to all residents of a community or district	Public tax funds	Local government's elected body appoints library board of trustees OR department of local government
SCHOOL: Elementary Secondary	Education Self-enrichment	Students and teachers of a school	Public schools - public taxes Private schools - tuition, endowments	School board, school administration
ACADEMIC: Colleges Universities Post-secondary schools	Education Research Information Preservation	Students, faculty, alumni Also, general public in publicly supported institutions	Public tax funds Tuition Endowment	Board of trustees, administration
SPECIAL: (Selective in clientele, subject coverage, materials, or format)				
Industry Business	Research Information	Specialized staff and clientele	Within budget of a business operating for profit	Board of directors, administrative officers of staff
Organization Association	Research Information Preservation	Membership in the organization or association	Within budget of a nonprofit organization	Board of directors, administrative staff
Institution	Recreation Information	Patients, inmates, etc.	Institution budget	Institution administration
Federal	All objectives	Specialized staff & clientele Tax-paying citizens	Federal tax funds	U.S. government

Governing authorities may differ in the administrative structure of their libraries, but they generally perform the same administrative functions. A governing authority is responsible for determining and adopting the mission, goals, objectives, and written policies of its library. It is also responsible for hiring a qualified and competent professional library administrator to direct the library's operations. The library administrator then hires a library staff that is legally accountable to this authority for carrying out the library objectives, policies, and services within the limits the authority sets. This means that the library director does not "run" the library alone. The director works with higher administrators or with a library board to develop library objectives and policies and to define the library budget. In turn, the governing body should not get involved in "running the library" or in making decisions about the library's daily operations. It should allow its library staff to carry out its policies. The concern of the governing authority should be to represent the library in the institution or community to which it belongs and to communicate and interpret the library's objectives, services, and problems to that community.

The manner in which the various governing authorities direct or control libraries under their jurisdiction can differ by type of library. Public libraries often are governed by state library laws that require governing bodies to appoint separate library boards of trustees. These boards of trustees represent citizen interest or control of the library and are often appointed by a mayor or county board chairperson and approved by the elected body. Thus, the appointment to these boards may be governed by political considerations rather than by what is best for library services in a particular community. Many of these public libraries are also considered to be departments within a city or county government. The library director may also be a department head reporting to a chief administrator, such as a mayor or city or county manager. (See figures 4.1 and 4.2.) In some cases, a public library may truly be a department within a local government where the librarian is appointed by and reports to an administrator rather than to a board of trustees. Sometimes, the library can even be a division within another governmental department such as a parks and recreation department.

Libraries within schools and academic institutions are ultimately controlled by a school board or governing board of trustees. This board designates responsibility for running the institution to the superintendent of schools or the president of the college or university. Usually, this individual delegates responsibility for the library or media department to one of the subordinate administrators such as an assistant superintendent, dean of the college, or academic vice president. The library director reports to this individual, and the library itself fits into the administrative pattern of the school or university. As a school or university department, the library works with the personnel department, business office, maintenance department, and other departments to conduct its operations. The library staff also fits into the staffing patterns of the parent institution, and professional librarians may be a part of the faculty. The clerical and technical staffs may be hired by the business or personnel offices with consultation from the librarians. (See figure 4.6.)

Special libraries usually are part of the administrative structure of their corporations, institutions, or governing bodies. In many companies, they may be part of the research and development divisions and report to the director of research or to a high-ranking officer or administrator. Special libraries that are also academic department libraries usually report to the library director. Other libraries may report to the chief administrator of a hospital, the executive secretary or director of an association, or even to the company president.

FINANCES

The library's finances may come from the governing authority in a variety of ways. Public libraries are financed by public funds from a particular governing unit or tax base, be it city, county, district, or regional. Sometimes these tax monies are supplemented by state or federal funds. Public libraries often will prepare a proposed budget and submit it to the governing authority for approval. When the budget is approved, the governing body will prorate the budgeted amount among the taxpayers and collect the taxes to fund the budget. School libraries usually receive their finances as part of the school budget adopted by the school board at the request of the school superintendent. Public school taxes are then collected from property owners based on a tax levy. Private schools get their operating funds from tuition, endowments, and gifts. Academic libraries usually request a budget from the university administration, which receives its funds from public taxes, tuition, student fees, or endowments. However, these library budgets may be based upon the prorated needs of the various university departments. In other words, the library may ask for a specific amount of money to support the English department or the science department.

Special libraries may carry this method one step further and develop their budgets based on a departmental charge-back system. Such a system requires each department to pay a percentage of the special library's budget based on that department's use of library and information resources and services. Other special libraries may simply submit a budget to the business office to be approved and included in the total institution budget. The funds for these budgets in special libraries come from drastically different sources than those for other types of libraries. Many special libraries are part of companies and businesses that operate for profit, and company profits determine the company's budget. Other library budgets depend upon membership dues in associations and organizations. The special library may have to prove that it contributes to the profits or to the well-being of the organization as a whole in order to get a workable budget. In any case, libraries of all types have usually found that the governing authority will question and change the library's submitted budget to correspond with the objectives and budget of the institution as a whole.

CLIENTELE

If there are so many different libraries governed by so many authorities, how are these libraries distinguished from each other and how do they keep from providing duplicate services and resources? Primarily, each library develops along individual lines to meet the particular needs of the individuals or patrons in the well-defined community it serves. Because these patrons may have many different needs, they may depend upon several libraries to satisfy these needs. Libraries may use a variety of techniques to determine their patrons' needs and the resources and services necessary to meet them. They may conduct surveys of their current and prospective patrons. Libraries may also study and evaluate library statistics and usage patterns. Finally, they will try to learn as much as possible about the community or institution they serve to coordinate their services with other agencies or departments.

Libraries have usually evaluated their community of patrons so well that several libraries can successfully serve the differing needs of the same person. For example, as a child grows into an adult, that person's interests and needs grow and change in many ways. When children first begin using a library, they usually want to listen to stories and look at picture books or other visual materials such as videotapes, movies, or filmstrips. As they learn to read, they will usually read fictional stories or view videotapes for pleasure. They will also read nonfiction books or watch informational videotapes on subjects that especially interest them. For all of these needs, children and young adults will usually be served by a public library. However, as young people enter school and need access to books and information for classes, they will usually find that school libraries provide more material to support these class assignments than do public libraries.

Adults also find that different libraries serve different needs. Students going to college turn to the college or academic library to provide information and resources for course assignments as well as for research projects. However, these same students may visit the public library for leisure reading or for information on subjects of personal interest to them. In addition, both adults and children may enjoy the activities and programs that the public library may offer for pleasure and entertainment.

Often, patrons may turn to special libraries to fulfill their needs for special subject information, for their hobbies, or for their work. These patrons may seek out genealogy or local history information in special collections in public libraries. They may also use the special libraries at their places of business. Some may even write to special libraries of professional associations or national organizations for information that may interest them. Thus, throughout their lives, patrons will usually turn to different types of libraries to satisfy their different needs.

MAJOR TYPES OF LIBRARIES

Each library usually serves the needs of a specific group of patrons based upon its objectives and its political and financial support. (See figure 4.8.) Since public libraries are financed by public funds, every individual who lives within the jurisdiction of the governing body is generally able to use the public library free of charge. The strength of the public library has been that it is freely available to all (in spite of the fact that many public libraries did not permit Black Americans to use their libraries until the 1960s and 1970s). Although the public library's mission has changed over the years, its purpose has generally been to satisfy the needs of all people for self-education, information, culture, and recreation. Public libraries all over the country, both large and small, have attempted to fill these needs by establishing specific goals and objectives to meet their patrons' needs. For example, a public library might develop a library collection of "quality" as well as of "popular materials" to meet its patrons' reading needs. It might also provide reference services to satisfy its patrons' informational and educational needs.

Fig. 4.8. Major types of libraries and their objectives.

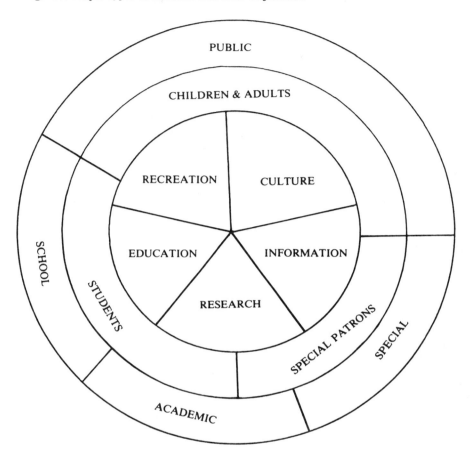

There is no one typical public library. Some public libraries are so small that they are only open a few hours a week. Other public libraries are among the largest libraries in the world. Public library materials collections can range from just 5,000 to 10,000 books to millions of books plus magazines and newspapers, maps, audiocassette tapes, compact discs, films, audio- and videotapes, and computers. The size of library staffs can also vary from 1 or 2 people to 15 to 20, or even 50 to 100 or more, depending upon the size of the community served and the importance of the library in the community. This importance in the community is usually directly proportional to the educational level of the community. The higher the average citizen's level of schooling is, the better developed the library services tend to be. Also, public libraries that are well supported tend to pay better salaries and to provide more levels of staffing than other libraries do. Finally, some very large cities such as Detroit and Memphis have even been able to develop pioneer library services such as information and referral (I&R) services and community advocacy to meet a community's total informational need.

School libraries or library media centers are part of educational institutions, and their major objective is to support the curricula of their schools. However, in recent years a second objective for school library media centers has developed as educators have come to realize that children need advanced skills to live in a technological society. Library media specialists have also recognized that children have interests outside of the class curriculum and need more information than the curriculum can provide. Thus, in addition to providing curriculum support, library media specialists have developed programs and services to help meet all the needs of the students.

Because school library media centers are parts of larger institutions, their clientele is usually restricted to the students and staff of a particular school. School library media centers are distinguished from academic libraries in that schools are defined as educational institutions serving kindergarten through high school grades. Although many schools have combined their print and audiovisual materials into a combined library media center, the size and scope of these centers can vary greatly depending upon the size of the school districts they are in. Small school districts serving small population areas may staff their library media centers with aides, clerks, or technicians who are supervised by a library media specialist at the district level. Medium-sized school systems may have both professional library media specialists and support staff at the building level. Large school systems often have several professional specialists in different areas who are supported by both technical and clerical staff. These large school systems may also provide collections of many varied types of media backed up by a centralized processing center.

Academic libraries serve institutions of higher education or post-secondary education, that is, schools beyond the high school level. Because these libraries are part of educational institutions, the mission of the academic libraries generally reflects the mission of the parent institutions. Thus, because these parent institutions are institutions of learning, one of the academic libraries' major objectives is to serve the educational needs of the students and faculty. When the parent institutions are publicly tax-supported institutions, the libraries may also make materials and services available to any member of the tax-paying community.

These academic institutions range from two-year and four-year schools, such as community and junior colleges, vocational and technical institutions, and colleges and universities, to graduate and professional schools, such as law schools and medical colleges. Each of these educational levels requires varying levels of library collections and services to support each type of institution. In the past, academic libraries in small junior colleges or four-year colleges tended to have library collections that mainly contained books and magazines. These libraries had collections ranging from 20,000 to 50,000 volumes and library staffs with a few professional librarians, a few clerks, and a number of college students. However, in recent years, most of these academic libraries have expanded their collections by adding automated technology and audiovisual materials. Larger academic libraries may have collections ranging from 100,000 to 1 million or more books and magazines, as well as other technologies and media such as maps, films, audio and video materials, and computer technology. Their staffs might include 4 or 5 librarians or as many as 10 to 20 and more, depending upon the services they might offer. Many academic libraries also provide extensive competency-based library instruction programs to achieve their educational objectives.

Many academic institutions, however, have broader missions than just the education of their students. Often, large colleges and universities are also centers of research that need the latest information and in-depth collections to support student and faculty research projects and reports. Libraries in these institutions must also support the need for research and information. To this end, our nation's universities have developed some of the largest and finest library collections in the world. Harvard, Princeton, Yale, the University of Illinois, and many others each have millions of books in their collections as well as many other types of materials. In addition, these large collections may be distributed into department or subject libraries that are larger than many library collections found in some small colleges. Many research projects may also depend upon historical and archival materials. Thus, these libraries must also fulfill the need for preserving materials from the past to be used by students and faculty in the present and the future. The academic library, therefore, tries to fulfill the following major objectives: education, research, information, and preservation.

Special libraries may significantly differ from one another. They have been defined as libraries providing special services to special clientele to satisfy special needs that sometimes cover special subject areas. Another definition might be that special libraries include those that are neither public, school, nor academic libraries. However, this could be an erroneous definition because many special libraries can be found within public and academic libraries. Special libraries do have particular characteristics common to most of these libraries.

First, a special library's governing body or institution most often is an organization, business, industry, association, institution, or government agency that restricts the use of the library to the members or employees of the parent organization. Second, these members and employees have special needs most often related to special subject interests, and a special library's collection will often be restricted to these major subject areas. Finally, libraries are primarily distinguished as special libraries when their primary objective is to provide individualized special services to patrons. The special library will generally serve each patron by locating information in library resources and forwarding materials directly to the patron. Such an individualized information service makes the best use of the time and energies of the personnel of the parent organization or institution. It is often so important to the special library that the library's name may be changed to that of an "information center."

Some of the most common types of special subject library or information centers are law libraries, medical libraries, business or commerce libraries, and scientific and technical libraries. Special libraries may belong to independent institutions such as business corporations and manufacturing companies, or they may be part of larger institutions such as hospitals, governments, and universities. Law libraries and medical libraries are not only special libraries, but they may also be department libraries of an academic institution and, therefore, also academic libraries. Other typical special libraries are those that serve the needs of special clientele. There are libraries to serve inmates in prisons and patients in hospitals and mental institutions. The U.S. armed forces have large library systems throughout the world to serve military personnel and their families. Some of these latter special libraries may provide services for their clientele that would be similar to services provided by public libraries for their patrons. However, the majority of special libraries are designed to fulfill patrons' need for specific information.

Special libraries may range in size and scope from small collections of a few hundred or thousand books and magazines to medium-sized collections of 5,000 to 10,000 books, magazines, and technical reports. Large special libraries may provide many thousands of books, magazines, technical reports, patents, and microforms. No matter what their size, almost all special libraries will provide some access to specialized automated databases.

Although every library is generally identified as belonging to a particular type of library, each library staff will often look to other types of libraries to help them meet their own library's objectives. Libraries will also join together in large cooperative networks to share access to their collections, their services, and even sometimes their staffs. Such sharing may be informal arrangements whereby public libraries provide liaison librarians to work with school libraries in their tax-supported unit, or special libraries may allow on-site use of their collections by other libraries' patrons. Other efforts may be formalized in cooperatives or consortia where school, public, and academic libraries share the costs of ventures such as computerized circulation, cataloging, instructional programming, and cable TV. Finally, some states have established and funded "multitype" library systems to provide the development of comprehensive coordinated activities such as interlibrary loan, continuing education, and consulting services.

STANDARDS

To help librarians in all types of libraries establish the best services for their users, many library associations have adopted national statements of purpose and standards of performance. These statements and standards identify recommended or acceptable levels of library service for that type of library. Each library can use them as a measuring instrument to indicate how well it compares with the recommended standards in providing quality library service. Standards have been developed by national associations and state agencies for such types of libraries as public libraries, school libraries, college libraries, junior college libraries, hospital libraries, and prison libraries. However, although these state and national standards may exist, they are usually advisory, and it is up to each librarian to determine how to use these standards in developing library services in each individual library.

Many factors influence how well an individual library measures up to its national standards. Because these standards are meant to be goals a library should strive to reach if it is to provide adequate library service, some libraries may already meet or exceed the goals for their type of library. However, these libraries would be the shining examples and exceptions rather than the rule. Most libraries strive for many years just to equal them. Recognizing the difficulties and problems libraries have had in meeting these ideal levels of service, many associations began in the 1980s to replace these standards with guidelines that libraries could use to identify their own levels of service they wished to reach. The guidelines were designed to encourage each individual library to assess its own community, adopt a mission statement, and develop goals and measurable objectives to meet its community's needs.

SUMMARY

More than 30,000 libraries have developed in the United States to provide library materials and services to meet the varying needs of their clientele. These libraries all serve the same basic function of acquiring and preserving information and making it available. They also share common administrative principles, practices, and activities in carrying out this function. However, libraries usually differ in the type of clientele they serve and the objectives they adopt.

Libraries serving similar clientele are described as belonging to one of four major types: public, school, academic, or special. Each type has similar characteristics that set it apart from other types. Thus, libraries in each type generally have organizational patterns or structures, governing authorities, finances, and objectives in common with each other. They have also developed similar collections, programs, and services to meet their patrons' needs. In this process, they have been encouraged by standards developed by library associations for each major type of library.

REVIEW QUESTIONS

1. Identify the four major types of libraries and the major purpose or objectives of each.

2. Identify the clientele served, the governing authority, and the source of financial support for each type of library.

3. Define *line* and *staff* levels of supervision and give examples of each.

4. Identify the major responsibilities of public services and technical services and three functions that could be included in each.

5. Identify one pattern of library organizational structure for each type of library.

6. Identify the organizational structure of two local libraries, including their place in their parent organization or institution.

SELECTED READINGS

Baughman, James C. *Trustees, Trusteeship, and the Public Good: Issues of Accountability for Hospitals, Museums, Universities, and Libraries*. New York: Quorum Books, 1987.

Berk, Robert. *Starting, Managing, and Promoting the Small Library*. Armonk, NY: M. E. Sharpe, 1990.

Martin, Lowell A. *Organizational Structure of Libraries*. Metuchen, NJ: Scarecrow, 1984.

Prytherch, Ray. *The Basics of Readers' Advisory Work*. London: C. Bingley, 1988.

Rochell, Carlton. *Wheeler and Goldhor's Administration of Public Libraries*. rev. ed. New York: Harper & Row, 1981.

Soper, Mary Ellen, Larry N. Osborne, and Douglas L. Zweizig. *The Librarian's Thesaurus: A Concise Guide to Library and Information Terms*. Chicago: ALA, 1990.

Webb, T. D. *Public Library Organization and Structure*. Jefferson, NC: McFarland, 1989.

White, Herbert S. *Library Personnel Management*. White Plains, NY: Knowledge Industry Publications, 1985.

Woodsworth, Anne. *Patterns and Options for Managing Information Technology on Campus*. Chicago: ALA, 1991.

Young, Virginia. *Library Trustee: A Practical Guidebook*. Chicago: ALA, 1988.

CHAPTER 5

PUBLIC LIBRARIES

Public libraries are the one major type of library that serves every citizen at every stage of life. Thus, public libraries serve more needs and objectives than other libraries do. They serve the leisure reading needs of persons from pre-schoolers to senior citizens as well as the information needs of first graders to scholars. Public libraries have even been termed the "people's university" because they can enable persons to pursue their own search for knowledge in the library's treasure house of literary works and scientific and technical information. Because they are so important in everyone's life, more than 15,000 public libraries exist in communities both large and small throughout the United States.

OBJECTIVES

As community needs have changed over the years, American public library objectives have changed to keep up with them. Robert Lee has identified the development of four phases of public library objectives.[1] He described the first phase, from 1850 to 1875, as a time when the education objective was foremost in the public library. The second phase covered the last quarter of the nineteenth century to World War I and added recreation and reference as objectives. At first, recreational reading was seen as a way to lead patrons to more serious reading, but this objective soon exceeded the education objective in terms of emphasis. This occurred because libraries were trying to reach the multitudes of people flocking to the cities from the farms and from other countries. To assimilate these people, society needed to popularize general knowledge. Libraries not only provided reading materials inside the library, but some libraries also took book wagons into the streets. Other libraries provided books and magazines in languages other than English for their foreign-language-speaking patrons.

In the third phase after World War I and up to 1957, some librarians tried to make education once more the dominant function of the public library. Franklin Roosevelt and his New Deal programs encouraged this objective. More public libraries began to function as adult education agencies and offer services and activities related to continuing education. In addition to helping individual patrons develop their own reading programs, many libraries sponsored discussion groups and educational programs.

The fourth phase began after the *Sputnik* scare in 1957 and lasted through the late sixties. During this period there was an increased emphasis on providing reference and information services. Less emphasis was placed on recreational reading because of new communication materials. The rise of television, the growth of news magazines, and the abundance of inexpensive paperback books allowed libraries to focus on other areas such as social needs.

A new fifth phase began in the late 1960s to meet the needs caused by changes in the American population. The baby boom after World War II produced more adults than were needed to run a mechanized American society. The centers of population grew bigger as many people moved from rural to urban areas or from the South to the North and West looking for work in the industrial and economic centers. Society no longer needed masses of unskilled labor, and these people did not have the technical skills needed to survive in their new environments. The antiwar years of the Vietnam era also produced social unrest and dissatisfaction with the established order. In response to the social and economic problems caused by this population upheaval, many minority and disadvantaged people who had remained outside the mainstream of American life demanded to become a part of it. In this social climate, librarians began to recognize that libraries had to satisfy a new need, that of social responsibility, and began to help poor and uneducated people fit into a highly scientific and technical society.

At the same time, the recessions of the 1970s and early 1980s began to affect the nation's economy and bring changes in this highly scientific and technical society. The gap between the "have" and the "have not" populations began to widen. At the lower end of the work scale, many families found they needed two incomes to make ends meet. At the upper end of the scale, single individuals with technological training and education, called "yuppies," received salaries that were larger than those of many two-income families. These changes also caused many people in society to reexamine their priorities and needs. For some, the 1960s' emphasis on a Great Society of federally funded social programs and "equal access for all" was replaced by an emphasis on individual achievement embodied in the yuppies of the 1980s.

These economic and societal changes also brought on a sixth phase of public library objectives. Economic recessions in the 1980s not only reduced local taxes; they also eliminated the state and federal aid upon which libraries had relied. Recognizing that they did not have sufficient funds to successfully carry out a large number of objectives, public libraries began to reevaluate their communities' needs. This reevaluation was outlined in the *Public Library Mission Statement and Its Imperatives for Service*, adopted by the Public Library Association (PLA) in 1979. This statement identified four roles in which the public library could make a unique contribution to society as a nontraditional educational agency, a cultural agency, an information agency, and a rehabilitation agency.[2] Each individual library was encouraged to analyze its own community to determine which of these roles it should select and to develop specific goals and objectives to satisfy them.

STANDARDS

The major direction for today's public libraries was set when the ALA published its postwar *Standards for Public Libraries* in 1943. These standards emphasized that a public library should provide free library service to the residents of a particular community. Each library should satisfy the needs of those residents for education, information, culture or aesthetic appreciation, recreation, and research. It should provide services for adult education and vocational education as well as services to the citizen, particularly the child and the young adult. This direction was expanded in 1966 with the publication of the *Minimum Standards for Public Library Systems*, which included the concept that "service to all" is the reason the library exists.

This expanded concept meant that libraries were looking beyond their typical library patron — the middle-class, educated, adult female who only represented a minority of the population. They were looking toward the unserved one-third of the population who had never used a library and to the millions of Americans who had no access to free public library service because they lived in rural communities or because of their race. For the first time, libraries recognized that all citizens had the same needs for information and education. Thus, the 1966 standards were based on the philosophy that "people need similar library resources whether they live in cities, in suburbs, or in rural areas."[3] The standards proposed that these resource needs could best be fulfilled by developing library systems based upon a population that was broad enough to financially support the type of library needed.

The 1966 standards suggested that library systems be developed to serve at least 150,000 people. This was felt to be the minimum population base that could financially and effectively support resources and staff and provide quality library service for the American public. The system was to provide local services within easy access of all persons backed up by a pool of in-depth regional and state resources and services. The local or community level would be served by branch libraries, small-town libraries, bookmobiles, etc., that could work jointly with schools and colleges to share resources. Supporting this level would be a systems center or headquarters library serving the entire region. This headquarters library would provide a comprehensive collection of materials that could be loaned to local units when needed. It would also provide specialized staff and services to help the local units. These services could include automated and centralized ordering, cataloging, and processing; reference library staff to provide reference support (perhaps via telephone and telefacsimile); staff specialists in children's and young adult work; public relations; administrative support; and guidance in developing community services. The headquarters library would also provide any guidance and direction the local library staff might request as well as in-service education for system staff members.

The next level of library service would be the state library agency that would provide resources, personnel, and support for the library systems. Many state agencies had already developed resource personnel and strong state programs as a result of the federal Library Services Act in 1956 and the Library Services and Construction Act (LSCA) in 1964. Through these acts, state libraries had developed state plans for library service and distributed federal funds to support library systems. Most state libraries had used these funds to develop and support those programs that would benefit the largest number of their citizens. Programs such as demonstration or model library services, statewide interlibrary loan networks, and contracts with large libraries to share their resources were initiated in many states. The 1966 standards recommended that a state library agency not only continue in these roles, but also assume the leadership for library development, coordination, and research within each state.

The emphasis in these standards for library systems was upon the quality of library service provided rather than upon the quantity of library materials. The standards required the public library to develop written selection policies and choose materials that are accurate, include opposing views, and appeal to all members of the community. Materials should be purchased and discarded on a planned basis. Services and programs should be developed to satisfy the needs of all individuals and groups. Standards for services to many of these groups, such as children, young adults, and blind and physically handicapped persons, were developed and published in separate standards by divisions of the ALA.

Although library systems are based on qualitative standards, librarians had long recognized the public relations value of stating these standards in quantitative terms. They found that government and community leaders could relate to standards that said "so much money per capita should be spent to support library services." Thus, the 1966 standards also included quantitative standards for such areas as services, materials, and staffing. These standards recommended that the local community library be open at least six days a week and that bookmobile services be provided to areas without libraries. Staff should include one-third professional and subprofessional and two-thirds support staff. Minimum numbers of staff were identified based on the population served. The number and types of materials were also identified by population served, and community library collections were to be backed up by a larger collection at the headquarters library. However, these quantitative standards were not meant to be definitive but were intended to be guidelines that libraries should strive to meet.

These quantitative standards were not met with equal levels of acceptance by librarians, community leaders, and state legislators. Many people felt threatened by the system concept and feared they would lose their local autonomy and control. Others enthusiastically endorsed them and established statewide regional library systems. The quantitative standards were considered to be too low and shortsighted by librarians in metropolitan and progressive libraries. Libraries in smaller rural areas considered them too high and impossible to achieve. Although some libraries quickly and easily reached the standards, many libraries took 5 to 10 years to reach them, and others had not reached them by 1980. That these standards were achieved in any measure was probably due to the perseverence and farsightedness of many librarians. State library agencies also contributed by providing state and federal funds as an incentive.

As librarians were striving to meet these quantitative standards, they also began to recognize that each library had its own unique characteristics that sometimes did not fit into any standard formula. Using the 1979 PLA mission statement to examine their own communities' needs, librarians began to look at the quality of services an individual library could provide. The PLA assisted librarians in this approach by publishing *A Planning Process for Public Libraries* in 1980. This process stressed that an analysis of an individual library and its community by community members, library board trustees, and library staff members could be used to help identify library needs and set directions for library services. Although this planning process was not new to librarians, they welcomed its strong emphasis on community involvement at a time of financial retrenchment when libraries needed as much community support as possible.

This planning approach for developing library services was further encouraged by the publication of PLA's *Planning and Role Setting for Public Libraries* in 1987. This document identified a menu of eight roles of library service. Libraries were encouraged to select and develop two to three roles to meet their own communities' needs. The roles of service included a community activities center, community information center, formal education support center, independent learning center, popular materials library, preschoolers' door to learning, reference library, and research center.[4] A description of each service role and its benefits for the community, critical resources, and suggested evaluation measurements were also provided. Librarians used this planning process to develop long-range plans of service that identified goals, measurable objectives, and specific strategies to fulfill these service roles.

Although many librarians welcomed this emphasis on local community needs, they still felt a need to maintain some quantitative standards against which they could evaluate their library's current level of services and materials. They recognized that many community leaders and governmental authorities were impressed by statistics such as the number of people who used the library and its materials and services. To help meet this need, PLA published another document, *Output Measures for Public Libraries: A Manual for Standardized Procedures, in 1987*. This manual was designed to be used in conjunction with the earlier PLA documents. It gave specific instructions for measuring library uses such as the number of library visits or reference questions per capita. Use of the collection was measured in circulations per capita and the "turnover" rate (the number of total items in the collection divided by the items checked out). Even the availability of library materials was measured to determine how many material requests were filled and how long it took to fill them. These "output measures" could be used in conjunction with more traditional "input measures" (such as the number of items added to a collection) to quantify a library's services. The results of such measures were collected on national and state levels by the Public Library Data Service and individual state agencies. Individual libraries could then use these national and state collections of statistical measurements. By comparing their own results with those from similar libraries, they could assess their library's effectiveness.

In addition to collecting output and input measures from public libraries, many state agencies also revised their own standards to incorporate these planning and measurement principles. They collected statewide input and output measures and identified planning standards that a local library should strive to achieve. (Figure 5.1, page 80, provides example minimum input measures adopted by two different states. Figure 5.2, page 80, provides example output measure results.) Many of these results are reported in "percentiles." For example, in figure 5.2, a library with a "circulation per capita" of 7.4 would have a circulation ratio greater than 50 percent of the state's public libraries. The "circulation per capita" for a library with a ratio of 9.8 would be greater than 75 percent of the state's public libraries. Using such statistical percentile measurements, libraries can compare their own statistics with those from similar libraries to assess their effectiveness. Many states provide aid to encourage libraries to improve their findings in these measurements.

Fig. 5.1. State public library standards: Example minimum input levels.

STATE OF ILLINOIS (1989)

Population	Book Volumes	Periodicals	Days/Hrs. Open
Under 5,000	10,000	40	5 / 25
5,001-10,000	20,000	90	5 / 48
10,001-25,000	35,000	150	6 / 56
25,001-50,000	85,000	280	6 / 67
50,001-75,000	140,000	560	7 / 71
Over 75,000	295,000	700	7 / 72

STATE OF WISCONSIN (1987)

Population	Book Volumes (based on per capita)	Periodicals	Hours Open
Less than 2,000	6,000-12,000	20	18
2,000-3,999	12,000-24,000	40-80	34
4,000-7,999	20,000-40,000	64-128	51
8,000-14,999	28,000-52,000	100-18	56
15,000-24,999	49,000-81,000	165-27	56
25,000-49,999	75,000-150,000	212-42	62
50,000 and over	125,000 + 2.5pc	350 + 7pc	68

(pc = per capita over 50,000 pop.)

Fig. 5.2. State public library standards: Example output measure results.

STATE OF ILLINOIS (1987)

PERCENTILE	50th	75th	90th
Output Measure:			
Circulation Per Capita	7.4	9.8	12.1
Turnover Rate	1.9	2.6	3.3
Program Attend. Per Capita	.2	.4	.8
Reference Transactions Per Capita	.6	1.1	1.8

STATE OF WISCONSIN (1985)

Output Measure:	Circulation Per Capita			Turnover Rate		
PERCENTILE POPULATION	50th	70th	90th	50th	70th	90th
Less than 2,000	9.8	12.8	18.8	1.6	2.0	3.1
2,000-3,999	11.1	15.0	19.9	2.0	2.3	3.0
4,000-7,999	11.8	13.4	16.5	2.3	2.7	3.4
8,000-14,999	10.7	12.3	18.7	3.0	3.4	4.2
15,000-24,999	8.2	9.2	12.9	2.5	2.6	3.3
25,000-49,999	6.7	9.3	11.9	2.5	3.2	4.3
50,000 and over	9.2	10.4	12.0	3.2	3.8	3.9

LIBRARY SERVICES

Once libraries had selected the roles of service they would strive to fulfill, they developed differing material collections, programs, and services within these roles to satisfy their individual communities' needs. Perhaps the greatest differences were in the variety of library collections developed to fulfill specific roles. For example, to fulfill the "popular materials library" role based upon the makeup of their communities, some libraries developed strong collections of popular materials, others developed strong children and young adult collections, and still others developed strong media and computer collections. In fulfilling the "formal education support center" role, many libraries provided public access computers, others provided multiple or reserve copies of materials needed by school children, and still others supplied supplementary materials to their local schools for classroom use.

In addition, libraries also expanded their collections to include a wide variety of materials. The traditional print materials of books, magazines, and newspapers were expanded to include large-print books and magazines, college catalogs, pamphlets, business reports, and updating reference or financial services such as Facts on File and Value Line. Audiovisual materials joined the mainstream of library services and were made available to patrons as readily as were print materials. Older audiovisual materials, such as films and records, were often replaced in the collection by Books on Tape, audiocassette tapes, CDs and laser discs, videotapes and discs, computers and computer databases, CD-ROM products, cable television, and newer materials as they became available. Many libraries also included these materials in their library programming. Sometimes, libraries even produced their own radio and TV programs or ran their own cable TV channels to reach all segments of their populations.

In addition to developing diverse collections to satisfy different roles of service, libraries established a variety of programs and services to meet the differing needs of various populations. For example, most public libraries by the 1980s provided collections, programming, and staff for children's services. When the baby boom began in the late 1980s, however, children's services were often expanded and strengthened in libraries that adopted the "preschool-door-to-learning" role of library service. Collections in these libraries usually included picture books, audio- and videotapes, filmstrip-cassette tape kits, puppets, developmental toys, games, and animals (both live and stuffed). Parents particularly welcomed the toys and games because they often were reluctant to buy such expensive items for such short-term use. These materials were sometimes housed in a separate preschool room where children could climb or play on "playschool"-type equipment or sit quietly looking at books. They could listen to stories read aloud by their parents, present mock puppet shows, or take part in a learning or craft activity without distracting other library patrons. Preschool story hours and puppet shows were presented to children at the library and at preschools, day care centers, and play groups. Parenting materials and child development programs also were sometimes provided.

Libraries that chose the preschool-door-to-learning role usually found that they also needed to provide programs and services for school-age children. These libraries would also adopt the "popular materials library" or "formal education support center" role depending upon their mission statement and goals. In many of these libraries, circulation of all children's materials could be as much as one-third to one-half of the library's total circulation. To further encourage such use, libraries extended their former summer reading clubs to year-round programs. They combined them with contests such as "battle of the books," which offered prizes and awards. Regular monthly programs often featured puppet shows, magic shows, animal acts, or visiting performers.

Libraries that chose to become formal education support centers established additional programs. Some of them established school liaison positions to coordinate with school library media services as well as with home-schooling programs. Sometimes library communities had large numbers of "latch-key" children or children who waited after school at the library for their parents to pick them up. These libraries often established homework services and other after-school programs to serve these children's needs. Library meeting rooms were often made available for library-sponsored youth activities such as drama and book discussion groups or for organized groups such as scout troops or youth service clubs.

Another group of library patrons who use the library heavily after school are young teenagers from 12 to 17. Beginning in the 1980s, libraries began to define this age group as "young adult" and tried to provide materials and services to satisfy their needs. (Before then, a young adult was described as a person aged 14 to 21, and young adult materials were "those adult materials which were of interest to young people.") Libraries found that serving these young adults was a little more difficult to do than serving elementary school children. Young adults were often more interested in developing social skills with their peers than they were in using a library's services. In some libraries, young adults made up a large part of their patrons. However, more often than not, these patrons came to the library to meet their friends rather than to study or use library materials.

Libraries tried to tap into this social need in several ways. They provided informational programs such as babysitting clinics, child development classes, and college entrance examination preparatory classes. Libraries also provided paperback collections containing multiple copies of books on topics of particular interest to young adults. These multiple copies allowed young adults and their friends to read and share the same stories and information at the same time. Some libraries hired young adult librarians and established young adult advisory councils or peer homework support groups to help channel and use some of this teenage group's energy. They were not always successful in this process, and by the early 1990s "library discipline monitors" were hired to supervise and discipline young adults and latch-key children.

To meet the information needs of most of their patrons, a majority of public libraries generally selected the "reference library" as one of their major roles of library service. In contrast, only the largest public libraries would select the "research center" role. Most public libraries developed reference material collections containing general reference encyclopedias, directories, dictionaries, yearbooks, handbooks, atlases, and indexes. Depending upon their communities' needs and interests, libraries might also develop specialized subject reference collections. These could be business and financial collections, genealogical and local history collections, or special interest collections such as art history or gardening and landscaping. In addition to books, many of them contained such media as weekly or daily updating services, periodicals on microform, online or CD-ROM databases, and local government archives. To help their patrons use these materials more effectively, libraries sometimes provided individual or group instruction or pathfinder tours of the library and its collections.

Libraries also provided reference staffs to help patrons locate information. Such reference assistance included telephone ready-reference service, assistance in using the library's reference tools, database searching, individualized help in locating answers to a patron's question, and information through interlibrary loan. The range of services depended heavily upon the library's size and resources. Large public libraries might have banks of telephones to answer many questions at one time using many special-subject collections. Small libraries might use computer and telephone links to headquarters or system libraries to locate answers to patrons' questions. In any case, whether or not a library chose the reference center as one of its major roles, almost half of its patrons might use these services when they came to the library.[5]

In addition to meeting these reference needs, libraries provided other services for adult patrons depending upon their selected roles. Libraries serving as popular materials libraries developed large collections of current fiction, multiple copies of best sellers, and genre books such as mysteries and biographies. They also promoted these materials with individual and group booklists, library displays, and merchandising techniques such as face-out display shelving similar to that found in bookstores. In addition to books, popular materials library collections also included feature videotapes, popular as well as classical CD recordings, art prints, and sculptures. Libraries also checked out equipment such as videotape recorders, projectors, Polaroid® cameras, or even household tools. Programs for adults ranged from book discussions and informational lectures, to how-to programs such as cooking or photography classes, to travel-film or feature-film programs. In addition, a library might expand its programming by encouraging community groups such as an astronomy club or a support group to use its meeting rooms as long as their meetings were open to the general public. Most libraries provided programming and services for persons with special needs such as senior citizens. Libraries also included materials and services for blind and visually handicapped individuals such as talking books (books recorded on audio for blind and handicapped persons), braille materials, and large-print materials.

Many libraries further served adults as "independent learning centers." In this role, libraries requested materials on interlibrary loan for adults taking college-level or adult-education courses. Librarians served as proctors for correspondence courses or made their meeting rooms available for private or group study. In cooperation with other educational institutions and community agencies, the library helped individual patrons study for credit courses or take equivalency tests for high school (General Education Degree or GED) or college (College-Level Examination Program or CLEP). Sometimes adult education classes were conducted at the library or videocourses were made available to library patrons. Also in this independent learning center role, libraries attempted to reach beyond their traditional middle-class educated patrons to their unserved populations. In keeping with the push for national literacy in the 1980s and 1990s, libraries encouraged individuals to participate in nontraditional educational programs. Many libraries participated in adult literacy programs by providing adult basic education materials and study rooms for literacy students and their volunteer tutors. Some libraries provided foreign-language collections for their foreign-speaking populations and offered classes in English as a second language. Sometimes, when the economic climate of their communities dictated it, libraries established job/career placement centers to help unemployed patrons.

outreach

In trying to meet the needs of their unserved populations, libraries also designed "outreach" programs and services for persons who could not get to a main or branch library. Bookmobiles traveled rural highways and city streets to bring popular materials to all ages. In inner-city areas, bookmobiles were repainted in bright, attractive designs and restocked with lower-level reading materials, paperbacks, and magazines to attract nonreaders. "Mediamobiles" toured inner-city areas bringing library programs to children and young adults on their own street corners. Libraries also developed specialized services for patrons who were unable to use the more traditional library facilities. Prefabricated kiosk-type libraries were erected in such diverse communities as a small rural hamlet or a sophisticated urban shopping mall to provide quick and easy access to library materials. (See figures 10.1 and 10.2, chapter 10.) Books-by-mail catalogs of paperback titles were sent to patrons in traditionally unserved areas such as rural areas and prisons. Patrons would select titles from the catalogs, submit a request for them to the library, and receive the books by mail. Although some books-by-mail programs successfully supplanted traditional bookmobile services, children sometimes had difficulty using this new service.

As libraries reached out to serve these formerly unserved patrons, they recognized their need to fulfill the "community activities center" role of service. Many libraries established storefront branches or placed materials collections in urban housing developments and local ethnic or senior citizen centers. They hired local community members to staff these facilities and foreign-language-speaking librarians to develop collections and services to meet the needs of the community's various ethnic populations. Some libraries even built branches in community action centers to better serve their population. In addition, libraries worked with other agencies to provide voter registration, notary publics, income tax forms, tax assistance for seniors and low-income people, and health-testing programs. Libraries made their meeting rooms available so that community and government organizations could present public information programs or cultural groups could present lectures, concerts, and art shows.

As libraries began providing these community services, they found that many patrons' needs could be met by other agencies within the community. Rather than ignore these needs, libraries selected the "community information center" role to meet them. In this role, libraries gathered information about community organizations, businesses, and governmental agencies, which they made available to the public. This information was often shared with other agencies, published in directories, or made available through computer databases such as "Maggie's Place" in Colorado Springs. Libraries worked with social service, health, educational, business, governmental, and economic agencies and organizations to design information and referral (I&R) services to provide information that individuals could not obtain on their own. As part of an I&R network, libraries were in unique positions as information-gathering agencies to bridge the information gap between the "system" and the individual. As information agents, librarians could locate and provide information to help people resolve health, housing, family, and legal problems. As referral agents, librarians served as advocates or ombudspersons who would present the available alternatives to the patron, bring the patron and chosen agency together, and sometimes serve as interpreter (both literally and figuratively) between the two.

For I&R to be successful, however, the entire library staff, rather than just a few specific people, had to be committed to providing I&R. Libraries such as the

Detroit and Memphis public libraries that made a total commitment to I&R found that such services provided an important new stimulus to library use. This stimulus made the library visible within the community as a viable and vital institution responding to and satisfying the public's needs. As former Detroit Public Library Director Clara Jones said, "By incorporating I&R into its traditional reference service, the public library can become a comprehensive community information center. This expansion into community-based, often 'fugitive,' information is necessary if the public library is to fulfill its claim as an institution basic to civilization."[6]

LIBRARY MANAGEMENT

Although the public library as an institution may be considered basic to civilization by many people, public library collections, programs, and services have always been affected by economic conditions. National and local economic recessions impact library services, as do the local community's political and social climates. Such pressures often force library boards and staffs to reevaluate their objectives and programs to be sure that they meet their communities' needs. For example, in the 1980s libraries had to curtail many programs and services that were begun with high hopes and funding in the 1960s and 1970s. To avoid the same fate in the 1990s, libraries began to refine their goals and objectives to be sure they were effectively fulfilling their selected roles of library service. No longer did they adopt additional objectives and initiate new services without first examining their current services and then carefully planning for their future needs.

In examining their present and future needs, public libraries were faced with one major dilemma, that of providing "service to all." As the only agency that serves all persons from birth to old age, public libraries in the past had tried to be all things to all people. Public library staffs had attempted to provide equal service to patrons in all age and interest groups who came to their libraries. They took great pride in being able to provide more services and materials on more subjects for their patrons than did other types of libraries. However, with the advent of the concepts of role selecting and goal setting in the 1980s, libraries in the 1990s began to reevaluate this need to provide unilateral library services. They considered the ups and downs of library economics, the availability of electronic technology, and the capabilities of networking with other libraries as they developed library programs and services to satisfy all their patrons' needs.

Of primary importance to public libraries in the development of their programs and services was their vulnerability to economic changes in their own communities. With their almost total reliance on public property taxes, public library revenues were controlled by governmental tax regulations. In some states and cities, the public library's ability to increase these tax revenues was limited by legal or political considerations. In others, libraries had to go to the voters to get approval for increasing their tax limits, and these elections were not always successful. To minimize their dependence upon these sources, libraries began to explore additional sources of income and develop creative and innovative ways to finance their services and programs. Public libraries in growing communities began collecting developer "impact" fees from real estate developers to help finance library services to owners of new residences. Libraries joined the Public

Library Foundation or similar investment pools to increase the interest on their library funds. Many libraries held used-book sales, conducted library auctions, or sold library items to raise additional funds. A few libraries even allowed profit-making ventures such as restaurants or friends-operated retail shops within the library.

Although the majority of the public libraries charged overdue fines, many libraries increased these overdue fines and began to charge higher or additional processing fees for lost items. To help ease their economic plight, some libraries began to charge fees for formerly free services such as reserves and interlibrary loans. Others also charged fees for expensive services such as database searches or the loan of expensive materials such as videotapes, best sellers, and equipment. These latter fees caused considerable debate within the library profession. Opponents of such fees felt that the income raised from them was not a sufficient reason to deny access to library materials and services by patrons who could not afford them. In the final analysis, the revenues raised from all of these various methods only accounted for a small portion of the average public library's budget.

A more positive effect on library budgets occurred as libraries joined together in library systems and cooperative library networks to share their resources and stretch their budgets. By sharing the costs of automation technology, even the smaller libraries found that they could afford to join bibliographic cooperatives with circulation, cataloging, and interlibrary loan capabilities. No longer did they have to provide access to all the information needed by their patrons at their own libraries. Instead, they participated in regional system and statewide resource networks to share their materials and information with other libraries. These materials were usually sent from library to library by van delivery systems and mail systems. However, beginning in the 1990s, these delivery systems were often supplemented by FAX and online computer transmissions. In addition to exchanging materials, libraries exchanged their patrons. Reciprocal borrowing agreements between libraries enabled patrons to visit and check out materials at other libraries throughout a regional system or state. In addition, patrons could use a computer in either the library or their homes to see which libraries had the materials they wanted and whether or not these materials were available. Because all types of libraries participated in these cooperative systems and programs, public libraries were able to more fully provide the desired "service to all."

In providing library service to all of their patrons, library administrators and their staffs took great care to develop policies and procedures that ensured everyone was treated alike, whether the patron was a city council member, a library board trustee, or a young child. They adopted the ALA *Library Bill of Rights* and *Freedom to Read and View* statements and instituted policies and procedures to protect the intellectual freedom of their patrons. (See chapter 12.) Such policies included free access to the library's collections by children and the protection of patron records from public inquiry. In addition to providing equitable services, libraries had to juggle the needs of the various programs and services within the library. Programs and departments such as public services, technical services, and children, young adult, and adult services competed for budgets and staffs. Balancing the needs of all these areas required library directors and their staffs to constantly evaluate their goals and objec.ives and establish criteria for performance and evaluation.

Libraries were forced to reevaluate the staffing needs of their services and departments. As libraries developed new roles and goals of service, their staffing needs changed. Libraries with a popular materials library role added adult readers' advisors to their staffs. Reference library staffs were required to be computer literate in database searching. Children's staffs were expanded to include specialists in preschool or young adult services who were knowledgeable about the growth and development of their patrons. A library's ability to fill these changing staff positions, however, was impacted heavily by social and economic conditions.

Some libraries had reduced their children's staffs in the 1980s as they felt the effects of zero population growth. However, by the 1990s, many of these same libraries faced the need to increase these staffs to serve the offspring of the "baby boom" generation. At the same time, fewer librarians were being educated to fill these positions. Reduced enrollments and finances in the 1980s had forced many library schools to close their doors. Libraries that turned to the traditional pool of housewives and students to fill their clerical and technical positions also found that these people were no longer willing to work for minimum wages. Thus, library staffing needs became one of the important areas of concern for libraries in the 1990s.

These library staffing needs varied greatly depending upon the size of a library and the roles it had selected. Public libraries could range from a 1- or 2-person branch to a main library staffed with 50 to 100 people. Medium-to-large-sized libraries usually had a large range of library positions at all levels filled with appropriately trained personnel. They might have many specialized librarians who were responsible for administration, reference and readers' advisory services, collection development, and programming. Library technicians or advanced library clerks might perform paraprofessional or supportive tasks in such areas as children's services, bookmobiles, outreach, and technical services. Smaller libraries might have only one or two librarians to handle reference and children's services. In very small libraries or branches and on bookmobiles, the staff members tended to be generalists who shared all the jobs from checking out materials to helping a person find a book. In these libraries, there might not be a great differentiation between library positions, and the person in charge might be a technician without formal library education.

As smaller libraries began to grow in size and complexity, their staff members tended to become more specialized in their responsibilities, and their job classifications became more distinct. Many of these staff members had advanced education, although they might not have masters' degrees in library science. Their education and training might be in specialties other than library science. Graphic artists, TV technicians, computer programmers, and specialists in information science or public relations were just a few of the varied types of personnel found in public libraries. Also, in these larger library systems, there was a very definite pattern of specialization among library personnel. It was not unusual in such libraries for library employees to work many years in one particular area of either public or technical services. For example, in the circulation department, one clerk might be specifically responsible for reserves, one for overdues, and other clerks for checking materials in and out. These clerks might be supervised by a library technician or librarian and supported by library pages or shelvers.

development
& specific
roles/functions

To organize these varied staff members so they could work most effectively, public libraries began to examine and evaluate their personnel policies and procedures. Library administrators recognized that they should take the personal needs of their staff members into account as they designed these policies. Nowhere was this need more evident than in scheduling staff for the public service desks. It was not unusual for a public library to be open from 9-9 Monday through Friday, 9-5 on Saturday, and 1-5 on Sunday. Library administrators and supervisors found it challenging to schedule these 60- to 80-hour weeks that required an equivalent of one-and-a-half to two separate staffs working 40 hours each. In addition to making sure the library was well staffed, supervisors tried to consider their staff members' personal preferences for the hours they worked. They knew that many people do not like to work more often than every other Saturday or Sunday, and most staff members only want to work a few nights a week. In addition, state and federal labor laws imposed restrictions on the number of hours a person could work and how much that person should be paid. To resolve these conflicting scheduling needs, libraries employed many staff members on a part-time basis in all areas of the library at all employee classification levels. They also provided flexible scheduling for their full-time employees as well as shared jobs in which the responsibilities might be split among several employees.

Libraries also made other changes in their personnel practices. They revised their pay schedules to provide more incentive for employees to stay with them on a long-term basis. Jobs were redefined to make them more interesting and give individuals some responsibility for their own work performance. Leave policies became more flexible, not only to conform to federal guidelines, but also to allow for an individual's personal or family needs. When it was possible, libraries also allowed educational leaves or paid tuition for library-related courses. Staff members at all levels were included in management work circles or department teams to help identify library goals and set library objectives. The distinctions between professional librarian and nonprofessional staff became less important as all library staff members began to work as one unit to meet their library patrons' needs.

Whether or not libraries will succeed in meeting these patron needs is conjecture. Visions of the public library in the year 2015 range from the library as a fully automated and robotized institution to one that completely disappears. Some library futurists see the library as a place where wondrous and exotic adventures may be experienced while others see it replaced by home access to information and entertainment.[7] However, whether or not the public library as we know it in the 1990s will survive until 2015 will depend greatly upon the effort, imagination, and perseverence of everyone connected with it, from the library board and director down to the newest library clerk.

SUMMARY

Public libraries serve all citizens at every stage of life, whether they live in a large city or in the most remote rural area. Public libraries have developed collections, programs, and services to help them fulfill their principle of "service to all." To guide libraries in this development, the PLA has established standards identifying eight major roles of service from which libraries are encouraged to select and develop two to three roles to meet their communities' needs.

Once libraries select their roles of service, they often develop unique collections and services to meet these needs. Thus, libraries that select the same roles do not necessarily develop the same services. Instead, each library examines its community to identify and provide programs and services that are coordinated with other community agencies and services. In this process, each library's success in meeting its own community needs will always be strongly affected by prevailing economic and political conditions at the local, state, and national level.

REVIEW QUESTIONS

1. Identify the roles of library service that a public library might select.

2. Identify some of the major services libraries provide to fulfill these roles.

3. State the underlying philosophy of library service for public libraries as presented in the PLA planning documents.

4. Identify the levels of input and output measures recommended by the state library agency for the state in which you live.

5. Visit a public library you have not visited before. Compare the objectives and services of this library with those discussed in the text. Also, compare the input and output measures in question number 4 above with the staff, collections, etc., of the library you visited.

NOTES

[1] Robert Ellis Lee, *Continuing Education for Adults through the American Public Library, 1833-1964* (Chicago: ALA, 1966), 116-19.

[2] Public Library Association, *Public Library Mission Statement and Its Imperatives for Service* (Chicago: ALA, 1979).

[3] Public Library Association, *Minimum Standards for Public Library Systems, 1966* (Chicago: ALA, 1967), p. 10.

[4] Charles R. McClure, et al., *Planning and Role-Setting for Public Libraries: A Manual of Options and Procedures* (Chicago: ALA, 1987), chap. 4.

[5] Glenn R. Wittig, "Some Characteristics of Mississippi Adult Library Users," *Public Libraries* 30, no. 1 (January-February 1991): 30.

[6] Clara Stanton Jones, *Public Library Information and Referral Service* (Syracuse, NY: Gaylord Professional Publications, 1978), 22.

[7] Bruce A. Shuman, *The Library of the Future: Alternative Scenarios for the Information Profession* (Englewood, CO: Libraries Unlimited, 1989), 116.

SELECTED READINGS

Future of the Public Library. Conference proceedings of OCLC Online Computer Library Center, Dublin, Ohio, 20-22 March 1988.

Giacoma, Pete. *The Fee or Free Decision: Legal, Economic, Political and Ethical Perspectives for Public Libraries*. New York: Neal-Schuman, 1989.

Ihrig, Alice B. *Decision-making for Public Libraries*. (Library Professional Publications). Hamden, CT: Shoe String, 1989.

Lee, Pat W. "Managing Public Libraries in the 21st Century." *Journal of Library Administration* 11, nos. 1 and 2 (1989).

McClure, Charles R., et al. *Planning and Role-Setting for Public Libraries: A Manual of Options and Procedures*. Chicago: ALA, 1987.

Palmour, Vernon E. *A Planning Process for Public Libraries*. Chicago: ALA, 1980.

Public Library Association. *Minimum Standards for Public Library Systems, 1966*. Chicago: ALA, 1967.

_____. *Public Library Mission Statement and Its Imperatives for Service*. Chicago: ALA, 1979.

Sager, Donald J. *Managing the Public Library*. 2d ed. Boston: G. K. Hall, 1989.

Shuman, Bruce A. *The Library of the Future: Alternative Scenarios for the Information Profession*. Englewood, CO: Libraries Unlimited, 1989.

Van Horn, Nancy, et al. *Output Measures for Public Libraries: A Manual for Standardized Procedures*. 2d ed. Chicago: ALA, 1987.

Webb, T. D. *Public Library Organization and Structure*. Jefferson, NC: McFarland, 1989.

CHAPTER 6

SCHOOL LIBRARY MEDIA CENTERS

In many of today's schools, a well-run library media center may very well be the most active room in the entire school. Children may come there on an individual basis to choose books, use computers, view videotapes, or listen to audio materials. Entire classes may come to learn how to use the media center or to locate information for their reports. Groups of students may come for help in making transparencies or producing videotapes for class projects. All of these students may be assisted by professional librarians or media specialists, media technicians, and clerks. These active media centers have shown how important they can be in a modern educational system. Yet, it is amazing that school library media centers have taken so long to become a basic part of the educational institutions of this country.

THE BEGINNINGS

Not until the 1950s did most secondary schools have libraries, and even in the 1970s many elementary school libraries were just getting started. What took the educational systems so long to recognize that libraries were necessary components of the educational process? The answer to this question lies in the schools' educational goals and methods. In the early centuries of our country's history, "school" consisted primarily of students memorizing information presented by the teacher. There were few textbooks, and students were not encouraged to question. In the nineteenth century and the early part of the twentieth century, emphasis was on subject content, which was mainly learned from textbooks. In the 1920s and 1930s, the emphasis shifted to the learner, and finally, in the 1940s, the emphasis was placed on life adjustment and the education of all youth for their future roles.[1]

However, the space race of the 1950s and 1960s placed new emphasis on subject mastery so that U.S. education would be equal to education in the Soviet Union. To achieve this end, the 1960s emphasized the education of individual students according to their needs and abilities to prepare them for participation in American society. Unfortunately, economics often prevented schools and libraries from meeting these commendable goals in the 1970s and 1980s. The situation became so grave that the U.S. National Commission on Excellence in Education published a report in 1983 that identified the United States as *A Nation at Risk*. This report determined that the United States had let its formal educational system deteriorate to a very dangerous level. In response to this report, librarians drafted *Alliance for Excellence*, a statement that identified the important steps school libraries should take to reverse this deterioration process.

These developments in education had a direct impact on school library services because school libraries always function within the school's goals and objectives. The first school libraries supported learning that came mainly from textbooks. These libraries tended to be just classroom collections of encyclopedias, older textbooks, and perhaps a few reading books. The major impetus for the development of centralized secondary or high school libraries came from the establishment of educational accreditation associations at the turn of the twentieth century. The purpose of these associations was to rate high schools so that colleges could equate graduates of one high school with another. Because libraries were included in the criteria listed by the associations, those schools that wanted to become accredited had to develop libraries that met the standards of the accrediting associations.

STANDARDS

In the 1920s, these associations and the ALA began to develop standards first for high school libraries and then for elementary school libraries. However, they did not become widely adopted. Instead, the major type of library service that schools provided (particularly below the high school level) consisted of traveling library collections from state agencies. In many cases, public libraries provided school collections to the classrooms and public librarians to visit the schools. Sometimes the public library was actually part of the school system or housed branches in the school buildings. These services seemed to be satisfactory for those school systems that still considered learning to be largely classroom oriented.

As educators in the 1940s began to recognize that students should be involved in the discovery of learning based on study and inquiry, the school systems began to experiment with new methods of teaching. These methods emphasized the need for library services and materials to support the expanded curriculum. To help identify what these library services and materials should be, the ALA published standards for school library service in 1945 entitled *School Libraries for Today and Tomorrow*. These standards emphasized that the school library was an integral part of a quality educational system. They also identified qualitative and quantitative standards for library resources and services that should be provided by a professional staff in a centralized library.

The typical school library that developed at this time was a high school library housed in one room about the size of two classrooms and located in a corner of the school. The collection consisted of books arranged on shelves that stood along the walls, and the staff consisted of one professional librarian (with perhaps a clerk) who only had time to manage the library and its collection. If the school provided audiovisual films and equipment, they were often housed in a closet near the library or administered by someone else in another part of the school building. Very few elementary school libraries were established, and on the whole, the concept of library services envisioned by the standards was seldom implemented.

To encourage library development, in 1956 ALA published a policy statement identifying the important role the school library should play in the school's total instructional process. For the first time, the library was envisioned to be a central school library that included all types of learning materials available to both students and teachers. The concepts of this statement were translated into new *Standards for School Library Programs* in 1960. The adoption of these standards was greatly facilitated by the country's interest in the educational system after *Sputnik* was launched in 1957. In addition, the National Defense Education Act (NDEA) of 1958 provided funds for schools to buy print and nonprint materials and equipment. Sometimes states also used these funds to hire school library supervisors at the state level to help local libraries purchase these materials. The 1960 standards, therefore, coincided with society's need for quality education.

The standards helped usher in a new era for library services. For the first time, educators began to recognize that these libraries were an integral part of the educational curriculum. Central libraries containing all types of learning materials began to develop in elementary, junior, and senior high schools. Librarians were recognized as teachers whose subject specialty enabled them to help students and teachers use such materials as books, audiotapes, records, films, filmstrips, transparencies, and programmed instruction. These materials were used equally in either the classroom or the library to help students learn. The concept of a library changed to that of an IMC, instructional materials center, where many learning activities took place.

In the IMC, students and teachers could listen to or view the library's media or even produce their own. Students and teachers also could work in the library on group projects, hold meetings in its conference rooms, or they could study independently in the quiet areas. Library technical and clerical staffs were hired to free librarians to provide instruction in the use of the library and its resources or to help students learn independently. Librarians were able to perform such professional tasks as offering in-service training to teachers in the use of audiovisual materials and equipment. They became active members of curriculum committees and teaching teams. The modern school library as perceived by librarians many years before had finally arrived in the 1960s in many school districts.

This phenomenal growth of school libraries in the 1960s was largely due to several important developments. Foremost among these was the constant change that took place in educational philosophies and systems. Educators began to recognize that their students had varying educational backgrounds, abilities, and needs. They recognized that to meet these needs schools and libraries must provide varied educational methods and opportunities for learning. The development of libraries also was encouraged by the influx of private funds, which was the second major development that affected school library growth in the 1960s. The Knapp Foundation funded a school library demonstration project. This project chose demonstration libraries to serve as model school IMCs providing effective library programs in accordance with the new standards. Librarians and educators from throughout this country and the world visited these IMCs, enabling librarians to show their superintendents and school boards how quality library services could be integrated into their own school systems. The Knapp Foundation also sponsored a School Library Manpower Project that delineated and identified the kinds of staffing needed to support such comprehensive library services.

The final major development affecting library growth during this period was the passing of the Elementary and Secondary Education Act (ESEA) in 1965. Title (or chapter) II and later Title IV of this act provided the monies, direction, and impetus to state school library agencies and local schools to develop library services. State agencies used ESEA funds to hire state school library consultants, provide guidelines for local schools, and direct and consult with schools in developing and improving library programs. The state agencies also distributed ESEA monies to local schools to purchase materials, hire staff, and develop innovative and model IMC programs. This influx of monies for school library services, combined with community interest in providing such services, heralded the arrival of quality school libraries/IMCs.

With IMCs well on their way to becoming a part of many local school systems, new standards were proposed in 1969 by the American Association of School Librarians (AASL) and the Association of Educational Communications and Technology (AECT), formerly the Department of Audio-Visual Instruction of the National Education Association (DAVI). These *Standards for School Media Centers* carried the IMC concept one step further. They proposed that schools develop media programs and services that integrated all types of media into the curriculum based upon their contributions to the educational program of the school rather than upon their formats. The standards also proposed replacing the terms *library*, *librarian*, *audiovisual center*, and *audiovisual specialist* with the new terms *media center* and *media specialist* to better identify the entities that would emerge from fulfilling these new standards.

FROM LIBRARY TO
LIBRARY MEDIA CENTER

The concept of a "media center" caused great consternation in the educational and library worlds in the 1960s and 1970s. Many school systems enthusiastically endorsed this concept and combined their library, audiovisual, video, and graphics operations and programs into one media department. Titles for such new departments varied from media center and library media center to learning resource center, instructional media center, instructional resource center, or just resource center. However, no matter what their titles were, they all attempted to provide the media services recommended in the standards. Other librarians and audiovisual specialists had difficulty adjusting to this new concept, which required them to alter their thinking and their focus. Often they, as well as many educators, believed that the standards were utopian rather than practicable. To add to this confusion, the economic crisis of the 1970s practically wiped out the federal monies that had been used to develop library services. To provide direction in this chaotic time, the AASL and AECT published new standards in 1975.

The 1975 standards, *Media Programs, District and School*, expanded the concept of media programs beyond the individual school to include services and facilities that could be provided at the district level. The standards were based on the principle that media were a central part of the learning process and that if schools were to meet students' needs, they must provide quality media programs. These programs were seen to be a combination of district-wide and building-level services that would be tailored to fit the educational goals and objectives of each individual school system. Although quantitative standards were included (see figure 6.1, page 96), the emphasis was on the qualitative aspect of the programs.

This emphasis was extended in 1988 with AASL's and AECT's publication of *Information Power: Guidelines for School Library Media Programs*. These standards responded to issues that had been raised in the U.S. National Commission on Excellence in Education's report, *A Nation at Risk*, and answered in librarians' *Alliance for Excellence* statement. In particular, *Alliance for Excellence* had identified important steps that school library supporters should take to develop quality library services and resources for every school library. For example, the statement said that libraries should incorporate their services and resource collections into their schools' curricula. They should provide access to, and instruction in the use of, information resources both within and outside the library. Each library should be well funded and staffed by well-educated and paid library media specialists. These library media professionals should be responsible for actively indoctrinating teachers and administrators in the appropriate role and activities of the school library.

Information Power provided the guidelines and directives to help library media personnel carry out these recommended steps. This publication described the library media program's vital role in helping students gain the information skills necessary to function in a learning society. *Information Power* was based on a planning philosophy and presented guidelines rather than standards that a local school and community could use to develop a library media center program to serve its individual educational needs. The document's primary focus was to help the building-level library media specialist develop a team partnership with administrators and teachers to identify and establish the best instructional programs.

The guidelines reinforced the role of the library media specialist as that of an information specialist, teacher, and instructional consultant working with teachers to fulfill curriculum needs. They also recommended that the library media program and resources become fully integrated into the school's educational program. In addition, physical access to in-house media resources was to be extended beyond the school day. Access to information outside the library would be provided via interlibrary loans, multilibrary networks, and electronic technologies. A strong emphasis on intellectual freedom and intellectual access to diverse viewpoints was also encouraged. Finally, extensive guidelines were presented for the development of library media facilities designed specifically to serve individual school and curriculum needs.

Along with these qualitative guidelines, *Information Power* also identified some quantitative guidelines. (See figure 6.1.) However, for the first time, these quantitative guidelines were based on survey results of actual services being provided by the nation's schools. The quantities in these guidelines were based upon reports from 571 out of 3,500 public schools that provided at least 75 percent of 22 library media services identified for the guidelines. (See figure 6.2, page 97.) Such statistics would be used as bellwethers for school library media programs in the 1990s and beyond. For example, other schools were encouraged to use these results to analyze and evaluate their own programs in their search for excellence. However, because these statistics were based on only 17 percent of the public school universe, cries of utopianism were again heard from many schools.

(Text continues on page 98.)

Fig. 6.1. Brief comparison of national school library media standards.

	1969 Media Centers	1975 Media Programs	1988 Information Power
OBJECTIVES:	Unified media program is recommended	Develop district program to meet individual student needs. Media program tailored to individual school's curriculum. Evaluation based on effectiveness in supporting school curriculum.	Provides planning guidelines for school library media program to meet individual school needs and expand access by students and faculty to information and ideas.
STAFF:	1 media specialist for every 250 students. 1 technician and 1 aide for media specialist in schools of 2,000 students or less. 1 graphics technician. Over 2,000 students, adjust ratio 2 to 1	1 specialist as media director. Staff varies by size of school: from 1 specialist, 1 technician, and 1 aide for 250 students to 3-4 specialists, 3-5 technicians, and 2-3 aides for 1,000. District services will affect school level needs.	1 media program director. Specific number of all staff determined by school programs, size, number of students, and faculty. Based on high-service program, school size and level: from 1.5-2 in elementary schools under 500 to 4.7-8 in high schools over 1,000.
COLLECTION:	Books: At least 6,000-10,000 titles representing 10,000 volumes or 20 volumes per student. AV: Each type of material enumerated.	School of 500 or less: Minimum 20,000 items or 40 per student. Books: 8,000-12,000; Magazines: 50-175 titles; AV by type: 5,300-12,200 total; District: Professional library; 3,000 films, lesser-used AV	Provide materials and equipment in all formats. Varies by school program, size and type: e.g., from 9,227 books and 1,690 other items in elementary schools under 500 students to 37,668 books and 40,925 other items in high schools over 1,000 students
BUDGET:	To maintain an up-to-date collection: NOT LESS than 6% of national average for per-pupil operational cost (PPOC) per year, per student. Funds used for individual school and system media center. Flexibility is desired. Usually one-half books, one-half AV.	Total district budget: Equal to 10% of national per-pupil operational cost per student as outlined by U.S. Dept. of Education.	Building-level maintenance budget based on formula using current budget, increase/decrease in students, need to replace by age or loss and inflation rate. FACILITIES: Flexible to meet school programs. Range from 3,900-8,100 sq. ft. based on school size and type.

Fig. 6.2. School library media services. (Reprinted with permission of the American Library Association from *Information Power: Guidelines for School Library Media Programs*, by AASL, 1988, pp. Appendix A, p. 116 © 1988 ALA.)

1. Offers a sequential program of library skills instruction.

2. Coordinates library skills instruction with classroom instruction.

3. Informally instructs students in the use of various types of materials and equipment.

4. Conducts inservice education for teachers in the effective evaluation, selection, and use of media.

5. Assists curriculum committee in selecting appropriate materials and media program activities for resource units and curriculum guides.

6. Helps individual teachers to coordinate media program activities and resources with subject areas, units, and textbooks.

7. Helps teachers to develop, select, implement, and evaluate learning activities requiring various types of media.

8. Provides teachers with information about new educational and media developments.

9. Provides reference assistance to teachers.

10. Assists students in locating information and resources valuable to their educational needs and to the growth of their personal interests and ability.

11. Helps students and teachers find and use relevant information sources outside the school.

12. Provides interlibrary loan services to students.

13. Provides interlibrary loan services to teachers.

14. Provides reading/listening/viewing guidance to students.

15. Helps parents realize the importance of assisting their children to understand the benefits of reading, listening, and viewing for pleasure as well as for gaining information.

16. Coordinates in-school production of materials required for instructional use and other activities.

17. Provides technical assistance to students in the production of materials.

18. Provides technical assistance to teachers in the production of materials.

19. Coordinates textbook selection, ordering, and distribution program in school.

20. Coordinates school-operated radio station.

21. Coordinates video production activities in school.

22. Coordinates cable or other TV transmission and utilization activities in school.

Implementation of these guidelines was affected by both the educational and economic climates. The majority of teachers continued to rely on lecturing that did not need strong library media support. In addition, many administrators and teachers did not expect much involvement by library media specialists in the school's educational process. In such an educational climate, some school library media specialists felt uncomfortable adopting these new roles and becoming agents of change. The economic climate was also not conducive to the development of such comprehensive school library media programs. Although *A Nation at Risk* had recognized the need for a strong educational program, local communities were often reluctant to finance such programs. To encourage these latter communities to implement strong school library media programs, most states had adopted statewide school library media standards by 1990. Many of these states required local schools to meet these guidelines if they wanted to receive state or federal monies. Strong regional accreditation associations also encouraged the development of strong library media programs through their accreditation standards and local self-study requirements.

LIBRARY MEDIA PROGRAMS

Although state and national guidelines had some impact on the development of school library media programs, such development was also strongly influenced by the philosophies, objectives, and economics of the individual school systems served. In many school systems, the library media programs not only did not grow during the late 1980s and early 1990s, but they even began to stagnate or shrink. In other school systems with excellent educational programs, outstanding library media programs were developed. These superior library media programs were no accident, however. The more successful and effective programs were based upon stated philosophies and objectives carefully designed by everyone concerned. Library media center staffs, administrators, teachers, students, and parents worked together, sometimes in advisory committees, to develop library media programs and activities to meet the needs of individual students.

Many of the resources provided in these library media centers included much more than the traditional print and film resources of the 1970s. Many books, magazines, newspapers, pamphlets, and catalogs were also available in foreign languages or in formats that developmentally handicapped students could use. Nonprint forms included not only the more common audiovisual formats such as art prints, realia, microforms, films, and videotapes, but also materials such as compact and laser discs. Technological advancements also enabled library media centers to provide access to information in new ways. Many library media centers provided computers for the students' own use as well as for computer-assisted instruction, CD-ROM access to expensive resources, and computer-based catalogs. Library media centers provided dial access or online access to local, regional, and national union library catalogs and national bibliographic databases such as DIALOG. Access to daily newspaper services such as Express Exchange X-PRESS was available as well. Some centers provided cable television, interactive video, and satellite distance learning programs.

To make these library media resources more readily available to students and teachers within the schools, library media centers adopted flexible scheduling to accommodate both classes and individualized instruction. They expanded their programs to include access to resources outside the school. Library media centers joined with other schools and other types of libraries in networks and consortia to share their resources through interlibrary loan networks, access to special collections such as film collections, and FAX transmissions of materials such as magazine articles. Access to other collections was extended through direct loans to schools, student access to other libraries, and cooperative collection development.

In addition, businesses and corporations became involved in local "adopt-a-school" programs to help schools and library media centers expand their programs. Some national companies such as Apple and IBM offered educational discounts and programs. Other corporations made news broadcasts such as CNN (Cable News Network) News and Channel One available to schools without cost. Through these and other cooperative activities, library media specialists found they could stretch their budgets. At the same time, this increased access to additional resources and information expanded the library media program's impact on the educational process.

This impact was further heightened by library media specialists who took on the roles of teacher, information specialist, and instructional consultant. As teachers and instructional consultants, library media specialists did not only teach library skills but also worked with teachers to integrate these skills into curriculum projects. Many of these specialists not only developed microcomputer resource center laboratories, but they also taught students, teachers, administrators, and parents how to use these resources. Specialists worked with students and teachers to develop such resources as independent learning programs or packages on specialized subjects using all types of media. They developed print and media productions of class projects such as oral history audio- or videotapes of local interest (similar to the Foxfire books[2]). Games and kits were developed and produced by students and teachers to encourage students to think. Finally, library media specialists worked as researchers to gather library and community resources for in-depth group research reports on subjects.

As information specialists, library media specialists also worked with teachers to emphasize literature and the enjoyment of reading. Programs such as reading incentive programs, reading clubs, battles of the books, and contests were developed with teachers, administrators, parents, and other libraries to encourage and reward students for increasing their reading. To further encourage participation in these programs and to disseminate information about the total library media program, media specialists also publicized their programs through newsletters and public relations campaigns.

In addition to these expanded resources and programs, the library media center itself also changed. Some school systems with more than one school had already established library media programs at the district level to assist the building-level library media center staff. In such systems, district library media centers often provided centralized services such as ordering, cataloging, and processing; graphic production and duplication; television or radio production; and the distribution of expensive media collections such as films, kits, and live animal exhibits. In the 1980s and 1990s, these services were automated and expanded to include the centralization of other library operations such as circulation, media bookings, and bibliographic and administrative support. The district library media staff also helped building-level library media personnel develop programs to meet the educational goals of their individual schools.

The organization of building-level library media centers depended upon the educational programs of the schools they served. Some library media centers were centralized in one geographic area while others had a central library media center supported by satellite subject resource centers. These satellite centers might be adjacent to the central facility or adjacent to their subject areas in other parts of the building. Some schools adopted an "open concept" of learning that produced media centers without walls. Others developed library media centers that included small rooms for study groups as well as classrooms large enough for coordinated library-subject instruction. However, it was not the pattern of organization alone that determined the quality of a library media program. It was the program's ability to become fully integrated into the school's curriculum that determined how effective such a program would be.

LIBRARY MEDIA PERSONNEL

The development of quality library media programs also depended upon the development of qualified library media staffs to direct and operate these programs. Based on state educational requirements that teacher-certified personnel must be in charge whenever children were present, the majority of library media centers were staffed by teacher-certified library media specialists by 1990. These specialists usually had either MLS degrees or master's of educational media degrees, and many worked under district media coordinators. Some media staffs also included other professionals with varied backgrounds and experiences. At the building level, media specialists often worked outside the media center as integral members of the educational staff. In fact, the success of the library media program in each school often depended upon the specialist's ability to become accepted by the other teachers as an important member of the educational team.

As library media specialists became more successful in this educational role, they began to turn the day-to-day operations of the library media center over to their support staffs. Encouraged by national and state guidelines, many schools had developed full-time media center staffs based on a ratio of one specialist to one technician and one clerk. At the building level, this meant that library media technicians often supervised clerks, students, and volunteers in checking materials in and out. Library media technicians also supervised building resource centers that were separated from the main library media centers. In some smaller schools, library media technicians ran building-level media centers under the direction of a system-wide media specialist.

In larger school systems, staff in the building-level library media centers were often backed up by district library media staffs who could provide further professional or technical expertise. Specialists and technicians in such specialized areas as graphics, television, cable, audiovisual production, and computer technology could be found in district library media centers. These staff members produced resource materials to be used in classrooms and building-level media centers. Districtwide processing centers provided centralized support staff to order and process materials for the individual media centers. Centralized booking services for films, videotapes, and computerized learning were usually staffed by clerks and/or technicians, as were many of the centralized automated services.

Although many of the technical duties in these library media centers required specialized skills (e.g., computer literacy), formal training was not usually a prerequisite for library media clerical and technical personnel. In some cases, this was due to the economic recession of the 1980s that saw the decline of library media technician training programs. In other cases, this was due to the constant availability in earlier years of a large pool of untrained but talented workers. These workers were usually homemakers willing to volunteer or work at very low wages to have work hours and vacations that coincided with their families' vacations. By the 1990s, however, the economic need for people to make more than the minimum wage had almost eliminated this worker pool. Thus, if school library media centers were going to meet their growing need for library media support staff with more specialized skills, they would have to change their hiring patterns. They would have to seek out and pay well-trained technical and clerical staffs to fulfill their schools' missions.

SUMMARY

The growth of school library media centers has been tied to changes in the philosophy of American education. When education was based on rote memory or straight lecturing, schools had few libraries or only small classroom collections of reference books. However, as society and its schools began to emphasize educating the individual student, libraries began to take their place as an integral part of the educational system. Supported by federal and state monies, library organizations developed standards to encourage the development of school library media centers. These centers developed strong library collections and services at the local level to meet individual schools' needs.

Library media collections grew to include all types of materials, from books to audiovisuals to computer technology. Their services became comprehensive and were integrated into the educational system. Libraries at the building level were supplemented by district-level support services. School library media centers cooperated with public and academic libraries to provide services such as inter-library and direct loans. In keeping with such expanded roles and services, school libraries have changed their names from libraries to instructional materials centers to media centers. Similarly, school librarians and audiovisual specialists have become media specialists supported by media technicians and clerks.

REVIEW QUESTIONS

1. Identify the major objectives of school library media center programs.

2. Briefly describe school library media development from the classroom library to school library to library media center.

3. Discuss the differences in philosophy between the 1966 and 1974 national school library standards.

4. Compare your own state's standards with the guidelines of *Information Power*.

5. Identify the kinds of media that can be found in a school library media center.

6. Describe some services and programs provided in successful library media programs.

7. Identify duties of the different levels of staff in the modern library media center.

8. Visit a school library media center and compare its objectives, staff, collection, and services with those described in this chapter.

NOTES

[1]Jean Key Gates, *Introduction to Librarianship* (New York: McGraw-Hill, 1968), 220-21.

[2]Foxfire books preserve the cultural heritage of Appalachia through published interviews with senior citizens.

SELECTED READINGS

AASL. Knapp School Libraries Project. *Realization: The Final Report of the Knapp School Libraries Project*. Edited by Peggy Sullivan. Chicago: ALA, 1968.

AASL/AECT. *Information Power: Guidelines for School Library Media Programs*. Chicago: ALA, 1988.

_____. *Media Programs: District and School*. Chicago: ALA, 1975.

_____. *Standards for School Media Centers*. Chicago: ALA, 1969.

ALA Yearbook: A Review of Library Events. Chicago: ALA, 1976- .

Kulleseid, Eleanor R. *Beyond Survival to Power: For School Library Media Professionals*. Hamden, CT: Library Professional Publications, 1985.

Liesener, James W. "Information Power: A Broader Perspective." In *School Library Media Annual, 1989*. Englewood, CO: Libraries Unlimited, 1989.

Loertscher, David V., May Lein Ho, and Melvin M. Bowie. "Exemplary Elementary Schools and Their Library Media Centers: A Research Report." *School Library Media Quarterly* 15 (Spring 1987): 147-53.

Parsons, Larry A., comp. *A Funny Thing Happened on the Way to the School Library: A Treasury of Anecdotes, Quotes, and Other Happenings*. Englewood, CO: Libraries Unlimited, 1990.

Prostano, Emanuel T., and Joyce S. Prostano. *The School Library Media Center*. 4th ed. Englewood, CO: Libraries Unlimited, 1987.

"School Libraries in the '90s." *Illinois Libraries* 72, no. 7 (October 1990).

School Library Media Annual. Vol. 1- . Littleton, CO: Libraries Unlimited, 1983- .

Standards for School Library Programs. Chicago: ALA, 1960.

CHAPTER 7

ACADEMIC LIBRARIES

Just as school library media centers have met the changing needs of public schools, academic libraries have met the changing needs and objectives of their parent institutions. Colleges and universities have changed since the 1700s and 1800s, and they are no longer institutions based primarily on faculty lectures and faculty research. As a result, academic libraries have changed from storehouses of books to learning centers providing access to information in all its varied forms. Nevertheless, it is difficult to describe one type of academic institution or academic library because of the variety of institutions this general term covers.

TYPES OF ACADEMIC LIBRARIES

The library world defines an *academic library* as a library in an institution providing education beyond the high school level. This level of education is also called postsecondary or higher education. By 1990, there were more than 4,600 libraries at this level in the United States. Academic libraries are more commonly found in colleges and universities, but community colleges, junior colleges, and technical institutions also have academic libraries. A *college* is an institution that offers bachelor's degrees and perhaps master's degrees in the liberal arts and sciences. On the other hand, a *university* is an institution that offers doctoral degrees and may contain a number of undergraduate colleges. The distinction between the two types is very important to library development.

College libraries are generally much smaller in size and scope than university libraries because they are not trying to support graduate education to the extensive degree that universities are. College libraries may have collections ranging in size from 50,000 to 200,000 volumes and are likely to be staffed by 5 to 10 professionals supported by clerical and student personnel. (See figure 7.1.) University libraries may have collections ranging from several hundred thousand volumes to millions of volumes. These larger libraries may be staffed by 25 to 100 or more professional, associate, technical, and clerical personnel supported by many student helpers. Also, university libraries generally have large collections in every subject area while college libraries tend to concentrate on the general arts and sciences with a strong emphasis on humanities, social sciences, and broad sciences.

Fig. 7.1. Typical academic library public services. (From U.S. Dept. of Education 1985 Survey of College and University Libraries. Statistics are given for Bachelor Degree Colleges and Research Universities. *Statistical Norms for College and University Libraries*, W. John Minter, ed.)

	COLLEGES		UNIVERSITIES	
	Public	Independ.	Public	Independ.
WEEKLY PUBLIC SERVICE HOURS				
50th Percentile	79	83	102	105
75th Percentile	84	92	108	112
REFERENCE TRANSACTIONS PER WEEK				
50th Percentile	175	100	2,106	1,477
75th Percentile	314	92	4,282	2,400
ATTENDANCE IN LIBRARY PER WEEK				
50th Percentile	2,907	1,669	31,420	25,627
75th Percentile	5,104	3,200	46,000	41,248
TOTAL ATTENDANCE PER FTE (Full Time Equivalent)				
50th Percentile	2	2	2	3
75th Percentile	2	3	3	4
LIBRARIANS				
50th Percentile	6	3	45	47
75th Percentile	8	5	64	75
LIBRARY STAFF: (Full Time Equivalent)				
Staff/Librarian Ratio				
50th Percentile	1:1	1:1	2:2	2:2
75th Percentile	2:1	2:1	2:2	2:2
Student Assistants - Percentage to total staff				
50th Percentile	33	40	27	23
75th Percentile	51	54	34	28

University libraries also provide such specialized subject collections to support graduate and faculty education and research that they become, in essence, research libraries serving primarily the needs of scholars. This research function is evident in the title of the Research Libraries Group (RLG), which was established by Harvard University, Yale University, Columbia University, and the New York Public Library. This function is also reflected by the academic library association's title, the Association of College and Research Libraries, rather than one of college and university libraries. Thus, although college and university libraries originally followed similar developmental patterns, they had begun to diverge by the 1980s.

Other common academic libraries are community college libraries, junior college libraries, and libraries in technical institutes. These similar institutions are primarily products of the twentieth century and primarily serve the same purpose, providing academic education equal to the first two years of college. Many of them also provide vocational or avocational education as well as adult education. Their impact on library development has been tremendous because these institutions house more than one-third of today's academic libraries.

DEVELOPMENT OF COLLEGE AND UNIVERSITY LIBRARIES

The majority of academic libraries generally began as mere adjuncts to the classroom, housed in small rooms and administered by part-time faculty members. They were seen as "collections of books" rather than as part of the education function. As society changed from an agrarian to an industrialized one, colleges and universities began to focus more on research and to offer new programs to meet the needs of new occupations. To support these programs, collegiate accreditation associations emphasized qualitative library collections and staff. Librarians from professional graduate library schools administered and developed these growing libraries. Because many librarians also became subject specialists, faculty departments became willing to give up control of their subject department libraries to the college or university library.

Further library development was accelerated by the rapid expansion of the world's known information. Such knowledge doubled from the beginning of the 1900s through 1950, and academic libraries expanded their collections accordingly. This expansion of known information helped influence changes in institutional philosophies and methods and helped spark the introduction of electives in academic programs. The large influx of students after World War II also placed heavy demands on libraries to provide materials in great quantities. To help satisfy this demand without bankrupting themselves, academic institutions began to join together in cooperative collection development programs such as the Farmington Plan. Under these programs, each academic library was responsible for collecting all of the published materials from a specific country or in a specific subject area. These materials were then made available for loan to other academic institutions. Thus, by the 1950s the academic library had become an important element in fulfilling the goals of its college or university.

A typical academic library of the 1950s would have contained only print materials — books, serials, and pamphlets — housed in an architectural monument named after some benefactor. In smaller libraries, the books were usually kept on shelves arranged into alcoves, where students studied at long reading tables. Separate rooms housed the reserve book collection where students read many of their course assignments. In other areas designed for browsing, students could sit in easy chairs and read leisure materials or perhaps hear a lecture. Separate rooms for rare books and maps might also be available, but these were often only accessible to "serious" students.

Universities often kept most of their collections in closed stack areas to which only graduate students and faculty members gained admittance. Undergraduates had to ask for books at a circulation desk and wait for the materials to be "paged" or delivered to them. Many universities attempted to help the first- and second-year students adjust to the wealth of library materials by providing separate "undergraduate libraries." These libraries contained duplicate materials in open stacks that were particularly useful for students during their first two years. The third- and fourth-year students usually had access to departmental libraries scattered throughout the campus next to the subject departments. However, all of the libraries were usually only open during hours that were convenient for library staffs rather than for student studying.

The primary objective of these libraries was to contribute to the goals and philosophy of the academic institutions they served. Because the academic institutions were still largely faculty, graduate student, and research oriented, library objectives also leaned in that direction. Of the functions Guy Lyle identified in 1949 for a college library to fulfill, only two were directly related to the needs of its students.[1] These two functions were to provide study and reference materials for supplementing classroom instruction and to encourage students to use books independently. Even in fulfilling this latter function, libraries were supposed to cooperate with the faculty to develop student interests rather than work directly with the students. Two other functions served the faculty: providing technical and specialized study materials to keep the faculty abreast of their fields and supporting the research needs of individual faculty members. Another function was to provide alumni and correspondence students with bibliographies and study materials needed for courses and institutes.

This final function encouraged cooperation with other libraries to strengthen library resources in the local area. However, the cooperative library efforts that developed up to the 1960s were still often research oriented. Although most academic libraries provided interlibrary loans, these were restricted to faculty and graduate students by the National Interlibrary Loan Code. Undergraduate students rarely had access to materials their college or university did not own. Undergraduates were also hampered by not knowing how to find materials the library did own because library instruction was often limited to an orientation tour for freshmen during their first week on campus. By 1960, the academic libraries, as well as the colleges and universities themselves, were generally not meeting the needs of their students. This problem increased as students inundated the campuses throughout the 1960s.

The 1960s were a time of plenty and a time of crisis for the academic world. Society's emphasis on "education for all" meant colleges and universities were flooded with students. However, a majority of these students had more varied interests, backgrounds, and needs than earlier students ever had. Colleges and universities found that their traditional courses and teaching methods did not serve these new students. At the same time, students were demanding a voice in developing relevant education. In this climate, many educators and progressive librarians began to look for new ways to provide programs, materials, and services that would enable students, many of whom had poor academic backgrounds, to learn.

The passage of the Higher Education Act in 1965 provided funds for institutions and libraries to experiment and develop new materials, services, and programs to satisfy students' needs. These funds also helped in the development of new philosophies of education and new concepts of what a college or university should be. Comprehensive public community colleges opened all over the country serving the academic, technical, vocational, and avocational needs of their local communities. These colleges provided educational opportunities for many persons to learn new skills, get high school diplomas, be exposed to cultural opportunities, and participate in general educational activities. Programs emphasized meeting each individual's needs, and independent study programs were initiated. Many community colleges, as well as other colleges and universities, developed new programs that extended beyond the traditional classroom/lecture hall. New terms, such as *external degree programs*, *nontraditional study programs*, *independent study*, *extended education*, and *open university*, were used to describe these programs. Many colleges and universities proved they were equal to meeting the educational crisis.

LEARNING RESOURCE CENTER PROGRAMS AND SERVICES

As their parent institutions changed, academic libraries also changed to support the new educational programs. Many libraries began to experiment and to expand their library collections beyond the traditional print materials. The media explosion that had hit the elementary and secondary schools expanded to include higher education. Some libraries began to incorporate all types of media into their collections and programs, including audiotapes, videotapes, microforms, transparencies, films of all forms, shapes, and sizes, programmed learning, and computer-assisted instruction. The library no longer remained a passive member of the institution; it began to reach out beyond its traditional confines to participate in the learning process. Libraries provided book stores, media and graphic production facilities, and equipment support for instruction, including listening labs, TV sets and cameras, and overhead projectors. Library staff members began to participate in the teaching process by working with teachers to develop bibliographic units or courses or by developing their own library oriented units and courses. Some institutions even developed into "library colleges" in which the library was a prime factor in contributing to a student's education. Some libraries truly became the "heart of the university."

These new libraries developed new names such as learning resource centers, media centers, and learning centers and became extended libraries to identify their new functions. Robert Taylor identified the five functions of these new college libraries as providing direct support to undergraduate instruction, supporting independent student honors work, giving minimal support to faculty and graduate research, providing space where students could study on their own, and providing a context within which the student could browse freely among all subjects and materials.[2] The library had become student oriented rather than faculty and graduate research oriented.

The growth and development of these new types of libraries and library services in the 1960s encouraged the development of new academic library standards in the 1970s and 1980s. Whereas previous academic standards had emphasized traditional library materials and services, the new standards emphasized quality learning resources programs and student access to all media within the library. When quantitative standards were stated, they were usually based upon formulas rather than upon absolutes. Standards for all types of academic libraries were adopted by the Association of College and Research Libraries (ACRL) in the 1970s and 1980s: "Guidelines for Two-Year College Learning Resources Programs" were adopted in 1973, revised in 1982, and followed by quantitative standards in 1979. "Standards for College Libraries" were adopted in 1975 and revised in 1986 and "Standards for University Libraries" were adopted in 1979. However, rather than setting the pace for library services as the school standards had done, these academic standards seemed to follow rather than lead the development of innovative library services.

By the end of the 1970s, it could no longer be said that there was one typical academic library. University, college, and community college libraries each had distinctive variations designed to meet their institutions' objectives. Perhaps community colleges were the one type of institution in which most libraries resembled each other. Because they were largely developed during the media revolution of the 1960s and 1970s, most community colleges developed learning resources programs that combined all print and media materials and services into one department or organization. Four-year colleges founded or expanded during this time also often became learning resources centers or library colleges. Other college libraries may not have changed their organization, but their objectives changed to serve the student rather than the faculty member. University libraries became the most diverse group of academic libraries; some developed learning resource centers while others maintained their traditional roles.

However, no matter what form the academic library took in the 1970s and 1980s, one student-centered philosophy developed. Library services and procedures were often changed to match students' needs. Many new university library buildings housed the major book collections in open stacks that were made accessible to undergraduates for the first time. The interiors of these buildings also changed. Books were shelved on free-standing stacks, and students found seating at individual study cubicles or "carrels" or relaxed in modern lounging areas throughout the library. Library hours became long and flexible with some libraries staying open until midnight or even 24 hours a day. Professional staff was often available for student assistance whenever the library was open, including during traditional holiday or semester breaks. The academic library had finally removed the physical barriers that had restricted student access to its collection.

Many libraries began to make their collections more usable by reclassifying them from the Dewey Decimal or other classification systems to the Library of Congress classification system. This reclassification enabled libraries to use one nationally standardized classification number so they could develop and share cataloging descriptions. This standardization for cataloging and classifying materials also paved the way for libraries to adopt Library of Congress MARC-base cataloging thereby reducing the need for large original cataloging departments in each individual institution. Indeed, the largest cooperative venture, OCLC (now Online Computer Library Center, Inc.), originally began as the Ohio College Library Cooperative network to develop and share a computerized database. This shared database became so successful that it quickly expanded nationwide and formed links with other networks such as ILLINET (Illinois Library Network) and SOLINET (Southeastern Library Network) to provide authoritative standardized cataloging to their network members.

Academic libraries also took advantage of the emergence of relatively reliable and affordable computer technology to develop automated systems for library operations. Some of these libraries were so successful in this development that they sold their products commercially under labels such as UTLAS (University of Toronto), BRS (Bibliographic Retrieval Services, State University of New York), and NOTIS (Northwestern University). As technology became more sophisticated, computer systems grew from single-purpose systems for internal operations such as circulation or cataloging to integrated library systems. Integrated library systems such as Illinois's LCS system included not only circulation and cataloging, but also online public access catalogs the student could use as union catalog/shared databases to borrow materials on interlibrary loan. Some systems included serials control systems (SILO), online search systems (BRS), and materials acquisitions systems that were also used for collection analysis and development.

In addition to providing automated services for the library, academic libraries took the lead in intracampus and intercampus networking. In some cases, institutionwide computer centers and programs were added to the academic library's role of service. Computer labs were made available in libraries for students' homework use, and some schools such as Carnegie-Mellon made computers available in students' rooms. OPACs were made accessible to students and faculty in their dorms, offices, or homes. Libraries promoted intercampus networking with linkups for teleconferencing and telecourses via satellite or TV and other electronic teaching methods. Libraries marketed their services to community business and economic leaders. Library services such as business library cards, journal photocopying services, computer search services such as DIALOG, and professional librarian consulting services were made available for a fee or in exchange for business donations. Many institutions made their resources available to any citizen either in the library or outside the library for a fee. An example of such comprehensive services is at the University of Southern Florida, where the library and information services department is responsible for the library, the computer center, all information flow on campus, and the use of campus information resources by the business community.

Academic libraries also took the lead in developing resource-sharing networks with other libraries. These libraries had recognized many years before that they must share their resources, both bibliographically and physically. This sharing originally began on an informal basis with academic libraries in the same geographic area sharing materials or allowing reciprocal borrowing among their patrons. As library budgets shrank and the publication explosion produced more materials than one library could buy, these informal arrangements became formal agreements for interlibrary cooperation and networks. The interlibrary cooperation took many forms and provided many varied services. Some academic institutions joined together in consortia to formally share their educational resources and prevent costly duplication of subject specialties. Other universities and colleges actually formed joint libraries that developed one major collection to serve several different institutions. The Joint University Libraries of Nashville and the Atlanta University Libraries are two examples of this type of cooperation. The Center for Research Libraries provided cooperative storage facilities for its university members, and regional bibliographic centers in Denver and Philadelphia provided regional union catalogs for interlibrary loans. RLG was expanded to include other academic and research libraries and made its union catalog (RLIN or Research Library Information Network) available.

In many states, the largest academic libraries were designated as resource libraries by state agencies and reimbursed with state funds for sharing their materials and resources throughout the state. Other regional and local cooperative efforts included the development of joint databases such as WisCAT in Wisconsin and LCS in Illinois. These databases provided CD-ROM or online access to the collection status of most of the academic library collections within the state. Once identified, many of these materials were delivered through document delivery services using photocopying, FAX transmission, and library van delivery. Students also could go themselves to nearby public or special libraries to use their collections. Many libraries joined together in cooperative collection development and preservation activities to share the burden of preserving the world's collective wisdom in print form. By 1990, almost every academic library in the country participated in at least one cooperative network that provided these and other services.

However, as libraries expanded their access to these resources and collections, librarians began to recognize that students must be taught how to find and use them. Librarians began to develop extensive "bibliographic instruction" programs to help students use library resources more effectively. In addition to giving orientation tours of the library, librarians developed computer and media programs that explained parts of the library or individual library resource tools. They also taught credit and noncredit bibliographic instruction courses. Progressive institutions developed competency-based library courses and examinations that students were required to pass to become upperclassmen or to graduate. Libraries also established programs to help nontraditional students overcome their reluctance to use the library as a learning tool. Some libraries developed ongoing programs to help retain these students and worked with high school enhancement programs or Upward Bound programs for underachieving students. Thus, the academic library tried to fulfill its educational role in the institution it served.

ACADEMIC INSTITUTIONS
IN THE 1990s

Unfortunately, although the academic library had entered the 1990s, the rest of the academic world had not made similar efforts to meet changing students' needs. Textbooks, lectures, and assignments from library reserved-book collections continued to be at the heart of most college teaching by faculty who felt only slightly at home in libraries.[3] It is understandable that a study by the Carnegie Foundation of 5,000 undergraduate students showed that 65 percent of them only used a library for four hours or less per week and one quarter of the students did not use the library at all.[4] A more discouraging commentary for libraries was that most of these students used the library as a place for quiet study. In spite of the efforts by academic library staffs to make their libraries important in their academic institutions, only a few of them had succeeded.

By 1986, the problems with the educational structure that had been identified for schools in *A Nation at Risk* (see chapter 6) had also spurred a reform educational movement at the academic level. The Carnegie Foundation was in the forefront of this movement when it published a 1986 study, *College: The Undergraduate Experience in America*. This study stated that the way to measure the quality of a college is by the resources for learning on the campus and the extent to which students become independent, self-directed learners. It included four library-related recommendations. The first recommendation was that all undergraduates be given bibliographic instruction and encouraged to spend as much time in the library as they did in class. Second, colleges should "sustain the culture of the book" through activities such as author visits and faculty seminars on influential works. The third recommendation was that financial support for the purchase of books be increased so that a minimum of 5 percent of the college's operating budget would go to libraries. Finally, colleges should work with local schools and community leaders to help strengthen library holdings.[5]

Although academic librarians welcomed this report's support for the importance of libraries in their academic institutions, they also believed the report was too conservative and limited. They urged their colleagues to be bold in developing and implementing new ideas and concepts if they truly wanted to become an integral part of the learning process in their academic institutions. Librarians were encouraged to strengthen connections with the administration and faculty by developing their own research skills and becoming active partners in the research process. In fostering this research process, academic librarians could become special librarians for the faculty. They could provide such services as database searching, full-text databases, and selective dissemination of information (SDI). (See chapter 8.) They could also work with faculty professors to integrate learning resources and methods, bibliographic instruction, and library use into the classroom curricula. Until this happens and the focus on campus is shifted away from textbooks, lectures, and reserves, the academic library may still remain outside the mainstream of academic life.

LIBRARY MANAGEMENT

To bring the library into the mainstream of the academic institution, library managers worked to revise its organization. Some libraries took on the information function for the entire institution; other libraries took on bibliographic instruction functions in library college environments. By the 1990s, the library director had generally become a dean of learning resources who reported to an academic vice president. The library dean was not only administrator of a large department and budget, but that individual was also active in the council of deans and the total university administration. This expanded administrative role often strengthened and solidified the library's place in the entire academic institution.

Another area in which the library's strength was solidified was in the development and reorganization of library staffs. In most academic libraries, the dean had a Ph.D. as well as an MLS degree, and librarians at all levels not only had MLS degrees, but many also had subject master's degrees. Librarian staffs were reorganized as many librarians became subject bibliographers or specialists. These subject specialists worked with department faculties and developed resource collections in their specific subject areas. They also provided reference and research assistance and formal classroom instruction in their subject specialties. Librarians were freed from supervising in-house library operations so they could serve on faculty and institution committees and work with their faculty colleagues. Supervision of in-house library activities was delegated to technical support staffs as libraries found that a few technicians could supervise many students in carrying out library operations. These developments gave impetus to librarians' demands for faculty status, tenure, and pay equity. Their success in achieving such demands depended upon their success in becoming integral parts of their academic institutions.

Library administration and staffing patterns were further affected by the introduction of automated library systems. The bibliographic capabilities of the automated systems enabled trained technical staff to handle much of the cataloging and interlibrary loan workloads that had formerly been performed by librarians. These librarians were freed to take on more professional responsibilities in collection analysis and development, reference and research search strategies, and other bibliographic areas. As these professional responsibilities could be more easily equated to academic responsibilities among the teaching faculty, librarians began to gain more faculty rank in the institution. Their titles began to change, and more and more librarian positions were designated as instructor and assistant or associate professor positions.

Within the library, these automated systems had a further impact on library staffing patterns. The statistical and clerical capabilities of such automated systems enabled libraries to combine single-purpose departments such as circulation, reference, acquisitions, and cataloging into larger public service and technical service departments. These capabilities also reduced the library's need to employ large numbers of employees or highly trained professional or technical personnel to perform a majority of the library's operations. In most of these areas, students performed library operations under the direct supervision of a technician, who in turn was under the general supervision of a librarian or library administrator. Thus, the introduction of automated systems in the academic library did not lessen the need for academic library staff members, but reorganized the kinds of staff members needed.

In addition to reorganizing their staffing patterns, libraries also evaluated and reorganized their total library operations. Beginning with their roles and objectives, academic libraries began to establish and use output measurements similar to those used by public libraries as they assessed their libraries' effectiveness. New library standards were established for all types of libraries from community and junior colleges to colleges and universities. Modern management techniques were used to evaluate and restructure library services and operations so that library resources and personnel were used as effectively and efficiently as possible. Library budgets were revamped to develop programs and collections to support the institution's major objectives rather than build up favorite areas of senior department chairmen. The ever-present scarcity of university funding caused libraries to institute cost-accounting systems and look beyond traditional funding sources in search of new revenues. Libraries sought monies from grants, endowments and gifts, and the sale of automated library services and resources to support their programs. Sometimes service fees were charged for heavy use of expensive services such as database searches or excessive interlibrary loan use.

The reality that funding for publicly supported academic institutions was based on political considerations was not lost on academic librarians. Many of them served on state higher education advisory committees. They joined forces with librarians from other types of libraries to lobby for recognition and funding from local, state, and national library and higher education governmental agencies. As important as funding will be in the 1990s for academic library administrators, however, "the greatest challenge facing academic libraries in the next decade is not funding or technology, but leadership and administrative ability."[6] Library leaders must be committed to making their libraries more productive, innovative, and entrepreneurial to fulfill their major roles of developing information-literate students, integrating libraries into the academic curricula, and providing access by students and faculty to all the information they need without regard for its location or format.

SUMMARY

Academic libraries have grown and changed over the years to meet the changing educational objectives of their parent institutions. This transformation process included the expansion and addition of so many library functions and services that many academic libraries changed their names to learning resource centers or library colleges. In these libraries, collections were expanded to include all media, and library services became more student oriented. Computer technology expanded library resources and services as well as added a new dimension to libraries. Some academic libraries even took on the function of providing computer technology to the entire college or university. Academic libraries joined networks with other libraries to acquire, preserve, and share their resources. Library staffs were reorganized to take advantage of these new functions. All of these capabilities enabled academic libraries to contribute to the educational objectives of their colleges or universities.

REVIEW QUESTIONS

1. Define an academic library and describe some of the major types of academic libraries.

2. Identify the objectives of an academic library.

3. Describe the changes in academic libraries from library to learning resource center.

4. Identify some of the major services academic libraries provide.

5. Describe the changes brought about in staff development by the installation of automated library services.

6. List some example cooperative academic library resource-sharing and networking programs.

7. Visit a local academic institution and compare it with the objectives and services discussed in this chapter and the standards identified for that type of library. If possible, visit two types of academic institutions, such as a community college and a four-year college or university, to compare and contrast their libraries.

NOTES

[1]Guy Lyle, *The Administration of the College Library* (New York: H. W. Wilson, 1949), 24-25.

[2]Robert S. Taylor, *The Making of a Library: The Academic Library in Transition* (New York: Becker & Hayes, 1972), 36.

[3]Patricia Senn Breivik and Robert Wedgeworth, *Libraries and the Search for Academic Excellence* (Metuchen, NJ: Scarecrow, 1988), 29-32.

[4]Breivik and Wedgeworth, *Libraries*, 7-8.

[5]Breivik and Wedgeworth, *Libraries*, 13-24.

[6]Allen B. Veaner, *Academic Librarianship in a Transformational Age: Programs, Politics and Personnel* (Boston: G. K. Hall, 1990), xiii.

SELECTED READINGS

Association of College and Research Libraries. "Guidelines for Audiovisual Services in Academic Libraries." *C&RL News* (October 1987): 533-36.

_____. "Guidelines for Two-Year College Learning Resources Programs." *C&RL News* (January, February 1982). Reprint.

_____. "The Mission of a University Undergraduate Library: Model Statement." *C&RL News* (October 1987): 542-44.

_____. "Standards for College Libraries, 1986." *C&RL News* (March 1986): 189-200.

_____. "Standards for Community Junior and Technical College Learning Resources Programs." *C&RL News* (September 1990): 757-67.

_____. "Standards for University Libraries: Evaluation of Performance." *C&RL News* (September 1989): 679-91.

Breivik, Patricia Senn, and E. Gordon Gee. *Information Literacy: Revolution in the Library*. New York: American Council on Education, 1989.

Breivik, Patricia Senn, and Robert Wedgeworth. *Libraries and the Search for Academic Excellence*. Metuchen, NJ: Scarecrow, 1988.

Lynch, Beverly P., ed. *The Academic Library in Transition: Planning for the 90's*. New York: Neal-Schuman, 1989.

Spyers-Duran, Peter, and Thomas W. Mann, Jr., eds. *Issues in Academic Librarianship: Views and Case Studies for the 1980s and 1990s*. Westport, CT: Greenwood Press, 1985.

Van House, Nancy A., Beth Weil, and Charles R. McClure. *Measuring Academic Library Performance: A Practical Approach*. Chicago: ALA, 1990.

Veaner, Allen B. *Academic Librarianship in a Transformational Age: Programs, Politics and Personnel*. Boston: G. K. Hall, 1990.

CHAPTER 8

SPECIAL LIBRARIES
AND INFORMATION CENTERS

Since the term *special libraries* was first used as an umbrella term to describe many different libraries, there have been many attempts to define what special libraries really are. The ALA thought the terms and objectives for these libraries were very vague when the Special Libraries Association was founded in 1909. What could a large scientific library with thousands of volumes and many paid staff members have in common with a small local historical museum library with 1,000 books cared for by volunteer staff members? What characteristics of these two libraries would enable one term to be used to define them both?

Of the characteristics that are most common to these libraries, the primary one is that their collections include materials relating to "specialized subject areas." Second, these libraries gather their collections and design their services to support and further the objectives of a "parent organization" rather than to support a curriculum as school and academic libraries do. Finally, these libraries are primarily concerned with actively seeking out and providing information the parent organization's clients or patrons need rather than just acquiring and preserving the information in a collection. In other words, special libraries provide "special and even individualized services" for their patrons. These three characteristics are key elements of any special library or information center, defined as "a library which provides special services in a specialized subject area or in a special format for special clientele."

There are almost 10,000 different libraries that fit this definition of a special library. They usually are libraries devoted to special subject areas, such as music and art libraries, libraries devoted to special forms, such as map libraries and archive libraries, and libraries devoted to special clientele, such as medical patient libraries and prison libraries. Special libraries can also be identified by their parent organizations or institutions, such as bank or insurance libraries, church libraries, and federal libraries. Finally, special libraries can be identified by their services as "information centers." However, these designations are far from comprehensive. If there is an organization, corporation, institution, or group of people with a special need for library and information services, a special library or information center has probably been developed.

The growth and development of special libraries has varied widely. Some libraries, such as independent research libraries, began in the 1700s, while other libraries, such as map libraries, developed primarily in the twentieth century. The development of library standards has encouraged the growth of some special libraries while others have not developed in spite of such standards. Yet, for all their variety in funding, type, subject, and clientele, special libraries and information centers continue to have more similarities than differences. Their financing, governance, resources, and services are more strongly affected by their importance to the health and welfare of their parent organization than in any other type of library. Unfortunately, such dependence on the wealth of the parent organization continues to be a problem.

RESEARCH LIBRARIES

Research libraries are some of our most important special libraries. Because they have been developed to support the research needs of the world's scholars, they have traditionally been more allied with academic libraries. Most are actually a part of large universities. Other kinds of research libraries are federal government libraries and independent research libraries. The New York Public Library has its own research library as its central library. (The branches are tax-funded public libraries.) Most research libraries were originally established and endowed by wealthy benefactors; financial support for them today often comes from further endowments or from university and public funds. Limited funds have forced most research libraries to limit and refine their subject interests, but through careful purchases many libraries have been able to develop definitive collections in narrow subject areas.

Independent research libraries are unique because they do not belong to any other institution and exist for their own sakes. They have generally been established by wealthy benefactors with their own boards of directors and their own facilities and endowment funds. Usually the board of directors will choose a particular subject interest area in which the library will specialize. These subject areas may be based on the private collection of the library's benefactor, such as the Folger Shakespeare Library, or they may be chosen to coordinate with other research libraries. For example, the subjects of the Newberry Library (humanities) and the John Crerar Library (physical and natural sciences) in Chicago were chosen to complement each other and those of the Chicago Public Library. Sometimes, these libraries may lose their independent status as the John Crerar Library did when it was added to the University of Chicago in 1984.

Some of the earliest research libraries were begun in the 1700s by scientific and historical societies. These libraries helped preserve priceless documentation of an era to save it for future historians. Each of these libraries has tended to "build on strength" by gaining eminence in particular historical periods or forms of materials.[1] For example, the American Philosophical Society Library contains over half of Benjamin Franklin's surviving papers and concentrates on all sciences in the colonies and the United States to 1850. The Boston Atheneum Library holds George Washington's personal library and is recognized for its strength in New England colonial books and pamphlets. It also has purchased and developed a valuable collection of Confederate literature and imprints. By establishing such subject parameters, research libraries have been able to develop coexisting rather than competitive collections.

Independent research libraries often provide similar library services. Like other research libraries, they primarily house noncirculating subject collections for the use of special clientele who are most often scholars doing research at the postdoctoral level. In addition to providing computerized access to their collections and physical facilities for research, some libraries also provide research funds to the scholars. Most libraries have publishing programs, and some have microfilming programs so they may share the unique information contained in their collections. Independent libraries have received government grants to serve as centers of research or regional libraries for other libraries. Although these libraries have been called independent research libraries, they have become necessary links in the developing network of national information resources.

FEDERAL LIBRARIES

Federal government libraries are another important link in our national information resources. These federally funded libraries represent the most varied kind of special libraries. They include such libraries as national health, agriculture, technical, and institutional libraries, as well as academic, school, and quasi-public libraries. However, all federal libraries are still considered to be special libraries because they serve the goals of their parent institutions and their users are usually members of these institutions. There are more than 2,500 federal libraries serving the various departments and agencies of the U.S. government. About 40 percent of these libraries are scientific and technical (including health and medical) libraries that serve the special objectives of providing information and supporting research. Another 35-40 percent serve as quasi-public libraries that serve persons in military installations, veterans' hospitals, and federal prisons. About 20 percent of all federal libraries serve the educational needs of personnel in U.S. armed forces, the military academies, and military-dependent schools overseas. The U.S. Navy alone had 844 libraries in 1989 and the Marine Corps had 195 ship-and-shore libraries.[2]

The universe of federal libraries is constantly changing, however, as libraries develop to meet new services or libraries are affected by budgetary considerations. For example, after the first White House Conference on Library and Information Services in 1979, the development of library services for Native Americans was encouraged by the addition of Title IV to the Library Services and Construction Act. This title recognized that libraries were an excellent means of centralizing tribal archives and records, preserving Native-American culture, language, and history, and stemming the tide of illiteracy. In contrast, the development in other federal libraries, such as armed services libraries, is often tied to the ups and downs of the parent department's budget. Cuts in defense department budgets could not only reduce library hours and materials, but they could also bring the closing of libraries when a parent military or naval base is closed.

Another budgetary influence on the development of federal libraries resulted from the Reagan administration policies begun in the 1980s. Efforts were made to "privatize" government information by awarding contracts to private for-profit companies to provide library and information services to federal agencies. In addition, efforts were made to restrict the public's access to the government's vast electronic files. These efforts triggered a major debate that raged into the 1990s between federal officials and library and information supporters. It remains to be seen whether this debate over government information as "an economic resource" versus "a public good created with taxpayer funds" will be satisfactorily resolved in favor of the public's good.

The importance of federal libraries to our national information resources is seen in the extensive research and subject collections found in the majority of federal libraries. Many of these collections became accessible through FEDLINK, a network of cooperative federal libraries and information centers that has become the largest network in the country. FEDLINK enables federal agencies to access the informational resources available in other agencies. It also provides training to meet the requirements of federal agency personnel. However, the most comprehensive federal collections are contained in the three national libraries: the Library of Congress (LC), the National Library of Medicine (NLM), and the National Agriculture Library (NAL). These three libraries not only provide extensive research collections in all forms of media, but they represent one-third of the total federal collections, one-half of all expenditures, and two-fifths of all the personnel in federal libraries. The Library of Congress alone has over 20 million volumes, 75 million pieces of research material, and a budget over $150 million, although budgetary cutbacks in the late 1980s have reduced the staff from 5,000 to 4,800 employees. These national libraries provide library services to the nation and serve as national information resource centers. The NLM and the NAL have developed subject collections in medicine and agriculture and their allied fields; the LC covers all the other subjects and has become the largest library in the world, providing more national library functions and services than any other national library.

Serving as a national library is still an unofficial function of the LC, although it has been steered in this direction by two important events. The first was the U.S. Congress's purchase of Thomas Jefferson's collection, which contained materials on a great variety of subjects rather than just legislative materials. Over the years, librarians of Congress continued to strengthen these subjects. The passage of the Copyright Law in 1870 required that two copies of every copyrighted work be given to the LC. This national library function was further enhanced in the early 1900s when the library began to sell its classification schedules and catalog cards and to provide interlibrary loan privileges. The National Union Catalog (NUC) and the Union List of Serials (ULS) also enabled libraries to share the LC's collection as well as the collections of the largest libraries in the United States. In addition, the LC made its extensive collections available to all citizens and promoted their use through such programs as the American Folklore Center, the National Translations Center, and the Center for the Book. Finally, the LC became the national resource for materials for blind and physically handicapped persons.

In spite of these services to the nation, the primary purpose of the LC is still to serve as a legislative library for Congress. Librarians of Congress have judiciously nourished this relationship, and their skillful public relations have helped gain unparalleled financial support for the library and its programs. This financial support has enabled the LC and the other national libraries to provide national leadership in the development of library automation programs of international significance. For example, in the late 1960s, the LC began providing computerized cataloging for its monographs under the MARC program. Since then, this program has expanded to become the accepted standard for cataloging all types of materials throughout the world. By the early 1990s, the actual LC catalog became available online to other libraries.

The LC was not the only national library that made its collection readily available to the world. The NLM developed MEDLARS, an online service, which had made 25 medical literature databases accessible to its 30,000 users by the early 1990s. The NLM's computerized cataloging information in the biomedical areas was made available to medical libraries on CATLINE. Citations and indexes to articles were made available through *Index Medicus* or online through MEDLINE for the field of biomedicine. Because many of MEDLARS's users were individuals, the NLM also provided "grateful med" software so that health professionals could have access to more than 13 million references and abstracts via their personal computers. In addition, the NLM provided document delivery to medical libraries and health professionals and established regional medical libraries throughout the country to serve as resource centers between the user and the NLM.

The NAL also took its place as a national leader in providing library and information services to the agricultural community. As early as 1970, the NAL had made its computerized database AGRICOLA (**AGRIC**ultural **On** Line Access) available to other libraries. The NAL was an active member of AGLINET, a voluntary association of 27 agricultural libraries. It also was active in USAIN (U.S. Agriculture Information Network), a national forum to discuss agricultural information issues. Because the success of any agricultural effort can often depend upon worldwide climatic conditions, the NAL also became an important part of the international agricultural information network. This worldwide network developed interconnecting resource centers that provided electronic access to data, documents, and computer files throughout the world. This network was made available so that both the scientist and the lay user could understand its information. As with the medical community, access to this international agricultural network was also made available via computer linkups to users such as farmers at the local level.

CORPORATE LIBRARIES AND INFORMATION CENTERS

The private world of business and industry has not lagged behind the government in developing libraries and information centers to support their research needs. Almost all businesses and industries, including banks, insurance companies, advertising agencies, chemical companies, and aerospace corporations, have their own libraries. Though these companies' products may vary considerably, their libraries and information centers are similar in that their collections and services are completely identified with the objectives of their parent organizations. Because the major purpose of the parent corporation is to make a profit, the major purpose of the corporate library is to collect, organize, and put to use the knowledge in its collections for the greatest efficiency of the corporation. It is this characteristic that distinguishes corporate business and industrial libraries from other special libraries.

The profit-making motive may be one of the most influential factors in the makeup of a business or industrial library. Some businesses such as law firms, communications media, advertising and marketing firms, and insurance companies are so dependent upon the quick retrieval of information that they always provide well-funded collections and trained staffs in their libraries. For example, law firms may subscribe to expensive legal databases that make current U.S. Supreme Court cases available within days of release rather than weeks later in printed form. Other types of businesses, particularly small businesses and industries, might consider information services as peripheral to their profit goal and cut their libraries' staffing, materials, and funding when profits begin to sag. Thus, a library's or information center's success in contributing to the parent corporation's profit motive will usually affect its existence.

The need to successfully contribute to the corporation's profit motive by providing information is so vital that corporate libraries have become *information centers* rather than libraries. These information centers are staffed by information specialists and staff with subject and library expertise and a solid grounding in the corporation's objectives and organization. Using this expertise, information specialists have developed collections that include resources in all their many forms. This information may be contained in externally published materials such as books, microforms, serials, patents, and conference reports or in internally generated materials such as research and technical reports, corporate and product indexes, correspondence, and market surveys. However, it is not the format of the information but its currency that is of primary importance in special libraries and information centers. In fact, the most important service any information center provides may be quick access to journal articles and research data through extensive serial collections or electronic databases.

To facilitate easy access to their special collections, information centers usually collect and index everything written or published, either externally or internally, about the corporation and its products. Because their collections are used by every division in the corporation, information centers also include information about the corporation's clients or customers, business indicators, economic factors, and business administration. In cataloging these materials, information centers have often devised simplified classification and subject-heading systems because many documents do not have the necessary information for standard cataloging. Information centers also provide in-depth indexing for book chapters, periodical articles, and specific subjects buried within a text. Access to these materials has been further enhanced by the technological advancements of the 1980s and 1990s. These advancements enable information centers to make their materials available through electronic, telecommunications, or CD-ROM technologies to any member of the corporation anywhere in the world.

Information centers also provide extensive information services to support departments that have identified a problem or a need. The information services staff will not only locate bibliographic citations in a particular area, but they also may obtain the documents, read and analyze them, and write a report for the requesting department. In some corporations, information specialists join with department teams to work as researchers on corporate projects. In this role, they not only provide research background and reports, but they also take an active part in writing or editing any departmental reports. Such active participation in a company's programs has helped prove the library's worth to many corporate executives.

The information specialist may also save valuable corporate personnel time by providing individualized and specialized services such as selective dissemination of information (SDI) and expert systems. SDI searches of current literature are tailored to an individual's or group's specific needs or profile. It can be one of the most productive services for keeping researchers abreast of new research developments in their fields. In SDI searches, information specialists usually interview the patron to determine what specific type of search or information is desired. The specialist identifies subject descriptors or subject headings that a computer accepts as instructions. These descriptors are used to access databases and identify and locate any appropriate citations. *Expert systems* are computerized software programs that mimic some of the problem-solving abilities of human experts to locate information in a given field. These expert systems use the computer's logic and Boolean searching to locate information in a structured database. Once the desired information is identified through either SDI or an expert system, the information center may obtain it in many ways, such as through a full-text database, telefacsimile (FAX) interlibrary loan, or commercial document delivery vendors.

In addition, information specialists have always been concerned with quickly disseminating all the information available within the information center or accessible to it. Most corporate information centers circulate books, route serials, publish and distribute bibliographies and acquisitions lists, provide abstracting and translating services, compile files of news clippings, maintain electronic bulletin boards, publish information bulletins, and provide copies of relevant articles or patents. Through these many services, the corporate information center attempts to improve the corporation's efficiency and profits by taking an active part in its day-to-day operations.

INSTITUTIONAL LIBRARIES

Other special libraries that also have an important part in the daily activities of their parent bodies are institutional libraries. Some of the more common institutional libraries are museum libraries, association libraries, and organization libraries. Within each of these areas, there are numerous variations based on the subjects or organizations or institutions a library serves. For example, about 3,000 libraries are in historical museums, art museums, science museums, and other museum-type establishments such as zoos, arboretums, and national parks. All of these libraries vary in size and are funded by both private and public agencies. Although a few of them have large collections and well-trained staffs, most have small collections (1,000 to 5,000 items) that may or may not be staffed by trained personnel. Museum-type libraries are primarily open during regular business hours to serve the staff and researchers at their institutions.

Professional association libraries also serve the needs of their parent organizations. The ALA, the American Dental Association, and the American Medical Association are just a few of the associations that provide libraries for their executive staffs and their members. State and local government agencies provide libraries to serve their staffs, although these are not as extensive as the federal libraries. Law libraries are in practically every county courthouse in the United States, as well as in municipal city halls and state capitol buildings. Access to archival materials is also made available by many governments, institutions, and organizations through limited reference service, photoduplication, and lending policies. Such library-like services are encouraged by the Society of American Archivists, which provides a voluntary certification program for archivists. As with the other types of special libraries, all of these libraries serve the major objectives of their parent organizations and institutions by providing both in-depth research and current information to their members as quickly and efficiently as possible.

One type of institution, the hospital or health center, is unique because it often has two types of special libraries or one library that provides two distinct types of services. One type of medical library is the patient library, which provides recreational and leisure reading for patients. These libraries usually have very flexible circulation routines, and services may be provided by volunteer staff rather than by paid technical or professional staff. The other type of medical library is the one that serves the research needs of the medical staff. Some medical libraries may also support the medical staff's continuing education needs by providing lectures and current medical information in video or electronic form. Medical libraries may have very large staffs and provide access to extensive medical collections through Index Medicus, MEDLARS, and MEDLINE, or they may be small and poorly staffed.

Two interesting services developed by medical libraries in the last decade have enabled librarians to become members of the medical team. *Clinical medical librarians* (CML) attend clinical rounds or patient conferences to identify the medical staff's information needs. Clinical medical librarians then perform manual or online searches to locate specific information doctors may need for patients' care. The second service is *bibliotherapy*, or the development of a selected list of materials for a specific patient to support the instructions and recommendations of the patient's doctor or psychiatrist. A natural by-product of bibliotherapy for medical libraries has been the extension of information services to patients, their families, and the community in general. Such consumer education can help a patient make an informed decision before treatment is begun. It can also help the patient adjust more easily to a medical condition or disease once it has been diagnosed. The final goal of all of these services is to enable the medical center to provide the best care for the patient.

Medical and hospital standards have been established by the Joint Commission on Accreditation of Hospitals to help ensure that medical centers provide the most up-to-date information for their medical staffs. Although these standards include library services as a key indicator for health care accreditation, fluctuations in hospital economics often preclude the standard from being implemented or expanded. Medical libraries that had expanded with their parent institutions in the 1970s were adversely affected by the retrenchment of these same institutions in the 1980s. Newer services such as bibliotherapy and clinical medical librarianship often fell victim to economic problems even when they were well received by the medical staffs. Medical librarians tried to stem this downward spiral by making themselves indispensable members of the medical team. As medical institutions and their libraries move ahead, medical library administrators are learning how to compete with other departments to receive sufficient financial and administrative support for their resources and services.

Among other institutional libraries, prison libraries serve their prison populations. However, the goals of prison libraries have varied throughout the years as the philosophy of prison reform has changed. The first prison library collections contained moral and religious works to help prisoners see the error of their ways. Next, prison collections became important in supporting the educational system in the prison, and finally, the library became a part of the prison's rehabilitative function. Some libraries have advocated bibliotherapy as a service that librarians should perform in this rehabilitative function. By the 1990s, literacy programs had become a major part of many prison library services in response to the outside world's emphasis on literacy. Whatever the function of prison libraries has been, studies have shown that more people in prison read than do people who are not in prison. This phenomenon occurs in spite of inadequate and poorly staffed collections in most prison libraries. The largest library growth in prisons has been in law library services. In the 1970s, federal courts said that prisons must provide adequate law libraries for inmates to research material for drafting legal papers and briefs. In response to this requirement, some prisons have developed their own law libraries. Others have contracted with state or local libraries to provide such a service. Some of these city and state libraries also provide deposit book collections, books-by-mail, and bookmobile service to serve the prisoners' informational and recreational needs.

Special subject libraries have developed and organized their collections and services around a specific subject that may be important to a parent institution. Many of these subject libraries are connected with universities and colleges, and they can be as numerous and as varied as the university departments themselves. Many special library associations have developed to support these libraries, including associations for art, architecture, agriculture, astronomy, documentation, film archives, geography and maps, law, medicine, music, social science, sound archives, and theater. In addition, there are religious library associations such as the Theological, Jewish, Catholic, and Lutheran Church Library Associations.

LIBRARY AND INFORMATION MANAGEMENT

The management, administration, and staffing of special libraries and information centers is probably more varied and distinct than that found in other types of libraries. More often than not, the administrator responsible for the library or information center is probably not a librarian but a director or officer of a major department or division. In business and industrial libraries, the directors of research and development or the vice presidents of marketing may be given responsibility for administering the library or information center. These administrators usually hire library and information staffs that support their own conceptions of library services. Thus, if a research and development (R&D) director considers library services important, that person will provide a sufficient number of well-trained staff members to support the R&D function. Such a library might have a staff of information professionals supported by technicians and clerks. If another R&D director considers the materials more important than the services, the library staff might only consist of clerical workers. If either director were replaced, the services in that library or information center might be changed to fit the new director's viewpoint.

The personnel working in special libraries and information centers usually have more varied backgrounds than do staff in other types of libraries. Ideally, personnel should have both library and subject expertise. The special librarian or information specialist may have a degree in a subject specialty as well as in library science, and the staff may also include subject and language specialists. In fact, this subject expertise may be so important to companies and businesses that they may prefer a technician with subject specialization to a professional with a master's degree in library or information science. Large libraries often include professional librarians or information scientists backed up by subject specialists, technicians, programmers, and clerks. Medium-sized special libraries usually have smaller staffs of just a few people, and the small special libraries may truly be one-person enterprises.

The reality is that many special libraries are small with minimal library personnel who may not be paid very well. Sometimes the only staff member in a special library may be a secretary who has been put in charge of a collection of books and magazines. In other special libraries, several clerks and technicians may be supervised by someone who is a librarian or information specialist in name only. This person may have a degree in the subject specialty of the parent corporation or institution but not have any knowledge of library or information science. Clerical and technical staff members may be paid clerk-typist or secretarial wages without taking into account the paraprofessional nature of the jobs they perform. In some cases, a technician may be offered a high wage to perform professional responsibilities. In other cases, professional librarians or information specialists may only be offered technician-level wages unless they can prove their professional value to the parent organization. Sometimes, professional librarians may be hired to set up a library, and once this is done, they may be replaced by less-expensive personnel. Thus, finances may strongly dictate a library's staff, resources, and services unless the special library can become very important to its parent body.

The personalities of the staff members themselves also may strongly influence the makeup of the special library or information center staff. In 1990, the Special Library Association (SLA) used the Myers-Briggs Personality Type Indicators to study its members. This study showed that special librarians and information specialists share strong personality traits that differ from the general population. (See figure 8.1.) The survey showed that the majority of responding special librarians prefer "introversion" over "extroversion," "intuition" over "sensing," and "thinking" over "feeling." In addition, the preference among females for "thinking" over "feeling" was significantly more so than in the general female population.[2] These special librarians and information specialists share a preference for asking "why" and "how," for planning, and for solving problems. They enjoy using their thinking and analytical abilities to work closely with corporate or organizational personnel. They also take great pride in contributing to the accomplishments or profits of their parent organizations. Special librarians and information specialists may feel isolated from other library colleagues at times. However, they enjoy the variety and flexibility of working in many areas of a library or information center rather than being limited to one area. For many staff members, this ability to use their thinking and analytical skills, combined with job flexibility and a feeling of importance to the organization, may be what draws them to this type of library.

Sometimes, rather than working in one special library, a librarian or information specialist may prefer to use these problem-solving skills to become an *information broker*. The information broker is an independent or "free-lance"

Fig. 8.1. Distribution of Myers-Briggs Personality Type Indicators for special librarians. (Reprinted with permission from *Special Libraries*, 81, no. 4, pg. 331, Journal of the Special Library Association.)

	General Population	Special Librarians
Characteristic:		
Introversion (I)	35%	65%
Extroversion (E)	65%	35%
Sensing (S)	68%	43%
Intuition (N)	32%	57%
Thinking (T)	48%	65%
Feeling (F)	52%	35%
Judgment (J)	55%	68%
Perception (P)	45%	32%

Breakdown of Special Librarian Profiles:

ISTJ	17.41%
INTJ	14.37%
ENTJ	8.85%
INTP	8.49%

librarian or firm who will search out and provide information on a profit-making basis. The information broker provides services ranging from searches of computerized databases to translations to market surveys. Sometimes business or industrial firms call in an information broker to establish or organize special libraries or information centers. An information broker's clients may include corporations and individuals who do not have access to information centers. Or, the clients may be libraries or information centers that need specific information outside the realm of their collections. The information brokers' ability to specialize and produce results in a short span of time has made them invaluable resources for libraries and information centers.

Information specialists have welcomed such resource support for their collections as many factors have hampered their ability to provide access to in-depth resource collections. First and foremost, the fluctuating budgets of special libraries and information centers have made it very difficult to follow consistant collection development plans. The tremendous explosion of print and electronic publishing during the last quarter of the twentieth century has aggravated this problem. For example, by 1990 more than 100,000 journals were available in the fields of science and technology, and these had been increasing at the rate of 2 percent a year. In the electronic publishing field, more than 3,900 databases and services in all fields were available through more than 575 online services by 1990. Over one-fourth of these services were full-text databases, with LEXIS for law and NEXIS for current news information the most heavily used. In just the scientific and technical fields, this electronic publishing rate has been increasing at the rate of 10 percent a year.

In deciding which of these many materials and services to provide for their patrons, information specialists must contend with paying skyrocketing costs for them. For example, the cost of online scientific databases in 1990 ranged from $60,000 to $150,000 per year for one database. The cost of legal continuation and loose-leaf services increased by 250-350 percent between the 1970s and the 1990s. Fluctuations in currency exchange rates could play havoc with an information center's serials budget because foreign serials could account for 48 percent of an information center's serials collection. By the early 1990s, federal administrative policy also had forced the U.S. Superintendent of Documents and NTIS (National Technical Information Service) to reexamine their publishing practices. The result was that libraries had to pay substantially more for documents that had previously been available at reasonable prices. Similarly, their parent companies had to pay higher prices for the licensing rights to properties from such federal agencies as the Departments of Health, Agriculture, Interior, and Commerce.

In response to such economic problems, information specialists began looking in many directions for solutions. To extend their materials budgets, they began to turn to information vendors such as Chemical Abstracts and University Microfilms. For example, information specialists found that the cost of commercially procured documents compared favorably with the subscription, processing, and staffing costs of in-house serials collections. Some libraries used these comparisons to revise their budgets and reduce their pre-demand purchasing to provide more on-demand delivery of all kinds of documents. Finally, most special libraries and information centers joined one or more cooperative library networks such as the Museum Computer Network to maximize their resources and dollars.

This constant financial need has forced special libraries and information centers to be creative. Libraries and companies that had developed unique and marketable in-house materials such as software programs or databases sold them to other users as Lockheed Corporation did with DIALOG. More and more special libraries were required by their parent institutions' accounting departments to charge back their services to the corporate department end user, such as the engineering or marketing departments. This change in funding encouraged many of these special libraries and information centers to develop marketing programs to justify the costs of such charge-back systems. These programs also stressed the contributions that library and information services could make to help each department meet its goals and objectives. Many libraries were very successful in establishing their worth within their parent institutions. Some firms, such as law and engineering firms, even began "passing through" or billing the costs of such library and information services to the end-user client.

In addition to these funding changes, by the 1990s special libraries and information centers had begun to extend their budgets by providing fee-based services to "external" corporate or individual users who were not members of their defined clientele. Fees were charged for services such as online searches, reference service, and document delivery. They often enabled a library or information center to provide additional services for its members that it might not otherwise be able to afford. In contrast with public and academic libraries that had to face freedom-of-access concerns when they charged similar fees, the special library or information center had to ensure that the benefits of providing such fee-based services did not reduce any services to its primary clientele. Another major concern was the effect of such fees on library cooperation. When charging such fees, libraries and information centers had to consider whether they would charge fees to other network members and whether or not such fees would violate any network agreements. In the final analysis, however, the policies and practices of every special library or information center will always be governed by the needs and goals of its parent organization rather than by library or information center goals.

SUMMARY

Special libraries and information centers provide special services in a specialized subject area or special format for a special clientele. These libraries have developed to meet objectives of parent institutions. They are more varied and distinct than any other type of library. Special libraries can be found in any institution where special clientele have special library needs. They have developed in almost every business and industry to contribute to the profit-making motive of a particular company or business. Special libraries have extensive information collections, staffs, and services to support the research needs of their parent organizations. Such services have become so important that many of these special libraries are now called information centers, and their staffs are information specialists and technicians.

REVIEW QUESTIONS

1. Identify the major objectives of special libraries and information centers.

2. Describe the relationship of a special library or information center to its parent institution.

3. Describe the scopes and services of the three U.S. national libraries.

4. Describe the kinds of materials usually included in corporate libraries and information collections.

5. List 10 kinds of special libraries or information centers.

6. Visit one or two special libraries or information centers and compare their objectives, services, and collections to those discussed in this chapter.

NOTES

[1]William Burlington, "To Enlarge the Sphere of Human Knowledge: The Role of the Independent Research Library," in *Libraries for Teaching, Libraries for Research* (Chicago: ALA, 1977), 174.

[2]Tobi A. Brimsek and Dolores Leach, "Special Librarians to the Core: Profiling with MBTI," *Special Libraries* 81, no. 4 (Fall 1990): 331.

SELECTED READINGS

Ahrensfeld, Janet L. *Special Libraries: A Guide for Management*. 2d rev. ed. Washington, DC: SLA, 1986.

American Library Association. *The ALA Yearbook of Library and Information Services: A Review of Library Events*. Vol. 1- . Chicago: ALA, 1976- .

Bulletin of the Medical Library Association. Vol. 1, no. 1- . Chicago: Medical Library Association, 1911- .

Larsen, John C., ed. *Museum Librarianship*. Hamden, CT: Shoe String, 1985.

Larsgaard, Mary Lynette. *Map Librarianship: An Introduction*. 2d ed. Littleton, CO: Libraries Unlimited, 1987.

Medical Library Association. *Minimum Standards for Health Science Libraries in Hospitals*. Chicago: Medical Library Association, 1984.

Russell, Keith W., and Maria G. Piza, eds. "Agricultural Libraries and Information." *Library Trends* 38, no. 3 (Winter 1990): 327-638.

Special Libraries. Vol. 1, no. 1- . Washington, DC: SLA, 1910- .

Strauss, Lucille J., et al. *Scientific and Technical Libraries: Their Organization and Administration*. 3d ed. Melbourne, FL: Krieger, 1991.

White, Herbert S. *Managing the Special Library: Strategies for Success Within the Larger Organization*. Boston: G. K. Hall, 1984.

CHAPTER 9

LIBRARY NETWORKS

Libraries of all types have always worked to acquire, preserve, and make available their information and materials to other libraries. Throughout history, libraries have joined together to provide access to their collections for the benefit of all. This sharing of materials began in the Middle Ages with libraries that loaned manuscripts back and forth so they could be copied. It has continued into the 1990s with the development of online shared bibliographic databases. These cooperative library efforts are referred to simply as *networks* in this chapter. However, they are often identified by such different names as library systems, networks, consortia, councils, and cooperatives. If they include more than one type of library, they might be further identified as intertype or multitype. By 1990, over 405 of these organizations had been established to meet the information needs of a particular geographic area or to provide information in a subject area or for a specific type of library. However, no matter what their titles or the basis for their memberships, their goals were the same: to share resources, exchange information, and use computer and telecommunications technologies to foster joint projects that would reduce needless duplication of effort and resources.

NATIONAL AUTOMATED
NETWORKS

Although libraries had worked together for many years, the coming of the computer in the 1960s made it even more advantageous for libraries to do so. Libraries of all types joined in cooperatives or networks from the 1970s to the 1990s to use these computer capabilities and share expenses. Several major areas of concern strongly influenced this development of computer-based automation systems in the library and information fields. The primary concern was that the costs of the first computer-based systems were so high that only large libraries were able to justify them. Sometimes only a few of these libraries could afford their own computers dedicated solely to library operations. As a result, some libraries in the 1960s began to develop computer-based systems that were shared with other departments within their institutions. As the institutional demands on these computers grew, however, these libraries found they had more and more difficulty gaining access to the computer. Another major concern was that there was very few standards to guide early libraries in developing their own software and automated library systems. Thus, these "do-it-yourself" library systems may have worked well for individual libraries, but most of them could not be transferred very easily to operations in other libraries. When the LC introduced its MARC program in 1966, libraries began to look to the LC for leadership in solving some of these problems.

The MARC program was the first important factor in the development of library automation for the 1970s. MARC began as a project to provide the LC cataloging data for English-language current imprints on computer-generated magnetic tapes. By 1980, MARC was expanded to include virtually all Roman alphabet language materials in many different media forms. Rather than developing their own formats, libraries began to purchase these MARC tapes, load them onto their own computers, and use them to provide cataloging information for their new library purchases. MARC became accepted as the worldwide standard for a computerized library bibliographic format. Libraries began to band together to use the MARC format to build databases, share them with other libraries, and develop compatible automated library systems. The result was that practically every library automated system was either based on the MARC format or was compatible with it.

The development of MARC as the standard library bibliographic format was followed by the second important factor that influenced library automation in the 1970s. Some library institutions and a growing number of private companies began to develop and market their own automated library systems. They became automation vendors that sold or leased their automated systems to libraries on a contractual basis for an affordable service fee. These systems were often developed as joint ventures with the companies providing the computer hardware and software and the library providing the bibliographic information. For the first time, many libraries could avail themselves of automated systems in all areas of the library, from acquisitions and book catalogs (Brodart), to circulation (CLSI), to cataloging (OCLC) and reference (MEDLINE and Lockheed's DIALOG).

One of these automation vendors, OCLC, Inc., provided the most significant development in automation since MARC. Begun in 1970 as a cooperative of academic libraries in Ohio (Ohio College Library Center), OCLC was soon incorporated as its own entity and by 1990 had emerged as the major shared cataloging system. Libraries in every state from coast to coast joined OCLC's system because it was one of the first and best-designed library automated systems available. It was also well marketed and fulfilled a need libraries had for getting library cataloging quickly, easily, and at reasonable costs. OCLC began its operations as a shared cataloging service. This meant that a cooperating library would use a computer in its own library to search for a cataloging record in the mainframe computer based in Columbus, Ohio. If the cataloging record for an item were found, the library could edit the information to fit its own needs or "profile." It would add its location symbol to the cataloging record and instruct the computer to print library catalog cards for this item. The cards would arrive in about a week and already be filed in correct alphabetical order. If the cataloging record were not found, the library itself had to catalog the item and enter the cataloging record into the OCLC database. As each item was cataloged, it was also added by OCLC to the individual library's MARC-based master tape. By the

1980s and 1990s, many libraries were using their OCLC/MARC-based computer tapes to establish online computer catalogs or CD-ROM catalogs.

Because many large libraries were adding thousands of volumes to their collections and thousands of records to OCLC's database every year, OCLC soon developed a very large database. In addition, many libraries received permission to do retrospective searching to add cataloging records for older items already in their collections. This two-pronged approach to building the database enabled libraries that joined OCLC to experience "hits" or locate records for 85-95 percent of their cataloging needs. Libraries not only were satisfied with this success rate, but also were happy that much of the cataloging on OCLC terminals could be accessed by trained paraprofessionals. Many libraries found they no longer needed to develop large professional cataloging staffs.

As OCLC developed into a national resource-sharing database, it began to expand in other ways. It expanded its governing body to allow for input by its many library customers from outside of Ohio. It also encouraged libraries to join through library networks rather than as individual members. Networks such as PALINET (Pennsylvania Area Library Network) and SOLINET (Southeast Library Network) provided instruction to and control over the libraries that joined OCLC in their areas. OCLC also expanded its operations into other resource-sharing areas besides cataloging. The OCLC database was used as a union catalog, and interlibrary loan programs were developed so that libraries could use their local OCLC computers to request materials from other libraries. Some library networks such as ILLINET (Illinois State Library Network) even required their member libraries to participate in this interlibrary loan network as a contractual condition for using OCLC. A serials database was also developed, and other communication systems were planned. By 1978, OCLC had become the national leader in library automation that many people had expected the Library of Congress to become.

The development in the late 1970s of several other viable automation networks challenged this national leadership. Stanford University's well-designed BALLOTS system joined with the Research Libraries Group (RLG) to form RLIN (Research Libraries Information Network). This system combined the powerful and versatile technical system of BALLOTS with the databases of the libraries in RLG. (See chapter 7.) It challenged OCLC's dominance by attracting many research and academic libraries to RLIN. The Washington Library Network (WLN) emerged in the late 1970s as another successful network. In fact, WLN became such a successful regional network that it changed its name to Western Library Network by the 1990s. Its sophisticated software packages were also transferred successfully to other library systems (even in Australia) to support shared cataloging and acquisitions as well as other library processes. In Minnesota, libraries joined together to establish SILO, a cataloging and interlibrary loan network for serial publications.

None of the automation networks developed in the 1970s, however, were able to provide the totally automated library operations and systems dreamed of in the 1960s. Instead, economic decisions limited the development of most automated systems to single-purpose systems. For example, OCLC developed a tremendous network for providing catalog cards and automated catalogs, but its lack of subject access limited its use for subject bibliographic searches. BALLOTS had subject access but did not have OCLC's strength as a cataloging database or as a union catalog. Neither network had developed feasible circulation capabilities. To fill this circulation gap, a variety of commercial vendors stepped in and developed automated circulation systems based on these databases.

By the 1980s and 1990s, technological advancements in computers, and their decreasing costs, had spurred the development of multiservice library automation networks to bridge this gap. More and more networks became full-service networks. OCLC added circulation and serials to its services. Other networks expanded to provide coordinated services that included automated cataloging, circulation, resource sharing, collection development, and interlibrary loans. Networks that had started out as full-service networks, such as WLN, began sharing access to their systems and their databases. National automated networks, such as OCLC and RLG, began discussions in the early 1990s to combine some of their services. Such coordinated network services should continue to develop as support for a National Research and Education Network (NREN) gains ground in the 1990s.

By the 1990s, the impact of these automated systems had generated several major developments in the administration of these automated systems. Computer cooperatives or networks developed among libraries that could not afford to buy their own automated systems. These libraries joined in local or regional networks to purchase one vendor's bibliographic system that they could all use. By 1984, more than 5,000 libraries belonged to such automated system networks. Within each network, libraries participated in governing boards or councils and adopted common computer parameters and regulations that applied to every library in the network. As these library automated systems became more complex and more costly, library network users began to demand more input into the product development of the systems they were buying. Many of them joined with other library customers in informal users' groups to form a strong collective voice as they presented their problems and concerns to the automation vendors. Library users also became active in vendor-appointed user councils (CLSI) or user-elected councils (OCLC) to formalize their input into the development of the services they were using. They found that this user input was especially vital in the development of programs and provision for services.

The 1990s has also generated several major concerns for libraries as they begin to use the products of the many automation vendors. One major concern involves the question of ownership of the information in the bibliographic databases. Claims of copyright ownership by OCLC and LC have not set well with libraries that had contributed their own bibliographic records to such databases. Libraries have also been concerned with the number and variety of computer systems available. Because many of these systems are not compatible with each other, libraries have often had to purchase additional equipment for one library's computer system to "interconnect" or "interface" with another library's system. If a library wanted to expand its bibliographic or system capacity, it often found that the costs of upgrading its equipment or "migrating" (changing) to another system had serious financial impacts. When these latter concerns affected individual libraries, they could usually be easily resolved. However, when they involved library cooperative networks, their resolution could be very complicated indeed.

LIBRARY NETWORKING

Perhaps the greatest impact that the development of national automated networks had on the development of libraries was their influence on library cooperation. These networks enabled all types of libraries in a geographic or subject area to join together and mobilize the total library resources of that area to meet all of their users' needs. By the 1960s, public, academic, school, and special libraries in both the public and private sectors had recognized that they could not economically satisfy all of their users' demands by themselves. They understood that they could serve their patrons' needs better by sharing their budgets and resources through cooperative library operations and services. Thus, libraries joined together in networks to provide new and creative ways of sharing resources and services and to develop an information network that was greater than the sum of its parts. The rapid growth of these networks and the variety of their activities attest to the fact that they had indeed met some previously unserved library needs.

Networks were successful for several important reasons. First, cooperative network ventures were based upon a spirit of cooperation that had been part of the library world for centuries. Libraries and their staffs were accustomed to sharing their materials through interlibrary loan and sharing their staffs' expertise with colleagues in other libraries. Many library staffs had years of experience in cooperative acquisitions, collection development, and resource sharing. However, they all looked forward to the additional benefits of networks. These benefits included cost-effective access to computer technology and shared cataloging information they could not afford on their own. Network benefits also included access to a greater variety of resources and provided a more formal extension of library cooperation that libraries could use to meet their own patrons' needs. Because membership in these networks was voluntary, libraries depended upon a spirit of cooperation and concensus or compromise among the members to enable these networks to reach their fullest potential.

A second reason for the success of networks was the attention library organizers paid to the establishment of such organizations. Recognizing that a network is only as strong as its weakest link, network organizers designed governance structures that built on the strength of each network member. These structures ensured that the autonomy of each member library would be maintained and that larger libraries would neither dominate the other libraries nor be exploited by them. In the beginning of network development, these governance structures were informal. However, as more libraries joined the networks and network services became more diverse, most networks established governing boards of directors and developed constitutions and bylaws. These governing boards might be made up of a representative from each network institution, or they might be elected from among participating institutions. Decisions were often made by simple majority votes following the rule of "one library, one vote." However, in cases of finances or governance, a two-thirds majority or unanimous vote might be required. Although such forms of network governance could be cumbersome at times, they did help ensure that a network would address the issues and needs that were important to the majority of its members.

Another major reason for the success of library networks came from their members' commitment to developing and participating in network activities.

Member libraries donated facilities, materials, and services to help networks get established as economically as possible. They were willing to donate a considerable amount of volunteer staff time at all levels to organize and direct network activities. Network members found that this commitment not only developed a strong network, but it also developed deeper commitments among the library staff members who worked on these network projects and committees. As the networks grew in memberships and services, however, they found that more time was needed to direct the network activities than the member libraries were able to provide. The commitment to cooperative library networks began to change. Half of the libraries began to view networks as professional partnerships, and the other half viewed them as contracted utilities. This change was reflected in staffing as many networks began hiring specialized staffs ranging from very large staffs of 10 or more professional, technical, and clerical personnel to very small staffs of one full- or part-time professional. These staffs worked under the direction of the network governing boards to direct and carry out the networks' daily operations.

The more successful networks shared several additional characteristics. These networks tended to be more solidly funded and to have leaders who shared a vision and willingness to explore new ideas. They were less often affected by the political and psychological barriers that could deter their libraries from becoming more fully involved in network activities. Finally, they were able to overcome one of the major political barriers involved in the governance of networks: a legal one. Although most networks had governing authorities, they did not usually have any legal basis for their existence. State laws were often either silent on the question or could be interpreted to exclude them. Successful networks were able to work around this barrier. The less successful networks often found it politically difficult to work with their members' governing bodies when the network had no legal basis from which to operate.

At other times, libraries were more concerned with "turf protection" than with resource sharing. Larger libraries were worried that their resources would be overused by other libraries; smaller libraries were worried that their needs would be overshadowed by the needs of the larger libraries. In the same vein, many politicians, administrators, and librarians feared they might lose their local authority or control over their libraries if they joined such networks. They resented being required to follow network-established policies and procedures to participate in cooperative databases and services even though they might have voted on the adoption of such policies and procedures. In some cases, libraries chose to retain complete control of their operations by remaining independent. However, in such cases, libraries could generally provide access to the network's bibliographic computer through "interconnect" or dial-access telecommunications.

Psychological barriers could also make libraries decide to either leave or not join library networks. Some administrators objected to donating volunteer staff time to such quasi-legal entities. Others resented the time required at all staffing levels for participation in network committee assignments. If these network needs became so time consuming that full-time staffs were hired, libraries were concerned that they would be unable to afford such additional costs. Some librarians felt threatened because they did not understand the needs of other types of libraries that differed from their own, and they were not willing to try to understand these needs. In some networks, librarians felt that the networks were not responsive enough to their own library's needs. Often, these political and psychological problems came to a head as networks began to expand or to merge with other networks.

In addition to addressing these political and psychological concerns, library networks found that economics had a great impact on their development. Decreasing costs of microcomputers and CD-ROM technologies made it possible for networks to purchase better equipment with greater storage capacity for less money, which enabled networks to save on telecommunication costs. However, networks still needed to finance computer equipment upgrades, software enhancements, and CD-ROM services. Also, the availability of cheaper, stand-alone systems combined with increasing network costs made it more economical for larger libraries to withdraw from networks.

To offset this trend, library networks began to address a growing need in the 1990s to develop more adequate financial support for network activities. In the beginning of network development in the 1960s, financial support for networks had come from a variety of sources. Many states had used their LSCA (Library Services and Construction Act) funds to encourage and fund the development of automated network databases. These funds were often supplemented by membership fees paid by the participating institutions, but these fees were seldom enough to support the total function of the network. This "soft funding," or money that depended on political and economic variables, began to erode in the economic crises of the late 1970s and 1980s.

As state libraries reduced their support for network services no longer considered innovative, networks established new sources of revenues to take up this shortfall. Networks began billing their costs to member libraries. This placed a hardship on those libraries that had come to depend upon the network for services such as cataloging and circulation without adequately planning for their increased costs. To resolve some of these problems, networks began to investigate additional ways to supplement their budgets. They began to assess their members for capital development funds that were set aside to purchase future equipment such as computer upgrades. They charged their members fees or premiums for differing levels of service. Networks generated additional revenues by selling library and automated services, publishing library materials, and charging fees to nonmembers for network programs or institutes. A few networks followed the lead of WLN and became nonprofit corporations to sell their services and products to nonmembers. Other networks expanded their memberships to include nonlibrary institutions or agencies that wanted to avail themselves of a network's services. Although all of these steps have helped, many members believe that the major task facing networks in the 1990s will be to develop solid funding for network operations.

LIBRARY SYSTEMS

Library systems can be distinguished from other types of networks in several important ways. First, the development of library systems has differed considerably from that of most other library networks. Rather than being developed by their members to fill some specific member needs, library systems were originally established as public library systems by state library agencies in response to the 1966 *Minimum Standards for Public Library Service*. Using LSCA funding, almost every state developed a plan to establish and finance a library system on a geographic basis so the system would cover every part of the state. Once all of these systems were developed, they would enable every state resident to have access to state-supported library service. For citizens to obtain such service, however, they had to belong to a local library that had joined the library system.

To encourage local libraries to join a library system, the state held out several carrots. Usually, the system services were totally funded by the state so there were no system costs to the local library. These state funds were used to develop system services such as interlibrary van delivery, computer automation, FAX communications, reference and cataloging support services, and consultant services to which most of these libraries would not otherwise have had access. The only requirement of the local library was that it agree to make its resources and facilities available to patrons from other libraries in the library system or any other system in the state. Most library systems were established as federated systems that allowed each library not only to retain its own autonomy, but also to have representation on the system library board. However, library systems that served large rural areas or that had only one library within their jurisdiction often became consolidated systems. These systems consolidated all libraries within the system boundaries into one unit with one governing board and one central library administration.

As library systems became better established and the importance of access to information took precedence over the source of the information, most library systems expanded from public library systems to multitype systems. The governance of these library systems changed to include representatives from all types of libraries. School, academic, and special libraries, both public and private, joined public libraries in these expanded systems for the same reasons they would join any other library network. All libraries recognized that without such cooperation they might never gain such affordable access to library resources and bibliographic online databases to enhance their institutions' or organizations' needs. The library systems' services also expanded to provide the same service to each library regardless of its type. There were some concerns at first from private academic and special libraries that their facilities or confidential resources might be exploited by patrons of the other types of libraries. To alleviate these concerns, provisions were made to protect private corporate and product information. Some systems and states also reimbursed larger libraries for excessive use of their resources. Generally, however, studies showed that these concerns were groundless, and libraries of all types realized they could gain more than they lost by participating in such library systems.

NETWORK SERVICES

The development of intertype library networks initiated many new and creative services that had not been possible before. One of the most appreciated of these new services was the development of reciprocal borrowing programs that enabled patrons from one library to check out materials from another network library. This innovation made many collections in special and academic libraries available for the first time to members of the public who had never been able to use them before. Reciprocal borrowing quickly became a favorite network service for patrons from all libraries. Patrons particularly appreciated having access to libraries where they shopped, worked, or attended school without worrying about which type of library had the information they needed. These programs were also successful from the libraries' viewpoint because they were supervised by the networks so that large libraries or special collections were not overused or under-compensated by other libraries.

In addition to opening up their collections to patrons from other network members, network libraries developed shared bibliographic databases. These union databases made the combined holdings of all member libraries accessible at one time. Network members could develop joint collection development, cataloging, circulation, and public access catalog systems online so that the holdings of any network library were accessible from every other library. This access to all the network holdings enabled libraries to maximize and extend their budgets. They developed cooperative collection development programs in specific areas or types of material. Bibliographic cataloging records were also established, usually in combination with national automated systems such as OCLC or WLN, under the watchful eyes of network cataloging authorities. These authoritative cataloging records reduced the need for original cataloging by each library at the same time that they increased the quality of the network's database. Online circulation systems enabled libraries to use shared circulation files and patron records to reserve items easily and check out materials to patrons from other network libraries. Patrons could use OPACs and CD-ROM catalogs to see all the bibliographic records of the network at one time and determine which items were checked out or which items were available "on shelf."

This public access to network databases was also important in the development of another major network service, that of resource sharing. As the public used these databases, they often uncovered subject strengths or unusual items in libraries they would not otherwise have known about. In addition, access to national subject databases and to the many CD-ROM indexes and databases made the public aware of resources that were not available in the local library. This need to obtain additional resources contributed to the development and expansion of network interlibrary loan (ILL) programs. Using network, regional, and national databases as union catalogs and union lists of serials, libraries located materials which they then requested from other libraries on ILL. Although networks usually established fairly flexible ILL regulations among their own members, state and national ILL loan requests were governed by state and national ILL codes. In recent years, most of these codes have been updated to take into consideration the development of networks as well as the advancements in technology that could affect the filling of such requests. For example, the national *Interlibrary Loan Code* was not only revised in 1980, but in 1990 it was amplified by the publication of *Guidelines and Procedures for Telefacsimile Transmission of Interlibrary Loan Requests*.

Libraries followed these ILL codes and regulations as they used hierarchical systems for interlibrary loan and reference requests. These codes generally required libraries to request information or materials from local or network libraries first and then from state or designated resource libraries before going to out-of-state libraries. The referral systems developed in Illinois and New York are typical of these hierarchical systems. Illinois's statewide network, ILLINET, uses the Chicago Public Library, the Illinois State Library, and the University of Illinois and Southern Illinois University libraries as back-up resource and reference libraries. The University of Chicago, Northwestern University, and John

Crerar Libraries serve as special resource centers. New York's NYSILL (New York State Interlibrary Loan Network) uses three referral libraries (Brooklyn, Rochester, and Buffalo-Erie County Public Libraries) and nine subject referral libraries to back up nine regional "3Rs" (reference and research library resources) systems. These 3Rs systems provide interlibrary loans, document delivery service, and reciprocal borrowing privileges. Once such statewide hierarchical systems have been exhausted, a library can use interconnecting links between regional or multistate library networks, the national automated networks, and the national libraries to obtain information from the nation's library and information resources for its patrons.

By 1990, this nationwide system of local, state, and regional networks had provided cooperative library services and resource sharing from coast to coast which librarians had only dreamed about in the 1960s and 1970s. Networks routinely loaned and borrowed materials in all formats using traditional same-day or overnight mail or van delivery services. In addition, networks had progressed to an advanced level of sophistication in resource sharing using the latest developments in electronic computer and telecommunication technologies. Networks used electronic, telecommunications, or FAX systems to speed up the transmission of ILL materials as well as for other network activities. The state of Wyoming developed one such FAX network that connected seven community colleges, half of the county library systems, and the state library for ILL activities as well as for communication and other networking functions. The state of Wisconsin developed WisCAT, a CD-ROM union catalog of all types of libraries throughout the state for use in ILL and bibliographic control. Many networks made their databases accessible via dial access so that patrons with a PC and a telephone modem could not only search a database, but they could also place reserve requests on items they wished to receive. Some networks, such as CARL (Colorado Alliance of Research Libraries), could respond to these computer patron requests by sending articles online or by FAX.

In addition to resource sharing, networks provided many other operations and services. Some networks developed cooperative library acquisitions and collection development programs so that unnecessary and costly duplications could be eliminated. Such networks might also develop cooperative periodicals centers or cooperative storage facilities for little-used or last-copy items. Other networks created strong continuing education programs that offered workshops and institutes for the education of their members. Some cooperative networks, such as CLASS (Cooperative Library Agency for Systems and Services), provided discounts on materials, databases, online services, equipment and supplies, CD-ROM products, etc. CLASS even offered a subject area technical service center for Asian language materials. Other networks such as CARL in Colorado and LCS (Library Computer Services) in Illinois were expanded from single-service to full-service networks. As networks develop these expanded services, they will review them to ensure that they meet their members' needs.

SUMMARY

Libraries of all types have worked together throughout the ages to acquire, preserve, and share their materials. The benefits from such cooperation have been greatly accelerated by the advent of computer and telecommunications technologies in the last quarter of the twentieth century. These technologies have enabled almost every library anywhere to join in some cooperative library network activity to provide increased access to materials to meet their patrons' needs. Such networks generally have been established to meet the information needs of a particular geographic area or to provide information in a subject area or for a specific type of library. Their success has largely been due to their ability to share resources, exchange information, provide computer and telecommunications technologies, and develop joint projects to reduce needless duplication of effort and resources.

Library networks have formed at all levels to provide these cooperative library services. Automated network utilities have developed at the national level to provide automated bibliographic databases. At the state level, locally controlled library systems provide library service to every state resident. At the local level, libraries of all types have joined together in cooperative networks to establish local union bibliographic databases and automated circulation systems. Many of these state and local networks have joined national automated network utilities. They also have developed local cooperative programs to reduce unnecessary and costly duplications. However, local networks are strongly affected by the financial, political, and psychological barriers of the libraries that make up the networks. How well these libraries can overcome these barriers will generally determine each network's success.

REVIEW QUESTIONS

1. Identify the important features of the national library automated networks, including MARC, OCLC, RLIN, and WLN.

2. Describe the major reasons for the success of library networks.

3. Discuss the political and psychological barriers to successful network participation.

4. Explain the differences between the two types of governance of library systems.

5. Describe the distinctions between library systems and other types of networks.

6. Identify 10 services a network might provide.

SELECTED READINGS

ALA Yearbook: A Review of Library Events. Chicago: ALA, 1976- .

Ballard, Thomas H. *Failure of Resource Sharing in Public Libraries and Alternative Strategies for Service*. Chicago: ALA, 1986.

California Conferences on Networking. Proceedings of the California Library Networking Task Force, Sacramento, California, 22-27 September 1988.

Future of the Public Library. Conference proceedings of OCLC Online Computer Library Center, Dublin, Ohio, 20-22 March 1988.

Martin, Susan K. *Library Networks, 1986-1987.* Boston: G. K. Hall, 1986.

The Report on Library Cooperation, 1986. Library Cooperation Committee. Multitype Library Cooperation Section Staff. Chicago: ALA, 1986.

Sager, Donald J. *Managing the Public Library.* 2d ed. Boston: G. K. Hall, 1989.

Townley, Charles T. *Human Relations in Library Network Development.* Hamden, CT: Library Professional Publications, 1988.

Wareham, Nancy L., comp. and ed. *Report on Library Cooperation.* 1st ed. In cooperation with chief officers of state library agencies. Chicago: Association of Specialized and Cooperative Library Agencies, 1976- .

CHAPTER 10

LIBRARY FACILITIES

If a library's resources and services have been influenced by computers, technology, and networking, their buildings and furnishings have been influenced even more so. As a result, libraries in the 1990s differ drastically from libraries built in the 1950s and 1960s. No longer are libraries just quiet reflective places for patrons to sit and read books from the library's storehouse shelves. Instead, libraries built since the 1970s have expanded and changed to take into account many technological, societal, and environmental developments that have affected their programs, resources, and services. New developments such as display shelving for books, computer catalogs and CD-ROM stations, television studios, and media in all their formats have necessitated changes in library spaces, furnishings, and electrical requirements for most libraries. As libraries move into the twenty-first century, additional technological changes will continue to influence the development of future library facilities.

INFLUENCES ON
LIBRARY FACILITIES

Beginning in the 1970s, librarians responded to a number of technological, societal, and environmental factors as they planned efficient and functional library facilities to meet their patrons' needs. First, newer technologies and media often required specific electrical and mechanical services that could not be provided in a current or traditional library building. For example, libraries that added mainframe or minicomputers to serve online computer catalogs often had to add climate-controlled rooms to house the computer and dedicated electrical lines for the catalogs. Second, demographic and census studies identified changing community needs to which libraries needed to respond. For example, a demographic study at a college could reveal that the campus had changed from a commuter campus to a residential campus and that students wanted the library open day and night even on weekends. Census figures might also show that a public library's community of senior citizens had been replaced by young home-owners with preschool children. A third factor that influenced the development of library facilities was society's recognition that handicapped people needed access to public facilities. This recognition, and the adoption of government regulations to ensure such access, prodded libraries into remodeling older facilities or designing new ones.

Perhaps the most important factor in the development of library facilities has been the cost of operating such facilities. Beginning with the oil crisis in the 1970s, librarians began to remodel and design their buildings to provide more energy- and cost-efficient heating and cooling systems. Older libraries had new energy-efficient lighting bulbs and fixtures installed. New buildings took advantage of solar-heating and energy-saving designs. In these energy-efficient designs, librarians also tried to plan sufficient mechanical and electrical systems to support their new technologies. At the same time, librarians recognized that what might be the latest technology in one decade could be out of date in the next. Thus, library buildings had to be designed and redesigned with a flexibility and capacity for change that would enable them to grow with any coming technologies as well as to support any innovative developments in library services.

PLANNING LIBRARY FACILITIES

The development of any functional, efficient, and aesthetic library facility is governed by the maxim that "good libraries don't just happen." The design of well-functioning library buildings with flexibility and future capacity requires a great deal of careful planning and attention to detail. Most of this planning and attention is generally provided by the library staff members because they are usually the first ones to notice any problems or concerns with the current library facility. These staff members can usually identify any problems with shelving library materials or providing services because they work in the facility everyday.

Library staff may also be the first to identify societal changes, such as population shifts, or environmental changes that may affect the future functions of the library. For example, public library staffs might notice if adult lounge areas were always crowded with senior citizens while children's areas were seldom used. They might also report that patrons had to stand in line at circulation stations during busy hours after school. Academic library staffs might notice changing study patterns of students that could indicate a need for varied study environments. For example, students might prefer individual study rooms and carrels or informal lounge-type areas to formal areas with tables and chairs. School library media center staffs might observe changes in teachers' educational approaches that required students to use the media center's audiovisual materials differently than they had in the past. Thus, library staff members can become vital sources of information when a library facility is redesigned or planned.

Once the persons involved with the decisions have determined that a library's current facilities do not meet the needs of its patrons, a library planning team is usually assembled to develop a space-needs plan. This planning team usually includes the library director, library board members or administrators, staff from the parent institution, members of the library staff, and representatives from the library's community (citizens, members, or faculty and students). This planning team will also usually include a library building consultant if the space-needs project is complicated or too time consuming for the library staff to take on. This building consultant will assist the team in identifying its space and service needs and ideally prevent errors in planning and building by ensuring that all important issues are considered.

As the planning team begins its work, all of its members should recognize that a library is not just a building that houses books and other graphic material. It is a building that satisfies the objectives, purposes, and functions of the library system it serves. Everyone involved in the planning team must first become familiar with the objectives of the library and the objectives of any institution to which it belongs. Then the team should study the community that will be served. This study should determine the community's needs and makeup and identify any changes that could affect the library's services. Any such changes in the library community's needs may have an important impact on the site or location of a library. Thus, the library site should be evaluated to ensure that its location will contribute to the library's objectives rather than hinder them. For example, public libraries should determine whether or not they should remain in a downtown location when their patrons have moved to the suburbs. A special library may find that researchers who were their major users are moving to a new location. More often than not, the best site for a library may have political ramifications or physical limitations that must be addressed and overcome in any building program.

Once the planning team has reviewed these objectives and community needs, it should use them to identify services, programs, resources, and needs that the future library building project should satisfy. This review of needs and objectives also provides an excellent opportunity for everyone to rethink the library's operations to consider any changes that could be instituted. For example, could the materials collections be better organized or arranged, or should online catalogs be placed in one area or scattered throughout the building? In determining these needs, members of the planning team will find it useful to visit other libraries to see what is being provided elsewhere. Once all of these steps have been taken and all of these factors considered, a *building program statement* should be written.

The library building or remodeling program statement is the heart and soul of any library building or construction project. It is a blueprint for future services, staffing needs, facilities design, and any restrictions or innovations that should be considered. This program statement should identify the ideals, goals, and dreams that the planning team expects the project to satisfy. It should include plans for the present library as well as specific plans for future services and expansion. Although this statement may have to be pared down at a later date, libraries that do not "dream big" may find they have built too timidly and conservatively and designed a building that does not suit their future needs.

In developing this program statement, the planning team should examine the effects of any identified societal or environmental changes to see if they will change the future functions of the library. The team should also examine the library's activities and design the building to function around them. For example, traffic patterns should be designed to fit library needs and not an architect's plan. Too many times, a beautiful library was designed first and the activities forced to function, poorly at best, within the building. As these library activities are examined, planners should remember that library programs and services may change in the future and that *flexibility* is the watchword. For this reason, many libraries have used quantitative library standards as guidelines rather than as requirements they should meet. Many libraries also have found that by adding new technologies or by joining networks they did not necessarily eliminate any library spaces but just changed the kinds of spaces needed. With the development of computer cataloging systems, some libraries found that they no longer needed large offices for cataloging staff. Instead, they needed climate-controlled rooms to house computer equipment. If developments such as these are taken into consideration when the building program statement is written, the resulting facility should be able to accommodate them without any major problems.

DESIGNING AND BUILDING LIBRARY FACILITIES

Once a library's activities have been planned and the building program statement has been written and adopted, an architect is usually added to the planning team. It is not wise for an architect to be brought onto the project before then because, too often, an architect's vision of the library's form can end up dictating the library's function. However, once the architect is a member of the planning team, the architect should follow two architectural maxims when designing the library facility: "Form should follow function" and "Form should follow imagination, form should follow the future." By following these two principles, the architect should be able to develop an aesthetically pleasing architectural form to satisfy the library's needs. It is in this stage that the planning team must give the architect full rein because it is the architect who will be responsible for the beauty and character of the building. However, once the building is designed, the planning team should critique it and adapt it to be sure that the planned building will truly satisfy the library's needs.

In designing a new or remodeled library facility, the architect must take several important library design factors into consideration. The first is that libraries have design requirements that differ from other types of institutions. A primary distinction is that, unlike some other businesses or institutions, libraries only want to have one public access entrance and exit to the library facility. Unlike regular offices that have one station for one employee, public service staffs might share workstations or need two workstations, one in the public area and one in the work area. Research and cataloging staffs may need enclosed offices that are conducive to concentration rather than open workstations commonly found in business offices. Library staff and patron workstations have a much greater need for electrical outlets than architects are used to providing for office secretarial stations. A typical library staff station for the 1990s might need electrical power, a LAN hookup, a dedicated circuit for an online computer terminal, and telecommunications access for telephone and FAX. In addition, library staffs who work so much with the public or work evening hours like to get away from the public's view at meal and break times. They enjoy relaxing in privacy in comfortable staff lounges and preparing hot meals in library kitchen areas.

A second design factor that an architect should consider is that different types of libraries have different design needs. For example, the majority of a special library's collection usually consists of periodicals in one form or another that will require specific shelving for each form. Such a library might require lounge-type seating near current periodicals shelving as well as seating for microform, computer, or CD-ROM equipment. A public library might need a separate preschool room for children and their parents as well as a quiet reading room where adults can get away from noisy children after school. A school library media center might need space for online computer terminals, CD-ROM stations, and video display units. Both school and public libraries might need meeting rooms for classroom instruction or individual or group study activities. Such meeting rooms are often separated from the rest of the library by soundproof glass walls to make supervision of these activities easier and let other patrons see how the library is being used. Academic and special libraries may also have to fit in with the architecture or environment of a parent institution.

A third design consideration the architect should take into account is the fact that there are functional differences among individual departments within each library. For example, public service workstations usually need convenient counter or desktop space for consulting with library patrons as well as space for library computers and shelving for ready reference resources. Technical services workstations usually need at least one computer for cataloging, desktop space for working with the items they are cataloging or processing, and shelves or book trucks to store the waiting materials. Children's departments need shelving to house different types of materials such as picture books, trade books, audio kits, videotapes, and toys within a child's reach. In the same vein, children's furnishings should be provided in several sizes for children of all ages as well as the adults who accompany them. Libraries with many audiovisual materials may intershelve them with books on open shelves, or they may store them in locked cabinets or in closed stack areas. Any of these functional differences should be described in the building program statement and confirmed by the architect with the library staff during the design stage.

A fourth major consideration is to design a library on a "modular" basis. The modular library is designed with as few columns and walls as possible. This design is based on the standard 3-foot-wide section of library shelving and multiples of this standard 3-foot section. The major portion of the library would have large open spaces, and any columns would be spaced at multiples of 3 square feet. Such a design would provide the maximum space for library shelving and avoid 1-foot or 2-foot gaps between shelving and columns. In addition, any library furniture or fixtures should also be based upon this same 3-foot multiple. Although some architects would prefer to custom-design their spaces and furnishings to other standards, this should be discouraged. The results of such designs can be quite striking and beautiful, but they can also be very costly to maintain or replace, and they can limit a library's flexibility.

Within the modular design library, inside walls should be non-load bearing and movable rather than permanent. These walls should reach to the ceiling to ensure privacy and cut down on the noise level of distractions to library staff and patrons. The inside walls should also be placed to allow for supervision of the library by a minimal number of staff. Glass walls are usually recommended for this supervisory purpose even though staff members sometimes feel as if they are living in a goldfish bowl. Walls of any type are preferable to other methods that are sometimes used to separate library functions. Features such as background music and "white noise" might be too disruptive or ineffective at blocking out noise to be useful in a library.

Finally, the architect should follow good architectural and environmental principles in designing the actual library facility and its systems. The architect's library design should take into consideration any unusual physical features of the site or any local ordinance restrictions that would affect its location, size, or design. Windows and lighting should be designed so that the activities of the library are best served. For example, some libraries may please their staffs by adding lots of windows that can be opened. Other libraries may have a few narrow windows to protect against vandalism and theft. In addition, each library function has its own lighting needs. Patron study areas, staff work areas, and collection shelving areas each have different lighting level needs. For example, lighting in areas for the major shelving collection should run perpendicular to shelving ranges and aisles rather than parallel to them. This ensures adequate lighting if shelving is shifted in the future.

It is the architect's responsibility to see that the library facility meets all building and government codes. These codes include all the mechanicals, such as electrical, plumbing, heating, and air conditioning, as well as fire protection and safety codes. If the library is a public building, it may have to meet more stringent government codes that require the inclusion of sprinkler systems, smoke and heat detectors, or even that the library have an alarm system hooked up to the police or fire department. The library may also need to meet environmental codes that protect against natural disasters such as earthquakes, floods, or tornadoes. Any new or remodeled library must meet codes for handicapped accessibility that dictate not only the width of doors, but also the width of the aisles between the shelves and, in some cases, the height of the shelves. Architects should also take the security of the staff and the collection into consideration when designing library spaces and avoid unlocked exit doors, secluded stack areas, and darkened hallways or parking lots. Additional security measures may include security doors with electronic keypads rather than keys and silent alarms hooked up to police or security services.

Good architects have been able to place engineering and mechanical systems so they could be changed or replaced easily while taking up a minimum of a library's usable space. Some architects are able to provide 75 percent usable space in the same square footage where others provide only 55 percent. Some buildings have kept this loss to a minimum by actually placing the mechanicals on the roof or outside the building. The better architects usually take great care in designing the electrical and mechanical systems such as the HVAC (heating, ventilating, and air conditioning), electrical, plumbing, and telecommunications systems. However, few architects have been able to design systems that consistently provide comfortable temperature control. To help resolve this problem, many libraries have installed electronic devices to monitor these operating systems. The architect should also make provisions so that future audiovisual, telecommunications, and computer technologies can be included easily in the building. The building itself should be placed on the library site according to its best location and traffic patterns, taking into consideration future construction that can be added easily and reasonably. Although these requirements seem stringent, many architects have followed them imaginatively and successfully.

Architects and librarians have teamed together to introduce many innovative developments in library buildings. Energy-conserving features and alternative sources of heating such as solar heating have reduced operating costs in many libraries. Library remodeling projects have redesigned Carnegie-type libraries (with fixed spaces and limited access) to provide barrier-free access for handicapped persons. Imaginative architects and librarians have successfully converted such buildings as fire stations, banks, post offices, service stations, and stores into attractive and effective libraries. One such statewide innovation was introduced by the West Virginia State Library Commission. This commission provided "instant libraries" by erecting prefabricated libraries in a few days on very small rural sites. These octagonal libraries were only about 30 × 40 feet and could provide small communities with 6,000 books and a place for library programs. These buildings were so popular that similar buildings have been used as information kiosks, shopping mall boutiques, and branch libraries. (See figures 10.1 and 10.2.)

Fig. 10.1. Porta-structure exterior. (Photo courtesy of Porta-structure Industries.)

Fig. 10.2. Porta-structure interior. (Photo courtesy of Porta-structure Industries.)

Libraries that did not have the funds to build new buildings have reexamined and redesigned their existing buildings to make better use of their space available. Some libraries installed movable compact shelving units to gain up to 50 percent more shelving capacity in the same floor space. These units move mechanically back and forth and reduce the need for aisle space. (See figure 10.3.)

Fig. 10.3. Compact movable shelving. (Photo courtesy of Spacesave Corp.)

Similarly, large libraries installed computerized off-site storage systems. These systems enabled library patrons to key in book codes at computer terminals and have books that were stored in completely separate buildings delivered to them at the circulation desk. Such building innovations show that although funds may have dwindled for library buildings, there has been no decrease in imagination and ingenuity when it comes to developing library structures.

Once the architect's building designs are approved by a library's planning team, the building and remodeling project moves into a new construction phase. This phase includes the awarding of construction bids to contractors and service providers for the building. If a library is lucky, these bids fall within the library's planned building budget. However, often the bids are over budget or a building referendum does not pass, and libraries are forced to go back to the drawing board to reduce the cost of the planned project. In this revision process, trade-offs and compromises naturally take place, and everyone involved must ensure that the best choices for meeting the library's functions result.

Because the construction of a library can run into millions of dollars, many libraries add a final member, an "owner's representative," to the planning team for this phase. The job of this owner's representative or "clerk of the works" is to monitor any construction as it progresses to ensure that plans are being followed and quality workmanship is being performed. If the library's construction project is part of a project by the parent institution, the institution's personnel might serve as clerk of the works. If the construction project is a remodeling or expansion project rather than a completely separate building, libraries may be faced with an additional concern. Because staff members often find it traumatic to work in the library during the construction process, libraries that can afford to do so may move to temporary quarters until the project is completed.

LIBRARY INTERIORS AND FURNISHINGS

Just as library buildings have changed since the 1960s, so have library interiors and furnishings. By the 1990s, most libraries were no longer painted in dull institutional colors, floored with shining marble or tile, and filled with rows of wooden tables and chairs. Instead, librarians had discovered that environmental factors were important in setting the psychological tone for their library services. They had found that, although die-hard library users would use a library no matter what its decor, many occasional or nontraditional library users were less threatened by environments that interested them. To appeal to these users, librarians hired library furnishings consultants to help them design new buildings and refurbish old ones. These consultants helped establish a "library mood" that reflected the public images libraries wanted to create.

These library images could take many different forms depending upon the library's objectives. Libraries that wanted to create a tranquil and efficient mood often decorated and carpeted their rooms in soft or muted colors. Such buildings sometimes had such soothing effects on their patrons and staffs that very few arguments or disturbances ever arose. Other libraries that wanted to project an active and vibrant "where the action is" image might choose brightly colored carpets and furniture and perhaps spread bright supergraphics across their vinyl walls. Sometimes libraries might be designed with special features and decorations to appeal to the ethnic interests of their patrons. (See figure 10.4, page 152.)

Fig. 10.4. Chicago Public Library branch for Hispanic community. Design by Carow.Architect.Planner. (Photo courtesy of Mark Ballogg, Steinkamp/Ballogg Photography, Chicago.)

At other times, buildings that had been converted from other uses might retain some of the original features as a conversation piece, such as a fireman's pole in a former fire station.

To further enhance their image, libraries began to add professionally designed, color-coordinated library signage systems in keeping with their decor. These signage systems provided information and directions in clear, consistent and logical language that a layperson could understand. Thus, signs might read "pamphlet file" rather than "vertical file" or "checkout counter" rather than "circulation desk." Many libraries added signs in braille or pictorial signs for the illiterate, and libraries in ethnic communities might have signs in several languages in addition to English. Because libraries tended to shift the location of their materials around the library or from range to range, many libraries developed their own in-house lettering capabilities or purchased interchangeable sign systems such as the Modulex Company's movable lettering system.

This great variety in library decor was also carried through in library furnishings, which began to reflect society's acceptance of a more relaxed and open environment in its public institutions. Most public libraries carpeted their public areas because carpet was quieter than tile floors and easier to maintain. These same public areas were often divided visually rather than physically into separate environmental areas for separate functions. Each of these areas might have its own type of furnishings for study, lounging, and group activities. For example, tables in quiet study areas might have chairs with comfortable padded seats rather than straight-back wooden ones. Study areas might also have individual study "carrels" or tables with high sides so that patrons had their own study cubicles. Lounging areas might have coffee tables and casual pull-up chairs of molded foam furniture and cushions. Many children's rooms had child-sized tables, chairs, and pillows to sit on or chairs made in the shape of animals or objects such as a baseball glove. Some children's rooms also had puppet stages, story pits, or special features such as decorated bathtubs or tree-house-like structures where children could read undisturbed by adults. (Figure 10.4 illustrates a Mexican tree in the library's story-hour section.) One such library had a life-size wooden trolley where children and their parents could sit down and read books together.

In addition to different seating arrangements, libraries also provided a variety of shelving arrangements to house their materials. Almost all library shelving is based upon a standard 36-inch wide shelf arranged in 42- to 90-inch high sections with three, five, or seven shelves. When these sections are joined together they are called *ranges*, and all of the ranges that house a collection are called the *stacks*. Ranges of three or five shelf sections are most often used in children's rooms or reference areas where easy access and clear visibility for supervision are priorities. Ranges of seven-shelf sections are most often found in areas for adult patrons. However, libraries are finding that the top two shelves are difficult for many adults and handicapped persons to reach. Aisles between these ranges can vary from 42 inches to provide access for the handicapped to 30 inches for ranges in "closed stacks" or areas that are closed to the public.

Like seating arrangements, shelving is being designed and selected to contribute to an inviting atmosphere. Depending upon the intended "library mood," libraries might select wood shelving, metal shelving with wood end panels, or color-coordinated shelving. Rather than use walls within the library, libraries might arrange shelving ranges to separate and define different functional areas. They might use "display-type" shelving that shelves the books or items facing outward, or libraries might use carousel display racks or child-size display bins. Sometimes libraries will add special shelving that has been custom designed in the shape of circles, semicircles, or serpentine curves. At other times, special shelving may be dictated by the needs of the material it will house. For example, audio-visual materials may be stored in specially designed visible shelving or display-type units. However, because these latter materials are often stolen more readily than other materials, many public libraries have tended to keep these materials under lock and key and require the staff to retrieve them for the patron.

In addition to seating and shelving, libraries include other kinds of library furniture. Library card catalogs, tables for online computer catalogs or CD-ROM databases and indexes, atlases, and toy cabinets must be selected and placed to contribute to a library's image. Libraries also have furniture in special areas available for special-purpose activities. Furniture and equipment for using audiovisual materials may be kept in small soundproof rooms. Or they may be arranged in lounge-type areas with headsets that enable each listener or viewer to "do his or her own thing." Furniture is needed to house either the library's or the patron's personal computers or typewriters singly or all together in separate soundproof rooms. This furniture may consist of "wet" carrels or tables with electrical and computer hookups. Group meeting rooms usually contain comfortable chairs and conference tables. They may also have podiums, kitchen facilities, projection screens, or even photoboards in lieu of chalkboards and easels. All of these furnishings should be selected and arranged so that patrons can be comfortable in any library activity.

In selecting the library's various furnishings, librarians and designers usually look for furniture that will be functional, durable, and attractive. Library furniture must not only be useful, but it should also last a long time with a minimum of maintenance. As with good building design, good furniture design should follow function. It should consider who will use it, how they will use it, and for how long they will use it. Often the best designs are simple ones with clean attractive lines that will not become dated. Library furniture and equipment should also be convenient and comfortable for the patron to use. If the study chairs do not provide enough leg room under the study table, or if the lounge chairs are too high or too low, patrons will not use them and libraries will regret their purchase. The height of such public service desks as circulation and reference should be comfortable for both staff and patrons to use without intimidating the patrons. Staff work areas need desks with adequate work surfaces for an electronic environment as well as proper seating, lighting, privacy, and freedom from distractions and noise. To be sure that these functional requirements are met, library planners should physically inspect and test any furniture before purchases are made.

Library planners should follow similar principles in selecting library equipment. Since the 1960s, the variety and complexity of library equipment has grown extensively. In addition to all types of audiovisual equipment such as projectors, audiocassette players, and videotape players and camcorders, many libraries have added computers, FAX equipment, complex copying systems, and hookups for cable or telecommunications networks. When purchasing such varied equipment, librarians have often learned the hard way that library equipment, even more than library furniture, must be functional and durable rather than attractive. They have been inundated with all kinds of technical equipment while maintenance problems and nonstandardization of equipment have made comparisons and choices among competing machines very difficult for the uninformed. Thus, librarians have welcomed the ALA's *Library Technology Reports*, which provide in-depth evaluations of library equipment, furniture, and systems.

A major technological development has become a standard feature in many libraries since the 1970s. Because of a growing security concern over the loss of many of their materials, libraries of all types began to add one of two distinct types of electronic security systems to their library facilities. The type of electronic security system an individual library might select was usually determined by its building configuration because the two systems had distinct architectural requirements. For example, the *bypass system* required that a checked out item be passed around an electronic sensing device at a staffed desk near the library's entrance. The *full-circulating system* required staff to desensitize an electronic tag when an item was checked out. This system allows patrons to check out books anywhere in the library and carry them through the sensing device at the door. Although these systems could be circumvented by a determined thief, they were successful enough in preventing casual losses and occasional thefts that some systems paid for themselves within three years.

All of these technological advancements in library equipment had a great impact on the library buildings that housed them. Most of the equipment mentioned required special engineering features, such as special wiring and air conditioning for the computers or video studios, special lighting to enable patrons to use the computer screens, and special telephone, coaxial cable, or fiber-optic hookups. Libraries learned to take these requirements into consideration when they purchased such equipment and built or remodeled buildings. Thus, the quality of the services libraries provide is strongly affected by the buildings designed to support them.

SUMMARY

The development of library facilities and furnishings since the 1970s has been influenced by many technological, social, and environmental factors. These factors encouraged libraries to reevaluate and revise their goals and objectives so they could develop modern, efficient buildings to meet their patrons' needs. To design these modern buildings, libraries established planning teams that included library administrators, board members, institution personnel, and representatives from the library's community. A building consultant would usually help this building team develop a building program statement to serve as a blueprint for the library's future service, staffing, and facility needs. A library architect would then use this statement to design a building that met the maxim, "Form should follow function." The architect would consider several important library design factors to ensure that the completed building would meet the library's needs.

This completed building would have a library interior and furnishings that reflected the "mood" or public image the library wanted to create. The style and design of a library's furnishings and equipment would also be selected because they contributed to this public image, in addition to meeting rigorous library performance criteria.

REVIEW QUESTIONS

1. Give three examples of outside influences that can have an impact on the design of a library's facility.

2. Identify the members of a library planning team and explain the importance of developing a building program statement.

3. Discuss the implications for libraries of the two maxims: "Form should follow function" and "Form should follow imagination, form should follow the future."

4. Describe the major design factors that architects should consider in designing a library.

5. Identify the major characteristics that should be considered when purchasing library furnishings and equipment.

6. From your library visits, describe good and bad examples of library architecture or furnishings that either meet or do not meet their library function.

SELECTED READINGS

Brown, Carol R. *Selecting Library Furniture: A Guide for Librarians, Designers, and Architects*. Phoenix, AZ: Oryx Press, 1989.

Cooper, Richard S. "A Library for the Fifteenth through the Twenty-first Centuries." *Bulletin of the Medical Library Association* 79, no. 2 (April 1991): 147-58.

Dahlgren, Anders C. *Planning the Small Public Library Building*. LAMA Small Libraries Publications, no. 11. Chicago: ALA, 1985.

_____. *Public Library Space Needs: A Planning Guide*. Madison, WI: Wisconsin Department of Public Instruction, 1988.

Fraley, Ruth A., and Carol Lee Anderson. *Library Space Planning*. New York: Neal-Schuman, 1985.

Holt, Raymond M. *Wisconsin Library Building Project Handbook*. 2d ed. Revised by Anders Dahlgren. Madison, WI: Wisconsin Department of Public Instruction, 1990.

Klasing, Jane P. *Designing and Renovating School Library Media Centers*. School Library Media Programs: Focus on Trends and Issues, no. 11. Chicago: ALA, 1991.

Konya, Allan, ed. *Libraries: A Briefing and Design Guide*. London: Architectural Press, 1986.

Leighton, Philip, and David C. Weber. *Planning Academic and Research Library Buildings*. 2d ed. Chicago: ALA, 1986.

Library Administration and Management Association. *Planning Library Buildings: From Decision to Design*. Chicago: ALA, 1986.

Library Technology Reports 1, no. 1- (1964-).

Metcalf, Keyes. *Planning Academic and Research Library Buildings*. 2d ed. Edited by Philip Leighton and David C. Weber. Chicago: ALA, 1986.

Mount, Ellis. *Creative Planning for Special Library Facilities*. New York: Hawthorn, 1988.

CHAPTER 11

AUXILIARY LIBRARY SERVICES

The library world has probably been one of the few areas of society that has successfully brought together the user, provider, governing authority, and supplier to work toward one common goal: providing better library services for all. They have joined together in associations such as the ALA, Friends of the Library, American Library Trustee Association, American Association of Publishers, and Library Binding Institute to combine their efforts in the interest of providing quality library services. Even when their concerns have diverged, all of these associations have striven to serve the welfare of the library world rather than their own interests.

LIBRARY ASSOCIATIONS

Librarians recognized long ago that they could benefit their libraries by joining together in professional associations to provide mutual encouragement and growth, exchange information, and promote libraries in society at large. They believed that their calling was a true profession because it was based on a service orientation and required highly specialized knowledge and skills. As a profession, librarianship needed an association that would promote library services and librarianship, set library standards, and encourage excellence among its members. Toward these ends, the first major library organization, the American Library Association (ALA), was founded in 1876. Within a century, ALA was able to achieve many of these goals.

The ALA has been largely successful because of its unique organizational structure. In addition to having individual professionals as members, as other professional associations do, ALA also encouraged libraries to join as institutional members. Thus, the interests of both the employee and the employer were represented in one organization. ALA's individual members also differed from members of other professional associations. ALA allowed anyone interested in promoting quality library services to join the organization as a personal member rather than restricting membership to professionally trained librarians. This membership policy brought interested citizens or "friends," trustees, library professionals, support employees, and library administrators together in the same organization. Although many librarians through the years have objected to this melting-pot approach, it has provided librarians with a much stronger voice in the marketplace and the political arena than they would have had otherwise.

The strident voice of the ALA has been heard on many issues in the last 100 years. It has been an active proponent of intellectual freedom, actively opposing censorship and supporting the freedom of individuals to read. It has also worked for the development of nationwide library services by publicizing the plight of the nation's libraries and lobbying in Washington and the state capitals for federal and state funds to support such services. ALA has pushed for a national library policy and was the guiding light behind the White House Conferences on Library and Information Services held in 1979 and 1991. Internationally, ALA has cooperated with other national library organizations to develop international standards for cataloging and other areas of common interest.

ALA has also helped promote library services within the libraries themselves. It has adopted a policy statement to encourage the education and utilization of library personnel. (See appendix A.) It has influenced library education by establishing accrediting procedures for graduate library school programs and guidelines for library/media technical assistant programs. ALA has also set standards through the years for all types of libraries. It has encouraged the development of services in specialized areas, such as children's services and adult education. It has established a comprehensive awards programs to recognize and publicize outstanding achievements in the library field. For many years, ALA has been strongly involved in the development of quality library collections by authorizing and publishing bibliographies and review magazines (most notably *Booklist* and *Choice*). As the national leader in disseminating library information and promoting library development, ALA has become a major publisher of library serials. (See figure 11.1, page 160.) Although these publications are usually free to organization members, their sale to nonmembers has been very profitable for ALA.

The ALA has been able to accomplish so much in 100 years because its leadership has been strong and its membership diverse and vast. In 1991, ALA had over 3,000 organization members and 47,000 personal members representing all types of interests in all types of libraries. The organization itself is run by elected officers and a council composed of members elected at large and members elected by the state library association chapters. This council governs the association, although its decisions can be put aside by vote of the membership (which has occurred several times). The operations of the association are carried out by a headquarters staff under the direction of an executive secretary. However, the committees appointed by the elected president perform a large portion of the policy-making and standard-setting functions of the association. Some ALA critics believe this structure does not allow for full member participation in its governance because new members find it difficult to serve on committees or on the council. However, many members have made effective contributions by serving on less time-consuming division or round-table committees.

ALA is divided into numerous divisions, sections, and round tables that enable members of similar interests to share their ideas and solve their problems. Each ALA division may itself be an association that ALA members may join. These associations may be based on the type of library such as the American Association of School Librarians (AASL), or a particular area, such as the Association for Library Services to Children (ALSC). (See figure 11.2, page 161.)

(Text continues on page 162.)

Fig. 11.1. ALA Publications.

ALA Washington Newsletter
  (ALA Washington Office)
ALTA Newsletter
  (American Library Trustee Association [ALTA])
American Libraries
  (ALA)
Booklist
  (ALA Publishing Service)
Choice
  (Association of College and Research Libraries [ACRL])
Choice Reviews-on-Cards
  (ACRL)
College & Research Libraries
  (ACRL)
Documents to the People
  (Government Documents Round Table [GODORT])
The Federal Librarian
  (Federal Librarians Round Table [FLRT])
Information Technology and Libraries
  (Library and Information Technology Association [LITA])
Journal of Youth Services in Libraries (formerly *Top of the News*)
  (Association for Library Services to Children [ALSC] and
    Young Adult Services Division [YASD])
Library Personnel News
  (Office for Library Personnel Resources [OLPR])
Library Resources & Technical Services
  (Association for Library Collections and Technical
    Services [ALCTS])
Library Technology Report
  (Library Technology Reports [LTR])
Newsletter on Intellectual Freedom
  (Intellectual Freedom Committee [IFC])
Public Libraries
  (Public Library Association [PLA])
RQ
  (Reference and Adult Services Division [RASD])
School Library Media Quarterly
  (American Association of School Librarians [AASL])
SRRT Newsletter
  (Social Responsibilities Round Table [SRRT])
Women in Libraries
  (SRRT)

Fig. 11.2. ALA Organizations. (These lists are by no means exhaustive. For names of other ALA-affiliated organizations, see the most current *ALA Handbook of Organization* [Chicago: ALA].)

DIVISIONS

American Association of School Librarians (AASL)

American Library Trustee Association (ALTA)

Association for Library Collections and Technical Services (ALCTS)

Association for Library Services to Children (ALSC)

Association of College and Research Libraries (ACRL)

Association of Specialized and Cooperative Library Agencies (ASCLA)

Library Administration and Management Association (LAMA)

Library and Information Technology Association (LITA)

Public Library Association (PLA)

Reference and Adult Services Division (RASD)

Young Adult Services Division (YASD)

STANDING COMMITTEES

Accreditation

Awards

Intellectual Freedom

International Relations

Legislation

Library Education

Membership

Minority Concerns

Pay Equity

Planning

Professional Ethics

Public Information

Publishing

Review, Inquiry, and Mediation

Standards

Women in Librarianship, Status of

ROUND TABLES

Armed Forces Library Round Table (AFLRT)

Exhibits Round Table (ERT)

Federal Librarians Round Table (FLRT)

Government Documents Round Table (GODORT)

Intellectual Freedom Round Table (IFRT)

Library Instruction Round Table (LIRT)

Library Research Round Table (LRRT)

New Members Round Table (NMRT)

Social Responsibilities Round Table (SRRT)

Staff Organizations Round Table (SORT)

ALA members may also join *round tables*, which are smaller groups concerned with more specific topics, such as the New Members Round Table (NMRT). Many of ALA's divisions are national associations in their own right that provide dynamic programs to serve their members' needs. Sometimes members of these associations have objected to this division status and attempted to leave ALA (as AASL members proposed in 1986). However, the majority of a division's members have usually elected to stay and work within the framework of ALA. ALA also has chapter affiliations with library associations in every state, although members who join one association are not required to join the other. Each state association also has its own state divisions and round tables so that members can become involved in the decision-making process at the state level if they wish to.

ALA also affiliates with many other national and international organizations. About 20 national library organizations such as the American Association of Law Libraries (AALL), Association of Research Libraries (ARL), and the Catholic Library Association (CLA) have affiliated formally with ALA as has the Council on Library Media/Technical Assistants (COLT). COLT's primary purpose is to represent the trained LMTA's interest within the field of librarianship. COLT achieves its goals by working with ALA as well as developing its own programs. ALA also works closely with several other organizations concerned with reading and literacy, such as Reading Is Fundamental (RIF), the Coalition for Literacy, and National Partners for Libraries and Literacy.

In addition, ALA not only sends representatives to other organizations, but the association itself also belongs to many other educational and social organizations. ALA is an active member of the International Federation of Library Associations (IFLA) and works with the Library Association (British) and the Canadian Library Association on joint projects such as the development of the *Anglo-American Cataloguing Rules*. Needless to say, ALA has maintained a very close relationship with the LC over the years, and units of both organizations have worked on many joint projects. Thus, the ALA has had a greater effect on the library world than its own membership activities would show.

Two other organizations that ALA has affiliated with in different ways are very important to the library world. The first, the American Library Trustee Association (ALTA), became a division of ALA in the 1970s and works closely with another division, the Public Library Association (PLA). ALTA is probably the only organization for employers that belongs to an organization controlled by its employees. Its major goal is to take full responsibility for helping trustees carry out their roles effectively and to develop quality library service. ALTA tries to fulfill this goal by working with other divisions and state library trustee associations to educate trustees through workshops and publications.

The other association that works closely with ALA and ALTA is Friends of Libraries USA. Members of this group are interested citizens who care about libraries and want to help libraries provide the best possible services. They have become excellent spokespersons for local library services. Originally, "friends" groups were more commonly found in public libraries. However, the economic climate of the 1970s and 1980s brought about the establishment of friends groups in all types of institutions from small elementary schools to the largest academic institutions. These friends groups have helped pass library referenda, raised funds for library buildings, materials, and services, and generally have served as library consciousness-raising groups in their local communities. Friends of

Libraries USA is affiliated with ALA through liaisons from ALA's executive staff as well as ALTA and LAMA (Library Administration and Management Association). Thus, ALA's close links with both employers and users of its services have helped forge a unified library world.

ALA has also formed affiliations with the major publishing associations to discuss mutual problems and issues. One of these associations, the American Association of Publishers (AAP), is known as the voice of the American book-publishing industry. It not only participates in joint programs with ALA, but it also conducts its own programs in areas such as copyright, the First Amendment, and library and educational funding. Originally begun as an association of print publishing firms, AAP expanded in 1982 to include publishers of multimedia products, including computer software and online databases. Other book-related associations such as the American Booksellers Association (ABA), the Children's Book Council (CBC), and the National Association of College Stores also work with ALA to improve the quality of publishing as well as to encourage the sale of books.

In other more specialized areas, ALA may not only affiliate with national associations, but their memberships also may overlap. For example, many ALA members may also be active members of more specialized associations such as the Special Libraries Association (SLA), the Association of Educational Communications and Technology (AECT), or the American Society of Information Science (ASIS). These association memberships can range in size from 4,000 members in ASIS to more than 11,000 members in SLA. The strength of these associations often comes from their local and regional chapters, which are primarily in metropolitan areas. These chapters enable persons with common special interests to informally share their problems, improve their knowledge, and sharpen their strengths. These local chapters and special interest groups are usually very active in developing and supporting workshops, institutes, and publications for their members.

As much as ALA and the other associations contribute to the library world, however, they do not truly serve the personal and professional needs of their librarian members. By allowing anyone to join ALA and including institutions as well as individuals as members, ALA has emphasized its purpose of promoting library services rather than the welfare of librarians. Over the years, many librarians have criticized ALA for not taking an active role in library employment, salaries, and working conditions. Although ALA has responded through informal channels, as an organization it has not been inclined toward following the lead of the American Nursing Association (ANA) and becoming a quasi-union for its members. To do so, ALA would have to change its organizational structure, and it would probably lose its tax-exempt status and some of its financing. Thus, librarians began to look elsewhere for an organization that would help them improve their employment conditions.

Beginning in the 1970s, librarians began looking to unions and other labor associations to protect themselves from the impact of several important factors. First, because libraries were becoming larger, more complex, and more bureaucratic, librarians felt excluded from the decision-making process. Second, the introduction of technology into libraries, combined with the loss of library revenues, brought about changes and reductions in library staffs. Finally, society's attitude toward professionals and public employees who joined unions had changed. Many laws were passed that allowed public employees to bargain collectively. Many professional associations such as the National Education Association (NEA), American Association of University Professors (AAUP), and the ANA became quasi unions and began bargaining collectively or demanding pay equity for all their members. In this climate, many librarians no longer felt "less professional" if they joined library unions such as the National Librarians Association (NLA), which was founded in 1975. NLA's membership was limited to professional librarians, and its goals were to protect and advance their concerns.

The 1970s and 1980s also saw a significant growth in the number of librarians and other staff members joining local union organizations. Library unions developed in large public libraries in areas where membership in unions in general was strong, such as the East, the Midwest, and California. These library unions were often composed of both professional and support library employees. They negotiated with government officials or library administrators for salaries and conditions of employment. Sometimes the staffs of an individual library would form local staff associations that negotiated for salaries and conditions of employment. Some library support staff joined public-service employee unions, such as the American Federation of State, County, and Municipal Employees (AFSCME) and Service Employees International (SEIU). Librarians who worked in school and academic libraries usually joined organizations that represented the other professionals in their institution, such as NEA, AFT (American Federation of Teachers), or AAUP. Special librarians might join a professional association such as the Newspaper Guild.

PUBLISHING

Libraries have been closely allied with the publishing field for many years. At state and national library conventions, publishers have been present and active not only as library exhibitors but also as partners in library programs and the awarding of library prizes. Publishers and librarians have cooperated in supporting intellectual freedom and the freedom to read. They have also encouraged the spread of reading and the use of libraries through the National Book Awards and National Library Week. Publishers have cooperated in establishing cataloging programs such as Cataloging-in-Publication (CIP), which includes printing LC cataloging in books as they are published. They have also worked together in developing International Standard Book and Serial Numbers (ISBN and ISSN) so that each edition or serial title can be easily identified. Despite these cooperative ventures, however, publishers and librarians have often had a love-hate relationship. At times, their vested interests have brought them into conflict on such subjects as library discounts, copyright laws, and fair-use violations of such laws.

In the early years of library development, publishers were originally afraid that strong library development and use would limit purchases of their publications. However, as libraries grew, publishers found that people continued to buy books. After World War II, they also found that reading was stimulated by the increases in population, income, and leisure time and by the increased interest in education. Contrary to expectations, book clubs founded in the 1920s and the growth of TV in the late 1950s and 1960s stimulated reading and book sales rather than diminished them. Also, the phenomenal sales of paperback books and magazines only seemed to increase, rather than compete with, the sale of hardcover books. In the late 1950s, publishers found that the availability of federal funds for libraries to purchase materials further expanded the publishing markets. Thus, the publishing industry had grown so extensively since its beginnings in the late nineteenth century that over 55,000 books a year were being published by 1990.

The publishing industry not only grew in size, but it also changed in form. The mass production of paperbacks and reprints helped revolutionize book publishing. Many publishers began to publish and sell paperbacks as well as trade books, and sometimes they published a title in trade and paperback editions simultaneously. Serial publications (primarily magazines or periodicals) increased from a few thousand titles in the 1950s to well over 100,000 by 1990. The bulk of the serial increases was due to the increase in scientific and technical journals rather than an increase among the specialized or "little magazines." These latter publications usually struggled for awhile and then quietly folded. As libraries became more hard-pressed to house all of these books and serials, they often turned to publications in other formats, such as microform or CD-ROM, to solve their libraries' storage dilemmas. To this end, publishers often published serials in both print copy and microform or CD-ROM. Some publishers even began to publish reference books and sources such as dictionaries, encyclopedias, and loose-leaf services in both print and computer-based form. When materials were available in several formats, publishers often protected their economic interests in each format. Some publishers required libraries to maintain subscriptions to the print serial or service if they wanted to purchase the title in microform or CD-ROM.

The growth in the volume of publishing since 1950 has also influenced the growth of publishing firms. Most publishing companies began as private firms run by individual families. They tended to publish books for special publics or on special subjects. So many of these family firms were merged with other publishers and companies in the 1960s and 1970s that many people (especially authors) became concerned about their anticompetitive implications. The purchase of such publishing firms as Praeger and Fawcett by CBS; Random House, Knopf, Pantheon, and Ballantine by RCA; and R. R. Bowker by Xerox caused librarians some concern. They worried that corporate profits might begin to replace literary expression as the guiding factor in book publishing. This could have been a distinct possibility because only about 200 out of 3,000 firms were responsible for over 70 percent of a year's publications.

However, as a contrast to this merging of companies at the top, many specialized and small presses began to develop and concentrate on quality literary publications. Other presses focused on particular subject publications, such as West in law and Mosby in medicine and nursing. The two venerable publishers of library science information, R. R. Bowker and H. W. Wilson, were joined by newer companies such as Gale Research, Scarecrow Press, and Libraries Unlimited. The publications of these specialized firms were designed to satisfy the needs of the library community for research and bibliographic materials. University presses and professional associations expanded their strong publishing programs. Originally designed to produce scholarly works of the highest caliber, these publishers began to expand their range to appeal to a broader readership. Finally, the U.S. Government Printing Office, which prints U.S. government documents, had become the largest printer in the world, producing titles under the imprint of many government agencies and organizations.

In addition to print publishers, there was a rapid growth in the production of media and "electronic publishing" by producers or publishers of audiovisual and computer-based materials and software. The explosion of these materials spawned new publishers and companies for each new format. For example, traditional film-production companies, such as Encyclopaedia Britannica Films and Weston Woods, were joined by newer publishers of CD-ROM and computer-based indexes and database services, such as Information Access and Silver-Platter. This growth was so explosive in the 1980s that there were more than 4,000 publishers or distributors of information in electronic form by 1990. The 1990s will probably see many of these publishers move beyond the concept of text-only materials (either online or CD-ROM) toward an ultimate goal of multimedia publications that combine text with audio and video.

With this phenomenal growth, however, came problems and issues that caused mutual concern among publishers and librarians. Beginning in the 1970s and 1980s, publishers began to face large increases in paper and production costs that caused book and serial prices to soar. For example, book prices that had increased 50-100 percent from the late 1960s to the mid-1970s doubled again by 1983. By 1990, they had increased another 30 percent to an average price of $39 for an academic book. Serials prices also rose 100-300 percent between the late 1960s and 1990 so that the average cost of an academic serial subscription was $125 by 1990. Increases in the number of books and serials that were published also rose so dramatically that overproduction became a problem. Inadequate distribution of these increased publications caused yet another problem. All of these concerns came to a head in the copyright controversies that arose between publishers, librarians, and copyright authors and artists in the 1980s and 1990s.

These copyright controversies centered around developments in photocopying, FAX, and electronic technologies that enabled any person to copy or reproduce any part of a book, serial, CD-ROM, or online database. Although much of the information available in the first online databases originally came from "public domain" or noncopyrighted materials, more and more of this information began to come from copyrighted sources. This development brought concerns in all publishing areas that the rights, responsibilities, and royalties due to the copyright owner should be protected. Some of these concerns were addressed in the U.S. Copyright Law of 1978 that acknowledged the *fair use principle*. This principle allowed the copying of a small number of pages from a serial or book within a specific period of time for the use of one individual without paying a royalty to the copyright owner (usually the publisher). Although libraries welcomed fair use as a way to share their library materials without being required to purchase every book or serial, publishers objected to it for the same reasons.

To help resolve these concerns, publishers of print materials established the Copyright Clearance Center (CCC) to collect royalties for any uses that were outside the "fair use" principle. Publishers and producers of other types of materials faced similar copyright concerns and adopted additional solutions to resolve these problems. For example, some publishers charged licensing fees or higher subscription prices for materials destined for library networks or multiple users. Others entered into agreements such as the Digital Audio Tape (DAT) Agreement of 1991 that added a royalty or user fee to the purchase price of each DAT tape or piece of equipment. Such a fee would be passed on to the copyright owners and artists, ideally to compensate them for any abuses of the fair use principle.

LIBRARY SUPPLIERS

Libraries and their suppliers have always enjoyed a close working relationship since the first library supply house, Library Bureau, was founded by Melvil Dewey in 1876. Library suppliers have provided library materials, supplies, equipment, furniture, and services that met library needs and specifications. These products generally could not be purchased locally for a reasonable price. By specializing in the library market, library suppliers have been able to design their products and services to meet the needs of this special market. On the positive side, this specialization has enabled suppliers to develop new computerized products in anticipation of, or in response to, changing library requirements. On the negative side, such specialization can limit a library's choices as it did when major suppliers discontinued stocking record albums and films. On the whole, however, the relationship between libraries and their suppliers has been a strong and healthy one that has had a positive effect on the library field.

Commercial "for-profit" library suppliers exist in every area of the library field. There are wholesalers or *jobbers* for books, serials, audiovisual materials, microforms, etc. There are library binders who bind materials to library specifications. There are suppliers who furnish specialized library supplies, equipment, and furniture. There are commercial services that provide library computerized services and cataloging services. Because all of these suppliers are generally interested in making a profit, they recognize that service is often the most important product they have to offer libraries. For this reason, many suppliers employ professional librarians on their staffs. These librarians and other trained salespersons are able to discuss problems with librarians in the field to offer suggestions and solutions. They are often consulted by librarians when library problems arise or changes are planned. Librarians also provide feedback to suppliers when they encounter problems with their supplies or products. Thus, it is this working partnership between libraries and library suppliers that has encouraged the development of many innovations and improvements in library supplies, equipment, and services.

Library wholesalers or jobbers have based their entire business on this relationship. They work on the principle of supplying libraries with books, serials, or audiovisual materials from many different publishers more reasonably or more easily than libraries could purchase these materials for themselves. Jobbers enable libraries to place one order, receive all or most of their materials from one source, and pay one invoice. Jobbers are able to perform this service because they maintain large stocks of newly published titles from many different publishers, and they can order other titles from many more. These services free librarians from ordering materials from thousands of publishers, large and small, American and foreign.

There are many different kinds of jobbers for many different materials. Book jobbers may be general jobbers supplying all book titles in all subjects, or they may specialize in one type of work, such as out-of-print books or one particular subject. Some book jobbers, such as Baker and Taylor (B&T), may specialize in stocking new book titles and shipping them out quickly. Other jobbers, such as Blackwell of North America (BNA), may specialize in providing special orders, such as foreign publications. Jobbers may also specialize by type of material, such as serial jobbers EBSCO and F. W. Faxon, or microform jobbers such as University Microforms International (UMI). With the advent of audiovisual materials in libraries, many major book jobbers such as B&T and Brodart began to sell other types of media, such as records, audiocassettes, and CDs.

No matter which kinds of materials a jobber may handle, however, they all generally provide similar services. Jobbers not only fill orders for requested items, but they may also provide preview announcements of new titles in stock or new titles librarians might want to buy. Many also provide approval plans (sending materials on approval for the librarian to review), collection development plans, and lease or rental plans for new and popular library materials. They will assist librarians in the bidding or billing processes and will usually fit into the libraries' acquisitions routine rather than requiring special ones designed to fit the jobbers' needs. Some jobbers provide computerized ordering services or make their databases available to their customers via CD-ROM or online. Once an item is ordered, many jobbers also provide cataloging services from catalog cards to CD-ROM catalogs to fully process each item according to an individual library's specifications. Jobbers will even provide "instant libraries" or "opening day collections" of books processed and ready to place on the shelves. Because of all of these services, many libraries of all types usually purchase their materials through jobbers of one type or another.

Although library binders are not true jobbers, they may sometimes function in that capacity. Many binders began to purchase books from publishers in the 1960s and 1970s, rebind them in "library bindings," and sell them to libraries. (This practice became increasingly more common with paperbacks as they became more popular among library patrons.) This prebinding service arose as libraries found that books that were library bound, or bound according to stiff library standards before they were circulated, were more durable than trade bindings. This development was possible because of the Library Binding Institute (LBI). Made up of library binding firms, the LBI had worked for many years with librarians to establish binding standards for many different types of materials. These standards became so much a part of the library world that the LBI standard for Class A library binding is generally used by libraries as a criterion in bid specifications. In addition to prebinding new books, library binders also bind serials and rebind old books. Although serial binding used to make up a large portion of the binding for many firms, it has decreased as libraries have purchased serials in microform or CD-ROM. Unfortunately, this decrease in business has also decreased the number of library binding firms. Thus, to retain as much library binding business as possible, the remaining library binders have provided many services to help libraries meet their material preservation needs.

Library supply houses or vendors have been working with libraries since both ALA and the first supply house, Library Bureau, were founded in 1876. These supply houses provide specialized library supplies, equipment, and furniture, which are often manufactured to their own and library specifications. They are generally mail-order supply houses, similar to Spiegel and Sears Roebuck, which make their materials available to libraries through attractive catalogs. These catalogs usually include the basic library supplies, equipment, and furniture that libraries need for circulation, cataloging, processing, etc. They also include new items their firms hope will become basic items in the future. Although the major supply houses such as Gaylord, Demco, Highsmith, and Brodart usually have only one distribution center, they can usually provide their items more reasonably and more quickly than local suppliers can. These vendors also sell furniture and equipment built to library needs and specifications as do Library Bureau, Buckstaff, Worden and other furniture manufacturers. Supply houses also have been very active in developing new library materials and systems, such as circulation and theft-detection systems. Without their important influence, most librarians might still be using outdated library supplies.

The library supply field itself has also changed and grown tremendously since the 1960s. Nowhere is this more evident than in the developments automation has brought. The availability of public-domain cataloging on MARC tapes (from LC) and public-domain Integrated Library Systems (ILS) (from NTIS) enabled for-profit companies, such as CLSI and GEAC, and not-for-profit networks, such as OCLC and WLN, to develop integrated automated library systems. These commercially prepared or "turnkey" integrated systems usually included online circulation, cataloging, acquisitions, public catalogs, and interlibrary loan programs. A library would purchase and install such a system to run a mini- or microcomputer that required minimum staff training and operational support. Smaller libraries might buy single-system microcomputer and CD-ROM based systems and products from vendors such as Gaylord. The rapid changes and growth in the technology of these systems, however, often required libraries to "upgrade" or purchase more advanced hardware and software programs to satisfy their changing needs. Usually the cost of such an upgrade would prohibit a library from "migrating" or changing to another vendor. However, developments in the 1990s may bring "open systems" that will enable a library to mix products from several vendors and match them to their individual library's needs.

Developments in automation also brought several other types of vendors to the library world. Library networks or bibliographic "utilities," such as WLN, CLASS, and AMIGOS, not only provided vendor-type integrated library systems, but they also provided products and services such as offline catalogs, retroactive cataloging, and discounts on their services. Connections to online reference services were provided by commercial information broker services, such as DIALOG and BRS (Bibliographic Retrieval Services), or telecommunication gateway vendors, such as AT&T and MCI. Print materials were made available through commercial document delivery vendors, such as UMI, NTIS, and ISI (Institute for Scientific Information). These document delivery vendors filled online requests for documents from their own large monograph and serial holdings. The costs for these services included payment of any copyright fees and were often less than a library might pay to purchase or borrow a document from traditional document delivery sources.

In using all of these library service companies and suppliers, the librarian and the library staff have always realized that the major purpose of these organizations is to make a profit. Thus, librarians may turn to these companies for advice, but they will not necessarily accept that advice as the final answer to their problems. Most librarians will talk with other librarians about supplies, services, and equipment before making their final decisions about any purchases. They may also check ALA's *Library Technology Reports*, which are in-depth evaluative reports on every aspect of a product or a system. Sometimes librarians will also hire library consultants with expertise in specialized areas such as automation or interior design. Only after such thorough investigation will most librarians commit themselves to the products or services of a particular jobber, vendor, or other type of library service company. Thus, by having a healthy respect for the strengths as well as the limitations of their library suppliers, libraries have been able to work with them over the years to develop and improve library procedures and services.

SUMMARY

The strength in library development has come from a close affiliation among all the various partners that make up the library world. Library friends, staff, management, governing trustees, publishers, and suppliers have established strong national associations such as the ALA and ALTA. These associations have not only furthered their own specific interests, but they have also developed cooperative programs to enhance the library world. Their success in these endeavors comes from the variety and strength of their association memberships. It also comes from a commitment by library associations of all types to work together to establish state and national programs and standards to benefit all libraries.

Library associations have been supported in these endeavors by publishers and library supply companies and associations. These latter organizations have generally been able to put aside their profit-oriented motives to cooperate with libraries in providing materials, programs, and services to meet library needs. In particular, library supply vendors have not only provided libraries with traditional library supplies and services, but they have also developed specialized library furniture, equipment, and automated systems. Such cooperative efforts among all persons and institutions concerned with libraries have combined to make the library world a united one serving one common goal: providing better library services for all.

REVIEW QUESTIONS

1. Describe the major purpose, organization, and governing structure of the ALA.

2. Identify the complete names of the following organizations: ALA, AASL, ALSC, ALTA, COLT, NEA, AFSCME, IFLA, AAP, and LBI.

3. Describe the major areas of cooperation and the areas of disagreement among publishers and librarians.

4. Identify the types of library suppliers or jobbers that serve libraries and list the kinds of services they offer.

5. Describe some of the services provided by library automation vendors.

6. Describe the evaluation process a library should follow when choosing a library supplier, jobber, or binder.

SELECTED READINGS

ALA Handbook of Organization, 1990/1991. Chicago: ALA, 1990.

Association of Research Libraries. Systems and Procedures Exchange Center (SPEC) Kit 118. *Unionization in ARL Libraries.* Washington, DC: Association of Research Libraries, 1987.

AV Market Place, 1991: Complete Business Directory of Audio, Audio Visual, Computer Systems, Film, Video Programming with Industry Yellow Pages. New York: Bowker, 1991.

Bowker Annual. Library and Book Trade Almanac. 1st ed. New York: Bowker, 1955- .

Kusack, James M. *Unions for Library Support Staff: Impact on Workers and the Workplace.* New York: Greenwood Press, 1986.

Literary Market Place, 1991: Directory of the American Book Publishing Industry with Industry Yellow Pages. New York: Bowker, 1991.

Matthews, Joseph R. *Directory of Automated Library Systems.* Library Planning Guide Series, no. 2. New York: Neal-Schuman, 1985.

Reed, Mary Hutchings. *The Copyright Primer for Librarians and Educators.* Chicago: ALA and NEA, 1987.

CHAPTER 12

THE DEVELOPMENT OF
GOOD LIBRARY SERVICE

Libraries throughout the ages have developed to satisfy specific needs within their societies. A library's importance within a society has often been determined by how well it has satisfied these needs. Libraries, such as those in Rome and in Renaissance Europe, flourished because they provided for the aesthetic, cultural, scientific, recreational, and educational needs of their patrons. They were able to provide for these needs by acquiring manuscripts and books, preserving them from harm and destruction, and making them available for patrons to use. Today's libraries no longer follow the examples of these earlier libraries by acquiring their books through ransacking other libraries or preserving their books by chaining them to the shelves for safety. However, they do still make their materials available for their patrons to use.

Over the years, this concept of availability of materials has evolved into a philosophy of library service that is made up of several important elements. These elements include access to information in all its forms, stated objectives, and policies and procedures that encourage and develop the best possible service for a library's public. How well this philosophy is being fulfilled by today's libraries, both generally and individually, will determine how important libraries become in tomorrow's society.

INTELLECTUAL FREEDOM

American libraries have provided access to information in all of its forms in response to the basic needs of a democratic society. In contrast to other societies, a democracy depends upon an educated citizenry that can make informed decisions. Thus, subscription libraries, public libraries, academic libraries, and school library media centers grew up over the years to satisfy their citizens' need for education and information. Libraries became repositories of information and culture that allowed citizens to read and examine differing philosophies and theories to make their own political decisions. From this need has evolved the principle that each individual has the right to freely obtain and read or view materials without restriction by others. This principle has been identified as *intellectual freedom* and has its basis in the First Amendment to the U.S. Constitution: "Congress shall make no law abridging the freedom of speech or of the press or the right of the people peaceably to assemble and to petition the government for a redress of grievances."

Although even the U.S. Congress has enacted laws at different times that have limited these rights, the public and the courts have generally upheld the concept of intellectual freedom. They have supported the belief that a democracy can only be strengthened if its citizens have access to all viewpoints on a subject. Our democracy has not fallen to foreign powers in spite of some people's fears that have led to attempts to silence government opposition. From the Sedition Act in 1798 through the McCarthy era of the 1950s, such fears have proven ungrounded. Even the opposition of citizens in the 1960s to the Vietnam War eventually resulted in open discussion of the subject that legally brought about changes in government policy. Thus, in the 200 years of the United States' existence, its citizens have proven that freedom of speech and freedom of the press can provide an educated citizenry capable of making informed decisions.

In contrast to this democratic principle, there are many would-be censors in today's society who believe they should be able to restrict these freedoms for others. They believe that there is only one correct meaning or interpretation of a literary or artistic work and that they are the ones who can determine this true meaning. These censors believe that if good literature or art is uplifting, then bad literature or art must be morally wrong. They do not recognize that people usually respond positively to those aspects of reading, viewing, and listening that reinforce their values and ignore or suppress aspects that threaten their values. Because the censors do not acknowledge that a work may mean different things to different people, they believe that ideas they disagree with or find offensive should not exist in the marketplace of ideas. Such censors are often acting upon very sincere beliefs that society will be debased or debauched if ideas they disagree with are allowed to circulate freely. They believe that distribution of even small amounts of such ideas will be like a chink in a dike that will slowly widen to bring a river of ideas that will threaten and destroy society.

What kinds of ideas do the would-be censors object to so much that they would limit others' access to them? These ideas range from explicit descriptions and pictures of nudity and sexual matters to the use of obscene language. Censors even object to language that may be acceptable in most societies. Some parents of small children have objected to the concept of "vomit" in a preschool children's book. Other parents have objected to pictures of the birth of animals in books for elementary school children. Parents and other citizens have objected to such subjects as drugs for teenagers in *Go Ask Alice*, a realistic portrayal of life in John Steinbeck's *Grapes of Wrath*, and a boy's growing up in that most censored of all books, J. D. Salinger's *Catcher in the Rye* (still considered by many to be the modern classic in young adult reading). For many years, political books such as those on communism were censored. In more recent years, members of minority groups have objected to racism in books such as *Little Black Sambo* or stereotypes such as those in Mark Twain's *The Adventures of Huckleberry Finn*. In the 1990s, some people have objected to language which they believe is not "politically correct." Others have objected to dictionaries such as the *American Heritage Dictionary of the English Language* because they disagree with definitions of specific words. Sometimes even governments have joined the censorship ranks by objecting to the unauthorized publication of materials such as *The*

Pentagon Papers, which officials felt were threatening or a danger to national security.

What has caused censors to be so concerned about all of these issues in the latter half of the twentieth century? First, censors began to fear that society as they knew it was being threatened and changed by technological and informational developments that were beyond their control. They disapproved of the information that was brought into their homes via rental videotapes, cable TV, and telephone lines. Second, many people were alarmed by changes in society that highlighted any moral, cultural, racial, political, and social or class differences. Finally, the traditional middle class had difficulty relating to the literature about the lower classes that was often expressed in very raw terms. Led by some religious organizations, censors began to look upon people who disagreed with them on social issues as enemies. They accused persons who did not speak out against such issues as child pornography, abortion, homosexuality, AIDS, evolution, and religion in the schools, of having atheistic and unpatriotic views that should be suppressed.

In their fear, many censors blamed these changes in society on such factors as the growth of "questionable" paperback books in the 1950s and the elimination of prayer from the schools in 1963. They objected to the "relaxed morals" of the permissive society of the 1960s and 1970s that allowed "obscene" materials to appear in books, films, music, and on television. This attitude was given impetus by a U.S. Supreme Court decision in 1973. In this decision, Justice Berger identified guidelines for setting community standards for obscene material in that "the work in question, taken as a whole, must appeal to prurient interest as determined by applying contemporary community standards and that the work, taken as a whole, lacks serious literary, artistic, political or scientific value."[1] *Prurient* has been defined as being obsessively interested in "improper" matters, especially of a sexual nature.[2]

By this ruling, Justice Berger authorized local communities to determine what they considered to be "of prurient interest and totally lacking in serious literary, artistic, political, or scientific value." Such a ruling is very difficult to defend in a democratic society if one considers its implications. Many of the world's greatest works of art and literature could be determined prurient by some local communities. This was particularly true for would-be censors who had trouble distinguishing between "obscene" and less-offensive "indecent" materials. For example, Michelangelo's nude statue of David could offend some people, while the Bible's account of David and Bathsheba could just as easily offend others. This local community standard posed another problem as local communities began to censor literary and artistic works that were distributed on a national basis. National artists, writers, musicians, and publishers often found themselves in the unenviable position of having to defend in one part of the country works that were completely acceptable in another part of the country.

These local censorship efforts gained ground during the 1970s and 1980s as the political mood of the country became more conservative and religious groups became more militant. Encouraged by organizations such as the Moral Majority, individuals such as the Gablers in Texas, and government regulations under the Reagan and Bush administrations, censorship efforts had increased dramatically by the 1980s. Literary and artistic materials including books, magazines, films, videotapes, records, and audio formats were subjected to censorship on a variety of grounds. Artistic performances and museum exhibits were often shut down by overzealous censors. Although the court systems often rejected these censorship attempts, significant victories for the censors came in other ways. For example, Mr. and Mrs. Gabler in Texas were so influential in censoring state-approved textbooks that publishers began to alter the content of textbooks sold not only in Texas but also throughout the country. Some publishers even began to react to such concerns before publication by "expurgating" or deleting words and ideas from previously published works when they were included in new anthologies. Other publishers responded to economic pressure and withdrew challenged works from sale when boycotts or controversies arose. Thus, although no authoritative studies or statistics had shown that censored materials caused any feared behaviors, censors were often successful in banning those literary and artistic works of which they disapproved.

Although no one would deny the right of anyone else to disagree with these kinds of materials and ideas, many people have objected to the manner in which these objections are often raised. Persons who object to "obscene" or "filthy" words and pictures usually have not read the complete book, watched the entire film, or listened to the complete song. They have judged the material guilty without evaluating whether or not "the work, taken as a whole, lacks serious literary, artistic, political or scientific value." Some persons concerned with obscenity have objected to the "obscene" language of such classics as Kantor's *Andersonville* or Lee's *To Kill a Mockingbird* without recognizing that the true obscenity is really man's degradation of his fellow man. In addition, censors who fear the ideas contained in the materials to which they object often assume that the defender of these materials must approve of them. This is not necessarily the case. Many defenders of a book, song, or film may not approve of its content, particularly if it contains images that may appeal to interests that some people consider to be prurient interests. However, defenders of a censored item realize that what is at stake is not an interest in obscene or prurient materials, but the "liberty to think." They believe that if the right to protect "works of serious literary, artistic, political or scientific value" is not fought in every case, a chink will appear in the dike that will let through an ocean of restrictive censorship.

Nowhere has this censorship, with its simplistic solutions to complicated problems, been more evident than in the world of libraries. With the complete range of all the world's ideas in its collection, the local library became an easy target for arrows shot by people of many different moral or political persuasions. (See figure 12.1, page 176.) As libraries came under attack, they moved to the forefront of the defenders of the rights of free speech and free press. They recognized that no library has existed for very long that only collected and made available those ideas approved by the ruling authority. Even the Roman Catholic Church's Vatican Library, one of the greatest libraries in the world, contains ideas and doctrines other than accepted church doctrines. Libraries in a democratic society could do no less. Throughout their history, libraries have fought against censorship and restrictions on the materials they could include in their collections. This fight was formalized in 1948 when the ALA adopted *The Library Bill of Rights*. (See appendix B.) This document was revised in 1967 and 1980 and has been adopted as formal policy by many libraries. It endorses the principle of intellectual freedom and recognizes that censorship of any materials in any guise eventually affects the library. The ALA has published the *Intellectual Freedom Manual* to provide libraries with principles for opposing censorship and promoting intellectual freedom in the broadest sense.[3]

Fig. 12.1. Most frequently challenged book titles. (Donna A. Demac, *Liberty Denied: The Current Rise of Censorship in America* [New York: PEN American Center, 1988], 10-11.)

1. *The Catcher in the Rye* by J. D. Salinger
2. *The Grapes of Wrath* by John Steinbeck
3. *Of Mice and Men* by John Steinbeck
4. *Go Ask Alice* (anonymous)
5. *Forever...* by Judy Blume
6. *Our Bodies, Ourselves* by the Boston Women's Health Collective
7. *The Adventures of Huckleberry Finn* by Mark Twain
8. *The Learning Tree* by Gordon Parks
9. *My Darling, My Hamburger* by Paul Zindel
10. *1984* by George Orwell
11. *Black Boy* by Richard Wright
12. *The Canterbury Tales* by Geoffrey Chaucer
13. *Slaughterhouse Five* by Kurt Vonnegut

The basic policies expressed in *The Library Bill of Rights* are only those that a democratic society would seem to support. However, there have been many people over the years who have objected to them. In the 1950s, many libraries were attacked for containing books written about communism or by authors such as Richard Wright and Howard Fast who were labeled as communist. These censors felt that such books should either be removed from the libraries' shelves, labeled as the works of communists, or purged of the offending paragraphs or pages. Sometimes they even demanded that libraries be prohibited from placing these materials on their shelves in the first place. Other censors have objected to materials being made available to young people that they consider to be for "mature" audiences. The latter objections have become particularly prevalent with the advent of extremely popular adolescent novels such as those by Judy Blume. The most vocal objections have been to sex-education books such as Goldman's *Show Me Yours* or *Our Bodies, Ourselves* by the Boston Women's Health Collective. Perhaps censors have felt most uncomfortable with the idea of making these latter materials available to children on a library's open shelves because of their belief that *all* such materials are "prurient."

In addition to censorship, libraries have also faced other obstacles in providing complete library service in a democratic society. Before desegregation, many white people in the South objected to black people entering their libraries. These libraries often responded by limiting their facilities to members of the white race; a few cities developed two public library systems, one for each race. (These duplicate systems were often combined into one system after the Supreme Court desegregation decision in the 1950s.) To help libraries respond to such obstacles, ALA adopted the *Freedom to Read* statement in 1953 and revised it in 1972. (See appendix C.) In 1979, a companion *Freedom to View* statement was drafted and adopted by the American Film and Video Association. (See appendix D.) These statements supported the principles of the *Library Bill of Rights* by defining "the rights and responsibilities of publishers and librarians in maintaining the freedom of Americans to read and view what they choose."[4]

Unfortunately, sometimes the very persons who should be defending intellectual freedom may themselves become censors. Not only parents and children, but also teachers, administrators, city officials, and school and library board members have complained at times about specific library materials. Librarians and their staffs have even contributed to censorship in several ways. Some librarians have not challenged the removal of library materials because they did not want to fight their administrators, boards, or communities. Other librarians have chosen not to purchase materials they considered objectionable for fear that members of their community would disapprove. This indirect censorship may be as harmful to a library's intellectual health as all of the other censorship attempts combined. This censorship of ideas could ultimately end in the reduction of many of our freedoms. To prevent this, supporters of intellectual freedom are constantly working to educate people and inform them of the importance of intellectual freedom in a democratic society.

In this education campaign, the Freedom to Read Foundation was founded in 1969 to give legal assistance to librarians and library boards in their struggles against censorship. ALA also developed supplementary documents to expand the *Library Bill of Rights* and the *Freedom to Read* and *Freedom to View* statements. These documents provided philosophical ammunition for librarians in these censorship struggles. ALA not only urged libraries to adopt all of these documents, but they also encouraged libraries to develop material selection policies based on their principles. Libraries were also urged to develop policy statements for the retention and reconsideration of library materials before the need for such policies arose. ALA recommended that these policies include a complaint form for the questioner to fill out. Such forms usually asked whether or not the person was responding as an individual or as the representative of a group, whether the entire work had been read, viewed, or listened to, and exactly what was being objected to. Libraries found that would-be censors were often reluctant to pursue their complaints when they were asked to put them in writing. As libraries followed these principles and policies, they found they were often able to eliminate such complaints or reduce and minimize their effects on the community.

Nevertheless, some would-be censors still worried that without their watchdog efforts libraries would purchase every published item regardless of its merits. These people did not understand that a library's selection policies would prevent such a practice from occurring. Librarians would still continue to make their decisions based upon established selection criteria. These criteria considered the accuracy of the material and whether the manner in which it was presented contributed to its literary, artistic, or scientific value. A library would also consider the importance of an item in relation to the library's budget. Professional ethics would prevent librarians from selecting only those materials that reflected their own personal preferences. Instead, librarians are obligated to select materials that include all issues and points of view. Thus, even if a librarian, staff member, or board member disapproved of a particular title or genre, that person would not have the right or authority to exclude such material from the library.

Although some librarians across the nation have practiced censorship either directly or indirectly, many more have spoken up and fought for intellectual freedom. Many librarians have worked with their staffs, administrators, or governing boards to develop a climate for intellectual freedom. They have discouraged censorship in their communities by advocating freedom of access to ideas. They have stood fast against forces that would restrict children's access to many library materials. They have also objected to service fees that would be difficult for poorer or younger patrons to pay. They have lobbied local, state, and federal authorities to pass confidentiality laws that would protect the rights of their patrons to freely use a library and check out its materials. When presented with censorship complaints, these librarians have stood firm, explained their positions well, and sometimes won over their opponents. In some cases, they have had to go to court or seek the assistance of ALA, the Freedom to Read Foundation, or the American Civil Liberties Union (ACLU), but they have often won these battles for freedom. As long as there are librarians, boards, and staff members who are willing to fight these battles, freedom of speech and freedom of the press should remain alive and well.

LIBRARY ETHICS

Intellectual freedom, freedom of speech, and freedom of the press will not survive for long in libraries unless they become integral parts of a library's philosophy of service. They should be reflected in a library's objectives, policies, and procedures or the library will not be fulfilling the needs of its patrons in a democratic society. In addition, librarians, administrators, staff members, and board members must be sure that their own personal attitudes and philosophies contribute positively to a library's philosophy of service. This positive contribution can be fostered if everyone connected with the library understands the ethics or rules and standards governing their conduct.

Library ethics refers to the personal conduct of an individual in relationships with others in libraries. These ethics are well defined in the _Statement on Professional Ethics_ adopted by ALA in 1981. (See appendix E.) Although this statement was written for professional librarians, the ethics it describes should also be followed by all library staff and board members. Library ethics govern an individual's relationship with library patrons, fellow library staff members, and library supervisors and administrators, including the governing authority. Although the ethics are prefaced here with the word _library_, they are really just refinements of the same moral and humanitarian principles that anyone in society is expected to follow. That they are library ethics means they are further based on the library principles adopted in the _Library Bill of Rights_ and the _Freedom to Read_ and _Freedom to View_ statements.

Library ethics require library personnel to provide the highest level of library service, protect the confidentiality of their patrons, avoid conflicts of interest, and ensure equal access to information. Because these requirements are also based upon commonly accepted practices of courtesy and library etiquette, they should not be difficult for any person involved in a library to follow. For example, both library etiquette and ethics would dictate that each library patron be treated as an individual. This would mean that a staff member should look at a patron who is talking, address the patron by name, and use correct "standard"

English rather than slang or library jargon. Questions should be answered pleasantly, rather than begrudgingly, no matter how many times a question has been asked, such as "When does the library close?" Referrals to other staff members should include the staff member's name and complete directions for finding the person. Such statements as, "Go see the librarian in reference," do not communicate very much to a library patron who does not know what or where "reference" is.

The first important area of library ethics concerns the relationships between library personnel and library patrons. Library ethics require library staff members to treat all patrons as fairly and impartially as possible. This means that a senior citizen and a small child in a public library would receive the same service as a board member. It also means that students' needs would be given the same consideration as teachers' and administrators' needs in schools and colleges. Too many times, library staffs have provided services to their patrons based upon who the patrons are rather than upon their needs.

Another important library ethic is also based upon common courtesy. That ethic is to treat a patron's question as a private conversation between the patron and the staff member. This would prevent delicate matters from being broadcast throughout the library. For example, a patron might not want others to know that he or she is interested in books on gay rights or abortion. Also, as in private conversations, the library staff member should not repeat conversations to others unless it is necessary to satisfy the patron's library need. If such confidential information is repeated, it not only might harm the patron, but it might also destroy that person's faith in the library's integrity.

An added advantage to treating every question as a private matter is that it enables the library to limit a citizen's complaint to the few people involved. Such complaints can often come from an "irate patron" who objects to a library policy such as having to pay an overdue fine. They can also come from a would-be community censor who is bent on challenging the inclusion of an item in the library's collection. In any case, when a library support staff member receives such a complaint, that person should immediately turn it over to a supervisor or librarian. The supervisor should explain the library's policies and procedures to the patron. If the complaint is about an item in the library collection, the library's policy for reconsidering materials should be followed. It can also be useful to let the patron read any relevant policies, such as the materials selection policy or the *Library Bill of Rights* and the *Freedom to Read* and *Freedom to View* statements. All staff members involved should remember to be courteous and to treat the complaint in an impersonal yet polite and serious manner. They should avoid giving any personal opinions about any questioned material. At all costs, they should not lose their tempers or get into arguments with patrons over the policy or material in question. By handling the complaint or situation in a professional and ethical manner, the library staff will be better able to resolve any issue or defend any questioned material.

Library ethics would also protect an individual person's right to use a library and its information without this knowledge being divulged to other sources. This concern has become more important to librarians as information searches and computer databases have made it easier to maintain records of such uses. In particular, this capability has encouraged outsiders, such as local police departments or agencies of the federal government, to increase their demands for access to such information. For example, in the 1970s, the U.S. Treasury Department demanded to review circulation records of public library patrons in several cities. In the 1980s, the FBI attempted to recruit librarians to report on library activities of particular types of patrons. In some libraries, similar attempts have come from principals, board members, or even the local police. Library staff members should recognize that these requests are unethical. They represent an invasion of the reader's intellectual privacy and should be fought whenever they occur.

Another aspect of this right to use a library and its information has come to the forefront in libraries during the past few decades. Since 1964, libraries have felt the impact of societal and legal changes in mental health care. These changes have returned many mentally handicapped and disturbed people to general society. Because many of these persons have nowhere to go, they often use the library as a day care or home-away-from-home facility. Joined by people who became homeless in the economic recessions of the 1970s and 1980s, they often use the library's furniture for sleeping and its restrooms as bathing facilities. Sometimes their behavior disturbs other library patrons or monopolizes the staff's time. When this happens, staff members begin, understandably, to consider them as "problem patrons." Library ethics technically require staff members to treat these persons with the same courtesy and respect that they would give to any other patron. Although staff members are not expected to approve of such behavior, it is "only when our concern for the other patrons' and staff's suffering outweighs our concern for the disturbing patron, that can we consider legal measures to oust him from libraries. Until that point, our primary concern should be to help him get the assistance he needs."[5]

In addition to such ethical considerations for library staff-to-patron relationships, a second area of library ethics concerns the relationships among the library staff members themselves. Although common courtesy is important in this area, more specific ethics and procedures also apply. First, although some library employees may become great personal friends, this is not necessary for library employees to get along in a friendly atmosphere. Such an atmosphere can develop if employees respect each other and accept the differences in work habits and job performance that each person brings to the job. This respect should enable employees from several different levels or backgrounds to work together harmoniously to accomplish the library's objectives and goals. Another consideration governing staff-to-staff relations concerns interdepartmental matters. Ethical considerations require that employees in one department not get involved with problems, policies, or procedures in another department unless their job performance is affected by such issues.

When differences of opinion or problems do arise between employees, a third ethical consideration requires the people involved to sit down and try to resolve them. (Complaining in the staff lounge to friends only aggravates the situation.) If such a discussion does not resolve the problem, the employee should then go to the immediate supervisor and explain the situation and what has been done about it. A staff member should not go to a higher supervisor or a supervisor in another department without first talking with his or her own supervisor. This procedure follows the line of supervision and is essential for keeping the communication lines open. If problems not solved at one level are taken to the next higher level, it is a good procedure to inform all of the persons involved. This practice will help staff members develop a spirit of trust and cooperation. Finally, if a library employee is concerned with a question about a policy or a procedure, that person should not just criticize it but should discuss it with his or her supervisor. In the discussion, the employee might learn more about the background or issues involved in a policy or procedure. Only then can the employee make a valid criticism or offer possible alternatives. Although no one likes to hear chronic complaints, most supervisors will welcome well-reasoned suggestions that follow these outlined steps.

The final important area of library ethics concerns the relationships of an employee with supervisors and administrators, including the governing authority. All employees in a library should understand the lines of supervision. They should know which persons have the authority to assign duties, change schedules, approve leaves, make evaluations or reprimands, and hire and fire the library staff. In most libraries, these duties are split among various levels of supervisors subject to final approval by a board. By understanding the authority and responsibility of each of these levels, a staff member could become a better employee. For example, an employee would better understand that a librarian might be unable to make desirable changes because the principal or library board disagreed with them. An employee would also realize that although he or she is a friend or a relative of a board member, no special privileges should be granted. Likewise, board members should also understand that, for ethical reasons, they should not get personally involved in matters that the librarians and staff should handle. All of the persons involved in libraries, including libarians, staff members, administrators, and board members, must accept these obligations to develop positive working relationships with each other. If they do, libraries will be better able to direct all of their energies into providing good library service.

Unfortunately, sometimes library staffs, librarians, and boards seem to be at odds with each other. Some library staffs seem more interested in maintaining the status quo than in initiating new library services the board desires. Some library administrators seem more interested in establishing themselves in the library world than in directing their library operations. Other boards and institution administrators are more interested in cutting budgets and keeping salaries low than in providing library services. Because libraries are service-based institutions, such conflicting attitudes can severely affect the levels of library service.

If this begins to occur in a library, all persons involved should take stock of their positions. Library staff members may find that a union will enable them to bring pressure upon a penny-pinching board. Library board members may find that working cooperatively with a staff association or union might help enlist support for new taxes, services, and ideas. However, if staff members find they cannot ethically work within the objectives and philosophy being carried out by the administration and board, perhaps they should resign. If board members find they cannot ethically agree with board-adopted library policies or the principles expressed in the *Library Bill of Rights*, perhaps they should resign. Only if all of the persons connected with a library are totally committed to carrying out its policies and procedures based upon library ethics will a library be able to fulfill its philosophy of library service.

GOOD LIBRARY SERVICE

The role of each library employee in providing good library service is vital if a library is to fulfill its goals and objectives. Librarians and boards set the policies and procedures that direct the library's operations. However, all staff members are responsible for translating these policies and procedures into library service. Because the average person walking into a library often assumes that the new clerk at the circulation desk is in charge, this can become a very important consideration in establishing library service. Each person connected with the library must understand the principles of library ethics and the *Library Bill of Rights*. It is the responsibility of each supervisor, particularly the circulation supervisor, to impart this knowledge to each person under his or her direction. In addition, each supervisor should ensure that each new employee is informed of the library's stated objectives and understands how these objectives relate to the employee's own job and to the library's philosophy of library service.

Once employees understand their role in carrying out the library's goals and objectives, each of them should be encouraged to adopt the philosophy of "service to the patrons" as their own. Such a philosophy should include recognizing that the public's needs should come before the convenience of the staff when procedures are being set up or policies revised. Good library service also requires employees to follow ethical library practices and etiquette in their communications and interactions with library patrons and other staff. It is a very sad fact that some library patrons have forsaken libraries forever because of the curtness or rudeness of a few library staff members. Library staff members should also remember that the library is still considered a place for quiet study by many of its patrons. All too often, library employees have become the noisiest persons in the library. They forget to carry on their conversations in quiet tones outside the hearing of their patrons.

Library staff members have another important function in developing good library service. When they are performing their duties, they should be on the alert for new procedures, new techniques, or new ways that could help improve this performance. All library employees, from a librarian or supervisor to a clerk or page, may see a new technique at a nearby library or a new process at a library convention that could improve their area and be useful in their own libraries. If this occurs, an employee could mention it to his or her supervisor. The supervisor and employee could investigate everything about the new idea, including its costs and any problems others have encountered with it. The supervisor could then present a written proposal to the library manager that includes the possible pros and cons for adopting the idea. The manager could review and evaluate this information and make an informed decision regarding the proposal. Thus, by providing background information for procedures or areas in which the manager is not directly involved, an employee can have an impact on library service.

Good library service does not just happen. It is consciously developed by all members of the library team working together to achieve a common goal. This service does not necessarily depend upon a library's ability to provide the most up-to-date equipment and materials. Instead, good library service depends more upon the concern, imagination, and interest of all those involved, including support staff, librarians, administrators, board members, and patrons. Although libraries may differ from one another in their materials, objectives, and services, successful libraries generally share the same common goals of "Good Library Service." (See figure 12.2.)

Fig. 12.2. Good library service.

GOALS

- A library should follow its stated objectives.
- A library should support and defend the principles of the *Library Bill of Rights*.
- A library should practice a philosophy of service to its public.
- All library activities and services should encourage and provide the best possible service to a library's public.

OBJECTIVES

1. Determine the needs of the library's public.

2. Provide materials, programs, and services to satisfy those needs and to support the library's objectives.

3. Present materials that represent all points of view and do not remove materials because of partisan or doctrinal disapproval.

4. Provide the right information to the right person at the right time.

5. Choose routines and procedures that facilitate rather than hinder an individual's use of the library.

6. Update these procedures and services to reflect current needs of the public.

7. Make the resources and services of the library known to its potential users.

8. Provide sufficient trained personnel to give personal attention to patrons' problems and needs.

9. Be polite and courteous to patrons.

10. Treat every patron as fairly and impartially as possible.

11. Protect the privacy of library patrons.

12. Show respect for all library employees and work with a spirit of courteous cooperation.

13. Make only constructive criticisms and channel these to the proper authority.

SUMMARY

If today's libraries are to remain important institutions in our democratic society, every member of a library's community must understand and support the principles and practices that make libraries so important to their users. These principles and practices are based upon the rights established in the First Amendment and the U.S. Supreme Court cases that have interpreted these rights. They are embodied in the concept of intellectual freedom that has been outlined in the *Library Bill of Rights* and the *Freedom to Read* and *Freedom to View* statements. Libraries have adopted these statements and supported intellectual freedom to combat censorship attempts within their community.

Libraries have also established policies and procedures that are based on professional library ethics contained in ALA's *Statement of Professional Ethics*. These library ethics govern the personal conduct of individuals in their relationship with others in libraries. In addition, each library should develop its own philosophy of library service based on the goals and objectives of good library service. Every library employee and board member has a duty to incorporate the goals and objectives of "Good Library Service" into his or her own personal philosophy of library service. Only then will libraries develop programs and services to ensure that they remain important community institutions.

REVIEW QUESTIONS

1. Define *intellectual freedom* and discuss its relationship to a library in a democratic society.

2. Discuss the relationship of the *Library Bill of Rights*, the *Freedom to Read*, and the *Freedom to View* statements to the materials that should be included in a library's collection.

3. Discuss the role of library staffs and board members in supporting intellectual freedom and discouraging library censorship.

4. Identify the basic elements of library ethics and etiquette as they relate to library patrons, fellow employees, and those in higher authority.

5. Describe the ethics and procedures a staff member and supervisor should follow when confronted by a problem or irate patron.

6. Develop a statement of personal philosophy of library service based on the goals and objectives of good library service.

NOTES

[1]Miller v. California, 37 L Ed 2nd 419.

[2]*American Heritage Dictionary of the English Language* (Boston: Houghton Mifflin, 1969), 1054. This dictionary has itself been the target of censorship by persons who objected to some of its words and definitions.

[3] American Library Association, Office for Intellectual Freedom, *Intellectual Freedom Manual* (Chicago: ALA, 1974), 10.

[4] ALA, *Intellectual Freedom*, 10.

[5] Charles A. Salter and Jeffrey L. Salter, *On the Frontlines: Coping with the Library's Problem Patrons* (Englewood, CO: Libraries Unlimited, 1988), 11.

SELECTED READINGS

American Library Association. Commission on Freedom and Equality of Access to Information. *Freedom and Equality of Access to Information: A Report to the American Library Association*. Dan M. Lacy, chair. Chicago: ALA, 1986.

American Library Association. Office for Intellectual Freedom. *Intellectual Freedom Manual*. 3d ed. Chicago: ALA, 1989.

Before and After the Censor: A Resource Manual on Intellectual Freedom. Lansing, MI: Michigan Association for Media in Education and Michigan Library Association, Intellectual Freedom Committees, 1987.

Burress, Lee. *Battle of the Books: Literary Censorship in the Public Schools, 1950-1985*. Metuchen, NJ: Scarecrow, 1989.

Creth, Sheila D. *Effective On-the-Job Training: Developing Library Human Resources*. Chicago: ALA, 1986.

Demac, Donna A. *Liberty Denied: The Current Rise of Censorship in America*. New York: PEN American Center, 1988.

Green, Jonathon. *The Encyclopedia of Censorship*. New York: Facts on File, 1990.

Hauptman, Robert. *Ethical Challenges in Librarianship*. Phoenix, AZ: Oryx Press, 1988.

Jones, Frances M. *Defusing Censorship: The Librarian's Guide to Handling Censorship Conflicts*. Phoenix, AZ: Oryx Press, 1983.

Lindsey, Jonathan A., and Ann E. Prentice. *Professional Ethics and Librarians*. Phoenix, AZ: Oryx Press, 1985.

Mintz, Anne P., ed. *Information Ethics: Concerns for Librarianship and the Information Industry*. Series edited by Jana Valejs. Jefferson, NC: McFarland, 1990.

Reichman, Henry. *Censorship and Selection: Issues and Answers for Schools.* Chicago: ALA and American Association of School Administrators, 1988.

Salter, Charles A., and Jeffrey L. Salter. *On the Frontlines: Coping with the Library's Problem Patrons.* Englewood, CO: Libraries Unlimited, 1988.

White, Herbert S. *Librarians and the Awakening from Innocence: A Collection of Essays.* Boston: G. K. Hall, 1989.

CHAPTER 13

ENTERING
THE LIBRARY WORLD

The library/media/information world today offers a great variety of employment opportunities for every individual. Each individual can choose from among a wide range of jobs at the desired occupational level in a number of different types of libraries. Once these choices have been made, an individual can search for a library position that fits his or her own needs and desires. Although this process might seem to be endless and unrewarding at times, the guidelines presented in this chapter may help applicants find the position they truly want.

WHAT KIND OF WORK
DO YOU WANT?

The hardest part about choosing a new job is first determining what type of work you truly want to do. Many times people have accepted what seemed to be ideal jobs, only to find out within a short time that they have made disastrous choices. Others have been very happy with positions their friends and associates thought they would dislike. Such discrepancies between a person's expectations and the reality of a situation are influenced by many intangible variables. These variables can be emotional, physical, psychological, or economic, and their importance at any one time can affect a person's job satisfaction.

Prospective employees should evaluate their personal, physical, and psychological strengths and weaknesses. For example, do you prefer working in a quiet area by yourself or do you like to work near other people? (One library technician took a position as the only full-time employee in the library of a local historical society. Within a month she was ready to quit the library field because she could not stand being alone so much of the time. After she moved to a busy public library, she was very happy.) Do you prefer working with a particular age group? (After doing her practice teaching in a junior high school media center, one librarian realized that she did not enjoy working with eighth- and ninth-grade students.) Finally, do you like to finish your work at the end of the day rather than have an ongoing workload? (In one library, an acquisitions clerk finally quit in frustration because she could never clear her desk of the constant orders and arrivals of new books.) By taking the time to analyze your own personality needs, you may be able to avoid mistakes.

A good place to begin is by examining your physical and psychological strengths and weaknesses. For example, do you have the dexterity or talent, in addition to the interest, to work with computer or media equipment and materials? Or are you too overwhelmed by computerized or mechanical objects to relax and allow yourself to become familiar with them? Do you prefer jobs in which you sit still most of the day, or do you like jobs where you can stand up and move around? Would you prefer sitting at a desk typing or using a computer terminal for much of the day, or would you rather interact with people at a circulation desk? In this evaluation of your strengths and preferences, you can gain additional insight by talking with friends or by taking stock of yourself through assessment instruments such as the Myers-Briggs Personality Type Indicators.

Many people also have personal interest preferences that may influence their choices. Some people might want to work in a small library because they like the flexibility of working in many areas of library services rather than being limited to one area. Other people may want to move to a particular geographic location and would be willing to accept any number of positions just to be there. Some people may want to work in special libraries because they take pride in contributing to the accomplishments or profits of the parent body. Some may even want to work in a particular type of special library such as a medical library and might turn down other jobs until such a job comes along. Such personal preferences may seem strange to others, but they are important to job satisfaction.

Finally, there may be outside considerations that affect a person's career choices. To some persons, having a well-paying position may be most important, while having a flexible schedule with summers off may be most important to others. Some people may want to work in academic libraries to get free tuition and continue their formal education. Sometimes, persons cannot relocate or commute to a job because of family responsibilities, and at other times, persons might prefer to do just that *because* of their family responsibilities. "You alone" must decide which considerations and variables, both personal and external, are most important to you as you begin to look for a job in the library world.

WHERE DO YOU WANT TO WORK?

Once you have taken an inventory of your own preferences and needs, it is useful to compare your interests with the kinds of library positions available. First, think about the library or school courses that were most interesting to you. Then analyze them to see what you liked about them. Particular subjects usually will indicate a library area that will most interest you. For example, if you enjoy science or music, you might like to work in a special library. If you enjoy story hours or children's literature, you might like to work in a school library or in children's services in a public library. If you prefer bibliographic searches and verifying citations, you might enjoy working in a reference and interlibrary loan department. If you like to meet people and enjoy variety, jobs in the public services areas (particularly in public libraries) might appeal to you most of all. Thus, by analyzing library jobs in light of your own needs, you should be able to identify a range of jobs that interest you.

Next, it is a good idea to observe persons working in such jobs. You might volunteer to work or serve a practicum in a library to see if you really do like the work. If libraries do not want volunteers (and some of them may not), ask if you can observe their library operations for several hours. For example, unless you have observed or worked in a school library media center, it is very difficult to understand the frustrations of working with a particular age group or the chaos that erupts when the bell rings. This firsthand experience will not only help you learn more about the library, but it also will let librarians and staff members know that you are available and are willing to work. Although such volunteer efforts do not necessarily lead to a paid position, they can.

WHERE ARE THE JOBS?

Once you have decided on the type of work you would like to do, you should begin looking for a place of employment. You should explore all types of libraries, including public, school, and academic (both public and private) and any special libraries in your area. However, libraries are not the only places where materials must be organized and distributed. Thus, you should also compile a list of all of the possible industries, businesses, and organizations that might need someone to perform these particular job duties. Too often, prospective library employees ignore these possibilities, bemoaning the lack of library opportunities because the local libraries or schools are "not hiring."

Businesses, industries, institutions, governmental agencies, private organizations, and national associations all provide job opportunities for library personnel. (See figure 13.1, page 190.) For example, such an opportunity exists in practically every hospital in the United States. Because hospital accrediting associations encourage hospitals to maintain and staff medical libraries, hospitals are excellent places to look for a job. Similarly, law offices and county law libraries may be able to use the talents of someone interested in researching and maintaining collections of legal materials. Companies that are expanding or have developed strong economic bases may be ready to have someone organize their company records.

Probably the most frequent question asked of someone who gets a new job is "How did you find out about it?" So many people believe that jobs appear as if by magic or because of "who you know" that they do not realize a person can obtain a job through tenacity and perseverance. It is less romantic, but much more realistic, to recognize that finding a job you want, particularly in a recession, might take lots of time and energy. A good definition to remember is that "luck is opportunity meeting preparation."

One of the first places you will probably look for a job is at the nearest library with the kind of job you want. However, you should also contact all possible nearby libraries. If you know someone who works in the library, you can ask if there are any job openings. However, you should also go to the library or institution and ask for an application form. (Applying for a job will be discussed in a later section.) Do not be discouraged if your friends or the library indicate that there are no job openings at the present time. Often there are unexpected turnovers in the staff that create an opening without warning. If the local library

Fig. 13.1. Sample want ads for library positions.

ASSISTANT MEDICAL LIBRARIAN
One of Chicago's most modern health care facilities has an immed. opening for an Asst. Medical Librarian. Duties incl. handling circ. & ILL, technical processing, assisting patrons with reference inquiries and computer equipment. Must work P.M. and weekends. The qualified individual should have bachelor's degree and some credit hrs. in basic library science or equiv. work experience. Interested candidates should send their resume to Jane Jones at St. Mary of Bethlehem Hospital Center, 3322 N. Halsted St., Chicago, IL 60622.

LIBRARY CLERK TYPIST
Detail-oriented individual required to check in journals for association library. Some library experience preferred. Light typing. Pleasant, near-north location. Call 450-3563. American Brewers Assoc. (EEO)

PART-TIME LIBRARY TECHNICIAN
sought for the Youth Services Dept. of Prairie Meadows Public Library. Bachelors' degree or LTA degree preferred. This position involves planning and executing programs for children aged 3-14 & readers' adv. to this group. 15 hrs. per wk., some weekends. Contact Jean Arnold, Youth Services Librarian, 295-5230. 320 Juniper Lane, Prairie Meadows, WI 54432.

LIBRARY PARAPROFESSIONAL
Lib. asst. to work with serials mgmt in an automated environment. Respon. incl. check-in & claims, coordinating a periodical routing service, infor. services to users, & assigned projs. Position reqs. prev. tech. serv. exp. using OCLC or an automated serials control system; attention to detail. typ. 35-45 WPM; 2 yrs. coll. (degree pref.) & abil. to work with public. Send resume to T. Morgan, American Health Assoc. Div. of Employee Res. 725 N. Lake Shore Dr. NO phone calls. An Equal Oppor. Employer.

LIBRARY TECHNICIAN
Responsible for document delivery function of a busy information resource center, coordinates all in-house photocopying, and ILL processes. Staffs IRC ref. desk as scheduled. Req: LTA degree or equiv. experience in a special lib. Must have strong interpersonal skills to deal with variety of patrons and vendors. Must have excellent data entry and organizational skills. Send resume to Diane Shimmel, Human Resources, Anagram Healthcare Corp. Rt. 50, Park Hill, IL 60256. Phone (708) 329-5660.

LIBRARIAN — YOUTH SERVICES
Enthusiastic and creative person for full-time position. 35 hrs. per wk. incl. some PMs and weekends. Acts. incl. programming, acquisitions, cataloging & reference. MLS req. Salary $20,000 per yr. Send resume to Mrs. J. Hall, Brookside Public Library, 5910 Grand Ave., Brookside, WI 53270. Deadline Feb. 20, 1992.

LIBRARY ASSIST. ACQUISITIONS
Preorder searching; book check-in; mgmt of acquisitions database. Familiarity with computers, accuracy, and great attention to detail req.; library and OCLC experience prefer. $18,900. EOE. Resume to: Head of Technical Services, JL Jones Library, 1200 N. 32nd St., Chicago, IL 60615. Open until satis. candidate found.

LIBRARY CAREER OPPORTUNITIES
Avail. in youth and corrections centers for professional and support staff. For more infor. call or write Ms. Thea Chesley, Coor. Libr. Serv., IL Dept. of Correc., School Dist. #310, PO Box 31960, Springfield, IL 62794. (217) 523-4322.

LIBRARIAN
for 75-attorney law firm. Must have MLS degree and 2 + yrs. working exp. Law office working exp. helpful. Good working conditions & benefits. Salary $28-32,000. Send resume & salary hist. to P. Jones, POB 64920, Fresno, CA 93779.

belongs to a library system, you can ask to see any system-wide job notices, or you can contact the system yourself and ask if there is a fee for receiving such notices.

After you have applied to the local libraries, you can begin job hunting in earnest by looking through the want ads of all available newspapers. (See figure 13.1.) Do not prejudge any newspaper because you think it is too small or too large to cover the area you are interested in. This review of newspaper ads can begin many months before you will be available for a job. Not only is this an excellent way for you to keep abreast of the jobs available, but it also ensures that you will not miss an opportunity. One library technician student found the job of her dreams by doing just that even though she had another year of schooling to finish before she graduated. By following up a local ad for the national head-quarters of a barber shop quartet singing society, she was able to combine her library interests with music, her first love.

In addition to checking out newspaper ads, you can also check out major library publications and joblines. The major national library publications such as *Library Journal*, *Library Hotline*, and *American Libraries* have want-ad sections for professional librarians, while *Library Mosaics* has want-ad sections for support staff positions. (If you cannot find the most recent copy of these magazines on a library's shelf, you may need to ask a librarian for them because they are often routed to library staff rather than made available to the public.) In addition, national publications in other professions and associations, such as the *Chronicle of Higher Education*, also have want-ad sections.

Other up-to-date sources of job openings are telephone "joblines" or "job hotlines" operated by many state and regional library associations. Each jobline contains recorded messages of job openings in a particular geographic area. Some joblines will list both professional and support staff positions. They are usually updated on a weekly basis, and the caller is charged for each phone call. In addition, there are several online databases for job openings, such as GRAPEVINE, which can be accessed by someone with a computer and modem. (See Myers, *Guide to Library Placement Sources*, in "Selected Readings" at the end of this chapter.)

School placement offices and government employment agencies are also useful places to learn about job opportunities. School offices not only have current job listings, but they will also let students and alumni register or file an application for future openings. At federal and state government employment agencies, you can often register for a particular geographic location and category of personnel. The agency may then notify you about job openings that fit your choices. All federal and state governments and some city governments have civil service employment systems designed to ensure that every applicant has an equal opportunity for being hired. Each applicant must successfully pass a civil service test or pass it with a very high score before being interviewed for a job.

Commercial employment agencies and temporary library service agencies also provide job opportunities. These latter agencies are particularly helpful if you are new to the library field or to a geographic area and are looking for work in any type of library or position. Any fees charged by these agencies are usually paid by the employer, but temporary service agencies will pay you a lower hourly rate than they will charge the employer for your services. When you apply to any of these offices or agencies, it might be very useful for you to attach a copy of your resume to your application form. This can later be copied or detached by the office and forwarded with an application or any test scores to the prospective employing library.

You can also look up information about libraries and companies in professional or trade directories. For example, *The American Library Directory* lists libraries geographically by state and then by city (a particularly useful feature if you are planning to relocate). Under each city, the names and statistical data are given for every library. This data includes the director's name, size of the staff and names of the department heads, annual budget, the total staff salaries, size of the collection, and other useful information such as any automated systems or special collections.

Other professional and trade directories may provide similar information about any companies that interest you. Your local library also may have annual reports on local businesses, industries, or hospitals. By reviewing all of this information, you may be able to choose several libraries, institutions, or businesses that could use your talents and abilities. You could then write letters to individuals at each library or company inquiring about any job opportunities and enclosing a copy of your resume. (See the section below on "Letters of Application.")

A final way to locate information about jobs is to talk with the people you know. You should not be bashful about letting those around you know you are looking for a job. This "network" of friends, relatives, teachers, fellow students, and friendly librarians may have heard about job opportunities and be happy to tell you about them. If this happens, you should treat each lead as a valid job opportunity and follow it up. Although some of the leads might be false ones, others could be very important. Also, the fact that you did follow the leads will encourage these friends and others to tell you about other opportunities as they hear about them.

HOW TO GET THE JOB YOU WANT

Before you write any letters or fill in any application forms, you should first evaluate and list your strengths and weaknesses. Every person has particular talents or abilities that would be important to a prospective employer. It is up to you to identify these in the job application process. This does not mean that you should be a braggart, but it does mean that you owe it to yourself to present the information in as favorable a light as possible. You can record any awards or honors you have received or list any special courses or programs you have taken or participated in. If you can indicate that you have directed or organized any special programs, the better your resume will look.

Because library employers are looking for staff members with specific qualities, they may be looking at your life experience as a whole rather than just at your academic credentials. To an employer, students who are active in library or school activities indicate an interest in others and a willingness to work. Adults who have spent years of volunteering their time for parent-teacher associations, scout work, and church work have also indicated that they can work with groups, help organize activities, and direct others. Therefore, if you have experiences such as these in your background, you should certainly include them in your resume and refer to them at the appropriate time in your interviews.

Resumes

A resume is a concise summary of your personal data, educational background, and occupational information. It provides a prospective employer with a thumbnail sketch of the background and qualifications that make you eligible for the position. A resume usually consists of one to three pages and contains all of the pertinent data a prospective employer would want to know when considering you for employment. Because employers tend to spend only a few minutes reading each resume, it is important to present yourself in the best possible light. To do this, vital information should be in an easy-to-read format that is simply written, legible, and accurate. The information should be selected with care and should indicate your activities and employment from high school up to and including the present time. Thus, your resume should highlight your activities and experience that can then be expanded upon in an interview. It is very useful to write down this information once, keep it up-to-date, and use it in the future as a guide for filling in application forms. (See figure 13.2, page 194.)

A resume is usually divided into four or five basic sections. The first section gives personal data, such as your full name, address, and phone number. It may also include other data that could be of interest to a prospective employer. For instance, because federal laws require the employer to record an employee's citizenship status, you might indicate your birthplace or your citizenship or residency status if you were not a native-born U.S. citizen. In other areas, a statement that you have three children would subtly explain a 10-year absence from the work force. If you live in another city, you could indicate a willingness to move to the library's service area. Although employers may not legally ask the latter personal questions, they will usually greatly appreciate your volunteering such information.

Other sections of the resume present your professional or career goals, educational background, occupational experience, community activities, and honors. The first of these sections should include a statement of your professional or career goals. These goals can highlight any experiences or qualifications that relate to the prospective job. For example, if you are applying for a technical services position, you should stress an interest in cataloging and working with detail rather than an interest in answering reference questions. The purpose of this section is to point out to the employer how well your qualifications and experiences match the qualifications and duties required for the position advertised. If you do not do this, you cannot expect the employer to make this match.

The educational section should indicate, in reverse order, the names and locations of the schools you attended, the years you attended, when you graduated (if you did), and any degrees you received. You can also indicate your major courses of study and might even list any library and occupational courses you had that might be important. If an employer might not be familiar with the degree or courses you took, you also might attach a list of the courses and include a short description of each from the school catalog. A transcript of such courses is not necessarily needed at this time, although it might be helpful if you had very good grades and no other work experience.

The occupational or experience section should list all of your major places of employments in reverse order beginning with your present job. You should include the name of the library or company, the dates employed (in whole years),

Fig. 13.2. Sample resume.

NAME:	JANE ELLEN (DOE) BROWN
ADDRESS:	1234 Green St. Milwaukee, WI 53201
TELEPHONE:	(414) 443-2610
BIRTHPLACE:	Milwaukee, WI

PROFESSIONAL GOAL: To use my *knowledge of library technology* and my *experience in working with young children* to help provide programs and services to children aged 3-14 in the PRAIRIE MEADOWS PUBLIC LIBRARY.

EDUCATION:
GATEWAY TECHNICAL COLLEGE,
    Kenosha, WI 1990-1992.
    Associate of Applied Science, 1991
    (Major: Library/Media Technical Assistant)
BUSINESS COLLEGE OF WISCONSIN,
    Milwaukee, WI 1979-1980.
    Secretarial Certificate, 1980
    Outstanding Word Processing Award
East High School, Milwaukee, WI, 1976-1979.
    Business Diploma, 1979.

EXPERIENCE:
Kearney and Trecker Co., West Allis, WI, 1980-1984.
    Clerk typist, 1980-1982, for Engineer Dept. (File clerk and typist for four engineers)
    Secretary, 1982-1984, for chief engineer (Secretarial and word-processing duties for chief engineer. Supervised clerical staff of Engineer Dept.)

COMMUNITY ACTIVITIES:
Congregational Church Cooperative Preschool, President, 1988.
Parent-Teachers Association, Secretary, 1989.
Brownie Scout Troop Leader and Cookie Sale Chairperson, 1989.

REFERENCES:
Barbara E. Chernik, Instructor LMTA courses
Gateway Technical College
3520 30th Ave., Kenosha, WI 53143
(414) 656-6324

Norbert Link, Instructor AV courses
Gateway Technical College
3520 30th Ave., Kenosha, WI 53143
(414) 656-6324

Connie Jones, Executive Director
Milwaukee Area Girl Scout Council
356 Wisconsin Ave., Milwaukee, WI 53201
(414) 442-3769

and your job titles. You do not need to list your reasons for leaving your job or give the names of your supervisors. If an employer wants this kind of information, it will be asked on the application form or in the interview. Also, you probably should not indicate any information about salaries unless the ad specifically requests this information. However, you can include brief descriptions of your duties in each of your jobs to help the employer form a mental picture of your abilities and capabilities. This may be particularly useful if you have held paraprofessional positions whose titles do not indicate the level of responsibility or performance your job required.

A final consideration in the section on experience is whether or not preprofessional or nonlibrary experience should be included. Because many librarians prefer to hire someone with experience for even an entry-level library position, it could be very important for you to list such experience. Thus, if you have worked as a page or a library clerk in a college or school library or even volunteered as a library mother, you can include this information. If you have any computer knowledge or experience, it might be useful to include this information.

A listing of community activities and interests can also expand the employer's mental picture of your abilities. Here you can indicate any activities, honors, skills, or special areas of knowledge you have that may be useful to a future employer. For example, working on the school or college newspaper or doing volunteer hospital work may indicate an ability in public relations or a strong interest in working with people. By the same token, membership in any friends of the library group will indicate a library interest that appeals to many prospective employers. You should also include any special talents or skills you have such as a speaking or reading knowledge of a foreign language or a working knowledge of an automated computer system. Sometimes these outside activities and skills can be just as important as a person's occupational experiences when the final hiring decisions are being made. They can also be especially important if they show that an applicant can bring an additional skill or ability to the job that the employer had not expected. For example, in one library, a custodian was selected from among several equally qualified candidates because of his artistic abilities and interest in helping with library displays and exhibits. Thus, your resume should include any activities or interests that can give you a hiring edge, particulary for employers who have a large applicant pool.

The final section of your resume is very important to the library world. This section should indicate the names of several "references" or persons who would recommend you for employment. These references should be acquainted with your work capabilities rather than serve as "personal character" references. They should not be relatives, close personal friends, or ministers because these people often cannot be completely objective about your abilities. Some examples of good references to use would be former library science or technology teachers, supervisors, librarians, and library staff with whom you might have worked. It is a good idea to include such people because, more often than not, a prospective employer may know your former employer or supervisor and ask him or her about you anyway. To be on the safe side, you should ask each person you list if you might use his or her name as a reference before you do so.

Once you have compiled your resume information, the most important thing to remember in writing your resume is that it introduces you to the prospective employer. If it is clear, concise, legible, and accurate, it will give a good impression of you. If it is sloppy, illegible, and incomplete, it will be an indictment against you. You should also be sure to include all of the essential elements of the resume that have been discussed. If you type a new resume or personalize one for each job you apply for, you must be sure to proofread every item for accuracy and consistency. The final product should be typed on white bond paper. If a computer printer is used, it should be a high-quality dot matrix or letter-quality printer. If you do not have this capability yourself, you may have to pay to have your resume commercially printed or duplicated.

Letters of Application

Once the resume has been prepared and duplicated, you can begin writing letters of application to send out as cover letters with the resume. These letters of application are very important because they give the employer a first impression of you and your abilities. You can send out these letters in response to ads, in response to a lead from a friend, or as blind letters to libraries or institutions you have chosen from the library or business directories. Such information can be gleaned from the job advertisement or announcement itself or from *The American Library Directory* and other business sources.

Each letter should show you in your best light by indicating how you can help the organization rather than vice versa. Each letter should be written individually to each employer and should be geared to that individual employer's needs. However, you should be sure to verify the names and positions of any persons you plan to contact if the sources you use are not current. You may also mention that you heard about a job opening either from an ad or a friend, or you can just state that their library's reputation has drawn your interest. (Your local library should have a number of books about writing such letters.)

Although you should write individualized letters to every employer, each such letter should include the same basic format and elements. First, be sure to write any letter from the employer's point of view and keep the "I's" to a minimum. Next, mention the title of the position you are applying for in the first paragraph because the employer may have several positions open at the same time. Because the basic purpose of such a letter is to interest the employer enough to ask you for an interview, you should use this letter as your one opportunity to explain how your background and qualifications relate to the position you are seeking. If you are not successful in this function, the employer may never even get to your resume. Next, you should be sure to include all of the information requested in the ad. However, if the ad asks what salary you desire, you can ask for a salary consistent with your abilities and background. Salaries in libraries may vary greatly depending on many factors, and you would not want to eliminate yourself from consideration because the salary you ask for is out of line with those of other positions. You should indicate that you are enclosing a resume that includes references that can be contacted. Finally, you should indicate your interest in obtaining an interview (or receiving an application), and you should be sure to give an address and phone number (including area code) where you can be reached. (See figure 13.3.)

In contrast to your resume, which is duplicated, each letter of application should be an original letter that is clearly written and accurately typed or printed. If you have difficulty with grammar, or English is a second language to you, it might be worthwhile to have someone review your letter for clarity and accuracy.

Fig. 13.3. Sample letter of application.

1234 Green St.
Milwaukee, WI 53201
March 15, 1992

Ms. Jean Arnold, Youth Services Librarian
Prairie Meadows Public Library
320 Juniper Lane
Prairie Meadows, WI 54432

Dear Ms. Arnold:

The opening for a Part-Time Library Technician in the Youth Services Department of the Prairie Meadows Public Library has interested me very much because of the opportunities it provides.

The responsibilities of this position sound very exciting as they would enable me to use my experience in planning and executing children's activities and programs. This experience was gained in working with Brownie Scout and preschool activities. In addition, my library/media technology course in children's materials would enable me to provide readers' advisory service for the various children's age groups.

If you have any questions or concerns about my background or abilities in these areas, you may feel free to contact my references on the enclosed resume.

I look forward to hearing favorably from you and would be available any afternoon for an interview. You may reach me at (414) 443-2610 if you have any additional questions or concerns.

Sincerely,

Jane Ellen (Doe) Brown

enc.

Each letter should be correctly addressed to the person indicated in the ad or to a specific individual, preferably the head of the library or the personnel manager. The care you take to find out such information can favorably impress the recipient of the letter. Your letter should be written in correct letter-writing form and be accompanied by a copy of your resume. You should be sure to put sufficient postage on the envelope to cover the cost of the letter and the resume. For future reference, you should keep a copy of every letter you send.

When you are sending out blind inquiries, it might be wise to send two sets of letters and resumes to large institutions. One set would be sent to the personnel office and another to the person in charge of the library itself. Thus, in a school system, the second letter might go to a school librarian or principal, and in a company it might go to the special librarian or the director of research. This duplication can be very worthwhile, especially in institutions that have centralized personnel departments and many employees.

In addition to sending out blind inquiries and completing applications for local libraries, it might be worthwhile to write letters answering several newspaper ads even if you are not entirely interested in the jobs. The experience of answering an ad and interviewing for a job will help you perfect your job-hunting skills. This experience will also help you develop your strengths, minimize your weaknesses, and learn to relax.

Application Documents

The application process usually involves filling out several different types of application documents. The purpose of these documents is to ensure that similar information is gathered from each applicant so that every individual has the same "equal employment opportunity." Such standardized documents and procedures are governed by federal employment laws and guidelines. They help reduce the impact of any personal preferences or prejudices by the persons involved in the employment process. Libraries and personnel offices have developed documents such as application forms, supplemental questionnaires, knowledge tests, and skill or ability testing. All of these are designed to provide information that can help employers make an informed, nondiscriminatory selection. If you are concerned that such legal requirements were not followed in any position for which you have applied, you can contact the local U.S. Equal Employment Opportunity Commission.

The standard application form is the most common application document you will encounter. This form may be a general purpose personnel application form for an entire institution or government, or it may be an application form designed specifically for one library. In any case, you should provide all of the requested information to the best of your knowledge. At this time, your resume can be very useful in providing names and dates you might otherwise have forgotten. It is very important to provide accurate information that agrees with your other employment documents. An employer can fire you for knowingly giving false information on an application form. You should take the time to be accurate in your grammar and spelling. You do not want to misspell such words as "library" or to make an embarrassing slip of the pen. To reduce such chances, be sure to proofread the application before you sign it. If any questions are asked that might cause you some problems, you should be as truthful as possible. If you have a medical condition such as epilepsy or heart problems, you could state this but also indicate that your condition is controlled by medicine. If you were fired from your last job, you could state that you are looking for more challenging work. If a job application asks for an expected salary level, you should indicate a salary that gives credit for your education and work experience.

In recent years, libraries have added additional steps to the application process to give them more information for their selection decision. This information has been particularly useful when they have received many applicants for one position. These additional steps can include supplemental questionnaires that require the applicant to solve or address library service questions. Such questionnaires are more commonly used for professional positions. Other steps that are more common for clerical and technical positions include knowledge or skills tests such as typing or computer-literacy tests. Sometimes libraries may use assessment centers or "in-basket" problem-solving techniques. (See "Interviews" section below.) However, in almost all of these cases, each employer will establish some sort of rating or grading system to evaluate each step in the application process. They will use these evaluations to help identify the top candidates for a particular position.

Interviews

Once your resume and application documents have been reviewed, you may be selected for an interview for the position. If so, you should take the time to find out all you can about the library or institution beforehand. On the day of the interview, you should dress for the business world in a skirt and heels if you are a woman or a suit and tie if you are a man. Also, be sure that your personal hygiene is above reproach. You should arrive for your interview early enough so that you can tour the library or just sit and relax if you are in a personnel office. Although you may be nervous, it is not a good idea to smoke or chew gum. By paying attention to these external details, you can help yourself relax and gain a measure of inner confidence.

When you meet the interviewer or interviewers, you should learn their names and titles. This will not only impress them, but it will also give you some indication of their areas of interest. As you answer any questions, you should give the impression that you want to work at *this* library more than at any other place of employment. You can indicate this by asking questions about the library and about the job for which you are interviewing. Interviewers will expect you to have some questions, but you should not limit yourself to questions about insurance, benefits, or work schedules. You should ask several questions that pertain to the job requirements and duties. You may also ask to see a copy of the position's job description, or you might ask to see a copy of the library's goals and objectives or its long-range plan.

Many library interviewers like to ask open-ended questions that indicate your ability to reason and express yourself. Favorite questions often begin with "Why," "How," and "What if," and the perennial favorite of all is, "How would you describe yourself?" You should be prepared to state your career or professional goals and your philosophy of service. (One librarian applicant made a very unfavorable impression on interviewers when he did not understand what was meant by "philosophy of service.") If you are asked illegal questions about subjects such as your age or marital status, you can field them as you wish. You may either answer them if you want to, or you can rephrase the question to determine the reason behind the question. Sometimes the interviewer is either unaware that the concern is illegal or only curious about the answer. For example, if you are asked a question about your ability to relocate, you can counter with a question about whether residency is required. Do not let yourself get sidetracked onto personal or nonlibrary-related topics. Also do not talk negatively about your present or former jobs. Finally, if you are given the opportunity to make a final statement, it would be useful for you to review your qualifications and describe how and why you have the best qualifications to perform the job well.

Sometimes libraries and personnel departments have expanded the interview process to include an assessment center concept. Such a center may provide simulated library situations for you to try. These situations might be face-to-face encounters, questionnaires, or "in-baskets" containing written problems and exercises. These latter simulations enable interviewers to observe your reactions and decision-making abilities in situations similar to those you would encounter on the job. In addition to simulations, libraries have also turned to telephone or video interviews to screen nonresident candidates. These interviews usually have a set group of questions that will be asked in sequence during a certain period of time, usually 20 minutes. If you are faced with such interviews, you might ask about the questions and time period to judge the depth of your answers. Just remember, if you are interviewed through any of these nontraditional processes, you should remain calm, try to forget any observers or questioners, and respond as normally as possible to the situations presented.

After the interview, you might want to write a brief thank-you note to the interviewer. Such a note could highlight any important points from the interview, review your qualifications for the job, and indicate that you are still interested in the position. If a timeline has been given to you for the hiring process, you can contact the interviewer by letter or phone after the hiring date to learn the outcome of the opening. Do not be surprised to learn that the process has been delayed and that you still may be under consideration. You may even learn that finances have changed the library's plan and the position has been frozen until a later hiring date.

If you are offered the job, you should weigh all of the factors surrounding it before you say yes or no. Once the offer is made, it is acceptable for you to negotiate for salary or benefits if these are important to you. The library would generally not rescind the offer if it could not meet your requests, and you would still be free to accept the original offer. Besides considering the salary offer, you should review the benefits that are included. These benefits are usually tax free and can sometimes represent a monetary value equal to one-fourth or one-third of your salary. You should plan to stay in the job for a minimum of two years. You should also consider any opportunities for advancement if this is important to you. If you will need to commute to the job, you must consider whether the expenses of commuting will be offset by the advantages of the job. Above all, you should decide if this particular job will satisfy your emotional and psychological, as well as economic, needs. If it does not, it would not be fair to either you or the employer for you to take a job. After you have considered all of these factors, you should be able to make a clear decision about the job. Then you should call or write and inform the employer with your decision.

BEGINNING THE JOB

Once you have accepted the job offer, you can begin to prepare for the job. First, you should find out what your work schedule will be and exactly what day and time you are to begin work. You should learn the name and title of your immediate supervisor and stop in to meet him or her if you have not already met. This supervisor will usually introduce you to others and give you an insider's tour of the department. At this time, it would be useful to find out about such basic employee information as which door to come in (especially if you begin work before the library opens) and where the staff members put their coats and purses. You may also observe how the other employees are dressed so that you can do the same. If you are in doubt as to whether jeans or slacks may be worn at the library, or if smoking is permitted, now is the time to ask the supervisor. Although these matters may seem inconsequential, your attention to them may save you some embarrassing moments as well as indicate to the staff that you are willing to learn. This attention to detail will also help you feel more at ease on your first day of work.

When you start your first day of work, you should arrive at your desk or work station on time or even a little early. Usually your supervisor will help orient you to your job or assign someone else to do so. In either case, you should ask if there are any policy or procedures manuals you could read to familiarize yourself with library operations. Because such manuals usually will be out of date, it would be wise for you to take notes when you receive instructions during the first few days or weeks. This will help you remember information as well as enable you to ask intelligent questions about those areas you do not understand. Your supervisor and fellow employees will usually appreciate this quality because they often find it so frustrating to train a new employee.

If you have a major problem with understanding part of your job, you have a responsibility and duty to bring this up to your supervisor as soon as possible. For other concerns, however, it would be more politic of you to observe and take notes about what you are instructed to do rather than to question or challenge. After you have reviewed your notes, you can ask "how" and "why" a certain operation is done. It would be wise, however, to wait awhile before you offer suggestions for changes unless that is an expected part of your job. When you do suggest any changes, you should be sure to bring them up objectively and diplomatically to your supervisor. You do not want to inadvertently antagonize someone because you have questioned a pet project. You also should try to avoid being drawn into office politics by listening to one staff member complain about another. If you maintain a pleasant manner toward everyone and are conscientious in learning your job, you will find that most library staffs are very congenial and willing to accept new members.

SUMMARY

If you want to work in the library/media/information world today, there is a wide range of jobs in a number of different types of libraries from which you can choose. You should first determine which type of work you truly want to do. Then you should evaluate and match your interests to the types of job openings currently available. These job openings can be found in libraries and other organizations and institutions that can use library skills and knowledges. Once you have identified a library position you would like to apply for, you should develop a resume or summary of your personal data, educational background, and occupational information.

This resume is generally submitted with a letter of application to a prospective employer. This employer may ask you to complete an application form and other application documents. If your qualifications seem to match the needs, you will probably be invited for an interview. In the interview, you will have an opportunity to learn more about the library while the prospective employer learns more about you. If this process has been successful, you may be offered the position you want and be invited to become part of the dynamic library/media/information world.

REVIEW QUESTIONS

1. Review your own personal needs and preferences and make a list of those needs that are most important to you in searching for a job.

2. Review the types of work available in libraries and identify the type of work you would most like to do.

3. Look through the local newspaper ads for two weeks and keep copies of those that interest you.

4. Write a resume for yourself following the guidelines identified in this chapter.

5. Select a job that interests you from your list in question 3 above and write a letter of application for this job. (Or write a letter of application for one of the jobs in figure 13.1 for the person whose resume is shown in figure 13.2.)

6. Visit a nearby library that interests you and ask for an application form. Fill out this application form.

SELECTED READINGS

American Libraries 1, no. 1- (1970-).

American Library Directory. New York: Bowker, 1980- .

Dewey, Barbara I. *Library Jobs: How to Fill Them, How to Find Them*. Phoenix, AZ: Oryx Press, 1987.

Kennedy, Joyce Lain. *Job Interviews: How to Win the Offer*. Cardiff, CA: Sun Features, 1990.

_____. *Resumes: The Nitty Gritty*. Cardiff, CA: Sun Features, 1990.

Library Hotline 1, no. 1- (1983-).

Library Journal 1, no. 1- (1876-).

Library Mosaics: The Magazine for Support Staff 1- (September/October 1989-).

Myers, Margaret. *Guide to Library Placement Sources*. Chicago: ALA, 1991, and in *The Bowker Annual: Library and Book Trade Almanac*. 35th ed. New York: R. R. Bowker, 1990.

LIBRARY EDUCATION
AND PERSONNEL UTILIZATION*

A Statement of Policy Adopted by the Council of
the American Library Association, June 30, 1970**

1 The purpose of the policy statement is to recommend categories of library personnel, and levels of training and education appropriate to the preparation of personnel for these categories, which will support the highest standards of library service for all kinds of libraries and the most effective use of the variety of skills and qualifications needed to provide it.

2 Library service as here understood is concerned with knowledge and information in their several forms—their identification, selection, acquisition, preservation, organization, communication and interpretation, and with assistance in their use.

3 To meet the goals of library service, both professional and supportive staff are needed in libraries. Thus the library occupation is much broader than that segment of it which is the library profession, but the library profession has responsibility for defining the training and education required for the preparation of personnel who work in libraries at any level, supportive or professional.

4 Skills other than those of librarianship may also have an important contribution to make to the achievement of superior library service. There should be equal recognition in both the professional and supportive ranks for those individuals whose expertise contributes to the effective performance of the library.

5 A constant effort must be made to promote the most effective utilization of personnel at all levels, both professional and supportive. The tables on page 2 (Figure 1) suggest a set of categories which illustrate a means for achieving this end.

---

*The policy statement adopted by ALA with the title "Library Education and Manpower." In the spring of 1976, the Office for Library Personnel Resources Advisory Committee edited this statement to remove sexist terminology.

**Throughout this statement, wherever the term "librarianship" is used, it is meant to be read in its broadest sense as encompassing the relevant concepts of information science and documentation; wherever the term "libraries" is used, the current models of media centers, learning centers, educational resources centers, information, documentation, and referral centers are also assumed. To avoid the necessity of repeating the entire gamut of variations and expansions, the traditional library terminology is employed in its most inclusive meaning.

Reproduced by permission of the American Library Association.

205

FIGURE 1   CATEGORIES OF LIBRARY PERSONNEL–PROFESSIONAL

TITLE FOR POSITIONS REQUIRING:		BASIC REQUIREMENTS	NATURE OF RESPONSIBILITY
LIBRARY-RELATED QUALIFICATIONS	NONLIBRARY-RELATED QUALIFICATIONS		
Senior Librarian	Senior Specialist	In addition to relevant experience, education beyond the M.A. [i.e., a master's degree in any of its variant designations: M.A., M.L.S., M.S.L.S., M.Ed., etc.] as: post-master's degree; Ph.D.; relevant continuing education in many forms	Top-level responsibilities, including but not limited to administration; superior knowledge of some aspect of librarianship, or of other subject fields of value to the library
Librarian	Specialist	Master's degree	Professional responsibilities including those of management, which require independent judgment, interpretation of rules and procedures, analysis of library problems, and formulation of original and creative solutions for them (normally utilizing knowledge of the subject field represented by the academic degree)

CATEGORIES OF LIBRARY PERSONNEL–SUPPORTIVE

TITLE		BASIC REQUIREMENTS	NATURE OF RESPONSIBILITY
Library Associate	Associate Specialist	Bachelor's degree (with or without course work in library science); OR bachelor's degree, plus additional academic work short of the master's degree (in librarianship for the Library Associate; in other relevant subject fields for the Associate Specialist)	Supportive responsibilities at a high level, normally working within the established procedures and techniques, and with some supervision by a professional, but requiring judgment, and subject knowledge such as is represented by a full, four-year college education culminating in the bachelor's degree.
Library Technical Assistant	Technical Assistant	At least two years of college-level study; OR A.A. degree, with or without Library Technical Assistant training; OR postsecondary school training in relevant skills	Tasks performed as supportive staff to Associates and higher ranks, following established rules and procedures, and including, at the top level, supervision of such tasks
	Clerk	Business school or commercial courses, supplemented by in-service training or on-the-job experience	Clerical assignments as required by the individual library

6 The titles recommended here represent categories or broad classifications, within which it is assumed that there will be several levels of promotional steps. Specific job titles may be used within any category: for example, catalogers, reference librarians, children's librarians would be included in either the "Librarian" or (depending upon the level of their responsibilities and qualifications) "Senior Librarian" categories; department heads, the director of the library, and certain specialists would presumably have the additional qualifications and responsibilities which place them in the "Senior Librarian" category.

7 Where specific job titles dictated by local usage and tradition do not make clear the level of the staff member's qualification and responsibility, it is recommended that reference to the ALA category title be used parenthetically to provide the clarification desirable for communication and reciprocity. For example:

REFERENCE ASSISTANT (Librarian)   HEAD CATALOGER (Senior Librarian)

LIBRARY AIDE (Library Technical Assistant)

8 The title "Librarian" carries with it the connotation of "professional" in the sense that professional tasks are those which require a special background and education on the basis of which library needs are identified, problems are analyzed, goals are set, and original and creative solutions are formulated for them, integrating theory into practice, and planning, organizing, communicating, and administering successful programs of service to users of the library's materials and services. In defining services to users, the professional person recognizes potential users as well as current ones, and designs services which will reach all who could benefit from them.

9 The title "Librarian" therefore should be used only to designate positions in libraries which utilize the qualifications and impose the responsibilities suggested above. Positions which are primarily devoted to the routine application of established rules and techniques, however useful and essential to the effective operation of a library's ongoing services, should not carry the word "Librarian" in the job title.

10 It is recognized that every type and size of library may not need staff appointments in each of these categories. It is urged, however, that this basic scheme be introduced wherever possible to permit where needed·the necessary flexibility in staffing.

11 The salaries for each category should offer a range of promotional steps sufficient to permit a career-in-rank. The top salary in any category should overlap the beginning salary in.the next higher category, in order to give recognition to the value of experience and knowledge gained on the job.

12 Inadequately supported libraries or libraries too small to be able to afford professional staff should nevertheless have access to the services and supervision of a librarian. To obtain the professional guidance that they themselves cannot supply, such libraries should promote cooperative arrangements or join larger systems of cooperating libraries through which supervisory personnel can be supported. Smaller libraries which are part of such a system can often maintain the local service with building staff at the Associate level.

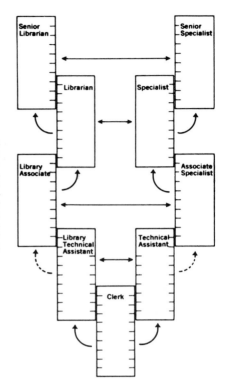

FIGURE 2

If one thinks of Career *Lattices* rather than Career *Ladders*, the flexibility intended by the Policy Statement may be better visualized. The movement among staff responsibilities, for example, is not necessarily directly up, but often may be lateral to increased responsibilities of equal importance. Each category embodies a number of promotional steps within it, as indicated by the gradation markings on each bar. The top of any category overlaps in responsibility and salary the next higher category.

Comments on the Categories

13 The *Clerk* classifications do not require formal academic training in library subjects. The assignments in these categories are based upon general clerical and secretarial proficiencies. Familiarity with basic library terminology and routines necessary to adapt clerical skills to the library's needs is best learned on the job.

14 The *Technical Assistant* categories assume certain kinds of specific "technical" skills; they are not meant simply to accommodate advanced clerks. While clerical skills might well be part of a Technical Assistant's equipment, the emphasis in an assignment should be on the special technical skill. For example, someone who is skilled in handling audiovisual equipment, or at introductory data processing, or in making posters and other displays might well be hired in the Technical Assistant category for these skills, related to librarianship only to the extent that they are employed in a library. A *Library Technical Assistant* is a person with certain specifically library-related skills—in preliminary bibliographic searching for example, or utilization of certain mechanical equipment—the performance of whose duties seldom requires a background in general education.

15 The *Associate* categories assume a need for an educational background like that represented by a bachelor's degree from a good four-year institution of higher education in the United States. Assignments may be such that library knowledge is less important than general education, and whether the title is *Library* Associate or Associate *Specialist* depends upon the nature of the tasks and responsibilities assigned. Persons holding the B.A. degree, with or without a library science minor or practical experience in libraries, are eligible for employment in this category. Titles within the Associate category that are assigned to individuals will depend upon the relevance of their training and background to their specific assignments.

16 The Associate category also provides the opportunity for persons of promise and exceptional talent to begin library employment below the level of professional (as defined in this statement) and thus to combine employment in a library with course work at the graduate level. Where this kind of work/study arrangement is made, the combination of work and formal study should provide 1) increasing responsibility within the Associate ranks as the individual moves through the academic program, and 2) eligibility for promotion, upon completion of the master's degree, to positions of professional responsibility and attendant reclassification to the professional category.

17 The first professional category—*Librarian,* or *Specialist*—assumes responsibilities that are professional in the sense described in paragraph #8 above. A good liberal education plus graduate-level study in the field of specialization (either in librarianship or in a relevant field) are seen as the minimum preparation for the kinds of assignments implied. The title, however, is given for a position entailing professional responsibilities and not automatically upon achievement of the academic degree.

18 The *Senior* categories assume relevant professional experience as well as qualifications beyond those required for admission to the first professional ranks. Normally it is assumed that such advanced qualifications shall be held in some specialty, either in a particular aspect of librarianship or some relevant subject field. Subject specializations are as applicable in the *Senior Librarian* category as they are in the *Senior Specialist* category.

19 Administrative responsibilities entail advanced knowledge and skills comparable to those represented by any other high-level specialty, and appointment to positions in top administration should normally require the qualifications of a *Senior Librarian* with a specialization in administration. This category, however, is not limited to administrators, whose specialty is only one of several specializations of value to the library service. There are many areas of special knowledge within librarianship which are equally important and to which equal recognition in prestige and salary should be given. Highly qualified persons with specialist responsibilities in some aspects of librarianship—archives, bibliography, reference, for example—should be eligible for advanced status and financial rewards without being forced to abandon for administrative responsibilities their areas of major competence.

Implications for Formal Education

20 Until examinations are identified that are valid and reliable tests of equivalent qualifications, the academic degree (or evidence of years of academic work completed) is recommended as the single best means for determining that an applicant has the background recommended for each category.

21 In the selection of applicants for positions at any level, and for admission to library schools, attention should be paid to personal aptitudes and qualifications in addition to academic ones. The nature of the position or specialty, and particularly the degree to which it entails working with others, with the public, or with special audiences or materials should be taken into account in the evaluation of a prospective student or employee.

22 As library services change and expand, as new audiences are reached, as new media take on greater importance in the communication process, and as new approaches to the handling of materials are introduced, the kinds of preparation required of those who will be employed in libraries will become more varied. Degrees in fields other than librarianship will be needed in the Specialist categories. For many Senior Librarian positions, an advanced degree in another subject field rather than an additional degree in librarianship, may be desirable. Previous experience need not always have been in libraries to have pertinence for appointment in a library.

23 Because the principles of librarianship are applied to the materials of information and knowledge broader than any single field, and because they are related to subject matter outside of librarianship itself, responsible education in these principles should be built upon a broad rather than a narrowly specialized background education. To the extent that courses in library science are introduced in the four-year, undergraduate program, they should be concentrated in the last two years and should not constitute a major inroad into course work in the basic disciplines: the humanities, the sciences, and the social sciences.

24 Training courses for Library Technical Assistants at the junior or community college level should be recognized as essentially terminal in intent (or as service courses rather than a formal program of education), designed for the preparation of supportive rather than professional staff. Students interested in librarianship as a career should be counselled to take the general four-year college course rather than the specific two-year program, with its inevitable loss of time and transferable content. Graduates of the two-year programs are not prohibited from taking the additional work leading to the bachelor's and master's degrees, provided they demonstrate the necessary qualifications for admission to the senior college program, but it is an indirect and less desirable way to prepare for a professional career, and the student should be so informed.

25 Emphasis in the two-year Technical Assistant programs should be more on skills training than on general library concepts and procedures. In many cases it would be better from the standpoint of the student to pursue more broadly-based vocational courses which will teach technical skills applicable in a variety of job situations rather than those limited solely to the library setting.

26 Undergraduate instruction in library science other than training courses for Library Technical Assistants should be primarily a contribution to liberal education rather than an opportunity to provide technological and methodological training. This does not preclude the inclusion of course work related to the basic skills of library practice, but it does affect teaching method and approach, and implies an emphasis on the principles that underlie practice rather than how-to-do-it, vocational training.

27 Certain practical skills and procedures at all levels are best learned on the job rather than in the academic classroom. These relate typically to details of operation which may vary from institution to institution, or to routines which require repetition and practice for their mastery. The responsibility for such in-service parts of the total preparation of both librarians and supportive staff rests with libraries and library systems rather than with the library schools.

28 The objective of the master's programs in librarianship should be to prepare librarians capable of anticipating and engineering the change and improvement required to move the profession constantly forward. The curriculum and teaching methods should be designed to serve this kind of education for the future rather than to train for the practice of the present.

29 Certain interdisciplinary concepts (information science is an example) are so intimately related to the basic concepts underlying library service that they properly become a part of the library school curriculum rather than simply an outside specialty. Where such content is introduced into the library school it should be incorporated into the entire curriculum, enriching every course where it is pertinent. The stop-gap addition of individual courses in such a specialty, not integrated into the program as a whole, is an inadequate assimilation of the intellectual contribution of the new concept to library education and thinking.

30 In recognition of the many areas of related subject matter of importance to library service, library schools should make knowledge in other fields readily available to students, either through the appointment of staff members from other disciplines or through permitting students to cross departmental, divisional, and institutional lines in reasoned programs in related fields. Intensive specializations at the graduate level, building upon strengths in the parent institution or the community, are a logical development in professional library education.

31 Library schools should be encouraged to experiment with new teaching methods, new learning devices, different patterns of scheduling and sequence, and other means, both traditional and nontraditional, that may increase the effectiveness of the students' educational experience.

32 Research has an important role to play in the educational process as a source of new knowledge both for the field of librarianship in general and for library education in particular. In its planning, budgeting, and organizational design, the library school should recognize research, both theoretical and applied, as an imperative responsibility.

Continuing Education

33 Continuing Education is essential for all library personnel, professional and supportive, whether they remain within a position category or are preparing to move into a higher one. Continuing education opportunities include both formal and informal learning situations, and need not be limited to library subjects or the offerings of library schools.

34 The "continuing education" which leads to eligibility for Senior Librarian or Specialist positions may take any of the forms suggested directly above so long as the additional education and experience are relevant to the responsibilities of the assignment.

35 Library administrators must accept responsibility for providing support and opportunities (in the form of leaves, sabbaticals, and released time) for the continuing education of their staffs.

Additional copies available from
　　Office for Library Personnel Resources
　　American Library Association, 50 E. Huron St., Chicago, Ill. 60611

8389-5482-0

Library Bill of Rights

The American Library Association affirms that all libraries are forums for information and ideas, and that the following basic policies should guide their services.

1. Books and other library resources should be provided for the interest, information, and enlightenment of all people of the community the library serves. Materials should not be excluded because of the origin, background, or views of those contributing to their creation.

2. Libraries should provide materials and information presenting all points of view on current and historical issues. Materials should not be proscribed or removed because of partisan or doctrinal disapproval.

3. Libraries should challenge censorship in the fulfillment of their responsibility to provide information and enlightenment.

4. Libraries should cooperate with all persons and groups concerned with resisting abridgment of free expression and free access to ideas.

5. A person's right to use a library should not be denied or abridged because of origin, age, background, or views.

6. Libraries which make exhibit spaces and meeting rooms available to the public they serve should make such facilities available on an equitable basis, regardless of the beliefs or affiliations of individuals or groups requesting their use.

Adopted June 18, 1948.
Amended February 2, 1961, June 27, 1967, and January 23, 1980,
by the ALA Council.

FREEDOM TO READ

The freedom to read is essential to our democracy. It is continuously under attack. Private groups and public authorities in various parts of the country are working to remove books from sale, to censor textbooks, to label "controversial" books, to distribute lists of "objectionable" books or authors, and to purge libraries. These actions apparently rise from a view that our national tradition of free expression is no longer valid; that censorship and suppression are needed to avoid the subversion of politics and the corruption of morals. We, as citizens devoted to the use of books and as librarians and publishers responsible for disseminating them, wish to assert the public interest in the preservation of the freedom to read.

We are deeply concerned about these attempts at suppression. Most such attempts rest on a denial of the fundamental premise of democracy: that the ordinary citizen, by exercising critical judgment, will accept the good and reject the bad. The censors, public and private, assume that they should determine what is good and what is bad for their fellow-citizens.

We trust Americans to recognize propaganda, and to reject it. We do not believe they need the help of censors to assist them in this task. We do not believe they are prepared to sacrifice their heritage of a free press in order to be "protected" against what others think may be bad for them. We believe they still favor free enterprise in ideas and expression.

We are aware, of course, that books are not alone in being subjected to efforts at suppression. We are aware that these efforts are related to a larger pattern of pressures being brought against education, the press, films, radio and television. The problem is not only one of actual censorship. The shadow of fear cast by these pressures leads, we suspect, to an even larger voluntary curtailment of expression by those who seek to avoid controversy.

Such pressure toward conformity is perhaps natural to a time of uneasy change and pervading fear. Especially when so many of our apprehensions are directed against an ideology, the expression of a dissident idea becomes a thing feared in itself, and we tend to move against it as against a hostile deed, with suppression.

And yet suppression is never more dangerous than in such a time of social tension. Freedom has given the United States the elasticity to endure strain. Freedom keeps open the path of novel and creative solutions, and enables change to come by choice. Every silencing of a heresy, every enforcement of an orthodoxy:

Reproduced by permission of the American Library Association.

diminishes the toughness and resilience of our society and leaves it the less able to deal with stress.

Now as always in our history, books are among our greatest instruments of freedom. They are almost the only means for making generally available ideas or manners of expression that can initially command only a small audience. They are the natural medium for the new idea and the untried voice from which come the original contributions to social growth. They are essential to the extended discussion which serious thought requires, and to the accumulation of knowledge and ideas into organized collections.

We believe that free communication is essential to the preservation of a free society and a creative culture. We believe that these pressures towards conformity present the danger of limiting the range and variety of inquiry and expression on which our democracy and our culture depend. We believe that every American community must jealously guard the freedom to publish and to circulate, in order to preserve its own freedom to read. We believe that publishers and librarians have a profound responsibility to give validity to that freedom to read by making it possible for the readers to choose freely from a variety of offerings.

The freedom to read is guaranteed by the Constitution. Those with faith in free people will stand firm on these constitutional guarantees of essential rights and will exercise the responsibilities that accompany these rights.

We therefore affirm these propositions:

1. *It is in the public interest for publishers and librarians to make available the widest diversity of views and expressions, including those which are unorthodox or unpopular with the majority.*

    Creative thought is by definition new, and what is new is different. The bearer of every new thought is a rebel until that idea is refined and tested. Totalitarian systems attempt to maintain themselves in power by the ruthless suppression of any concept which challenges the established orthodoxy. The power of a democratic system to adapt to change is vastly strengthened by the freedom of its citizens to choose widely from among conflicting opinions offered freely to them. To stifle every nonconformist idea at birth would mark the end of the democratic process. Furthermore, only through the constant activity of weighing and selecting can the democratic mind attain the strength demanded by times like these. We need to know not only what we believe but why we believe it.

2. *Publishers, librarians and booksellers do not need to endorse every idea or presentation contained in the books they make available. It would conflict with the public interest for them to establish their own political, moral or aesthetic views as a standard for determining what books should be published or circulated.*

    Publishers and librarians serve the educational process by helping to make available knowledge and ideas required for the growth of the mind and the increase of learning. They do not foster education by imposing as mentors the patterns of their own thought. The people should have the freedom to read and consider a broader range of ideas than those that may be held by any single librarian or publisher or government or church. It is wrong that what one can read should be confined to what another thinks proper.

3. *It is contrary to the public interest for publishers or librarians to determine the acceptability of a book on the basis of the personal history or political affiliations of the author.*

   A book should be judged as a book. No art or literature can flourish if it is to be measured by the political views or private lives of its creators. No society of free people can flourish which draws up lists of writers to whom it will not listen, whatever they may have to say.

4. *There is no place in our society for efforts to coerce the taste of others, to confine adults to the reading matter deemed suitable for adolescents, or to inhibit the efforts of writers to achieve artistic expression.*

   To some, much of modern literature is shocking. But is not much of life itself shocking? We cut off literature at the source if we prevent writers from dealing with the stuff of life. Parents and teachers have a responsibility to prepare the young to meet the diversity of experiences in life to which they will be exposed, as they have a responsibility to help them learn to think critically for themselves. These are affirmative responsibilities, not to be discharged simply by preventing them from reading works for which they are not yet prepared. In these matters taste differs, and taste cannot be legislated; nor can machinery be devised which will suit the demands of one group without limiting the freedom of others.

5. *It is not in the public interest to force a reader to accept with any book the prejudgment of a label characterizing the book or author as subversive or dangerous.*

   The ideal of labeling presupposes the existence of individuals or groups with wisdom to determine by authority what is good or bad for the citizen. It presupposes that individuals must be directed in making up their minds about the ideas they examine. But Americans do not need others to do their thinking for them.

6. *It is the responsibility of publishers and librarians, as guardians of the people's freedom to read, to contest encroachments upon that freedom by individuals or groups seeking to impose their own standards or tastes upon the community at large.*

   It is inevitable in the give and take of the democratic process that the political, the moral, or the aesthetic concepts of an individual or group will occasionally collide with those of another individual or group. In a free society individuals are free to determine for themselves what they wish to read, and each group is free to determine what it will recommend to its freely associated members. But no group has the right to take the law into its own hands, and to impose its own concept of politics or morality upon other members of a democratic society. Freedom is no freedom if it is accorded only to the accepted and the inoffensive.

7. *It is the responsibility of publishers and librarians to give full meaning to the freedom to read by providing books that enrich the quality and diversity of thought and expression. By the exercise of this affirmative responsibility, they can demonstrate that the answer to a bad book is a good one, the answer to a bad idea is a good one.*

The freedom to read is of little consequence when expended on the trivial; it is frustrated when the reader cannot obtain matter fit for that reader's purpose. What is needed is not only the absence of restraint, but the positive provision of opportunity for the people to read the best that has been thought and said. Books are the major channel by which the intellectual inheritance is handed down, and the principal means of its testing and growth. The defense of their freedom and integrity, and the enlargement of their service to society, requires of all publishers and librarians the utmost of their faculties, and deserves of all citizens the fullest of their support.

We state these propositions neither lightly nor as easy generalizations. We here stake out a lofty claim for the value of books. We do so because we believe that they are good, possessed of enormous variety and usefulness, worthy of cherishing and keeping free. We realize that the application of these propositions may mean the dissemination of ideas and manners of expression that are repugnant to many persons. We do not state these propositions in the comfortable belief that what people read is unimportant. We believe rather that what people read is deeply important; that ideas can be dangerous; but that the suppression of ideas is fatal to a democratic society. Freedom itself is a dangerous way of life, but it is ours.

This statement was originally issued in May of 1953 by the Westchester Conference of the American Library Association and the American Book Publishers Council, which in 1970 consolidated with the American Educational Publishers Institute to become the Association of American Publishers.

Adopted June 25, 1953; revised January 28, 1972, January 16, 1991, by the ALA Council and the AAP Freedom to Read Committee.

A Joint Statement by:
American Library Association
Association of American Publishers

Subsequently Endorsed by:
American Booksellers Association
American Booksellers Foundation for Free Expression
American Civil Liberties Union
American Federation of Teachers AFL-CIO
Anti-Defamation League of B'nai B'rith
Association of American University Presses
Children's Book Council
Freedom to Read Foundation
International Reading Association
Thomas Jefferson Center for the Protection of Free Expression
National Association of College Stores
National Council of Teachers of English
P.E.N. - American Center
People for the American Way
Periodical and Book Association of America
Sex Information and Education Council of the U.S.
Society of Professional Journalists
Women's National Book Association
YWCA of the U.S.A.

FREEDOM TO VIEW

The FREEDOM TO VIEW, along with the freedom to speak, to hear, and to read, is protected by the First Amendment to the Constitution of the United States. In a free society, there is no place for censorship of any medium of expression. Therefore these principles are affirmed:

1. To provide the broadest possible access to film, video, and other audiovisual materials because they are a means for the communication of ideas. Liberty of circulation is essential to insure the constitutional guarantee of freedom of expression.

2. To protect the confidentiality of all individuals and institutions using film, video, and other audiovisual materials.

3. To provide film, video, and other audiovisual materials which represent a diversity of views and expression. Selection of a work does not constitute or imply agreement with or approval of the content.

4. To provide a diversity of viewpoints without the constraint of labeling or prejudging film, video, and other audiovisual materials on the basis of the moral, religious, or political beliefs of the producer or filmmaker or on the basis of controversial content.

5. To contest vigorously, by all lawful means, every encroachment upon the public's freedom to view.

The statement was originally drafted by the Freedom to View Committee of the American Film and Video Association (formerly the Educational Films Library Association) and was adopted by the AFVA Board of Directors in February 1979.

Endorsed by the ALA Council January 10, 1990

Reproduced by permission of the American Film & Video Association.

STATEMENT ON PROFESSIONAL ETHICS, 1981

INTRODUCTION

Since 1939, the American Library Association has recognized the importance of codifying and making known to the public and the profession the principles which guide librarians in action. This latest revision of the CODE OF ETHICS reflects changes in the nature of the profession and in its social and institutional environment. It should be revised and augmented as necessary.

Librarians significantly influence or control the selection, organization, preservation, and dissemination of information. In a political system grounded in an informed citizenry, librarians are members of a profession explicitly committed to intellectual freedom and the freedom of access to information. We have a special obligation to ensure the free flow of information and ideas to present and future generations.

Librarians are dependent upon one another for the bibliographical resources that enable us to provide information services, and have obligations for maintaining the highest level of personal integrity and competence.

CODE OF ETHICS

I. Librarians must provide the highest level of service through appropriate and usefully organized collections, fair and equitable circulation and service policies, and skillful, accurate, unbiased, and courteous responses to all requests for assistance.

II. Librarians must resist all efforts by groups or individuals to censor library materials.

III. Librarians must protect each user's right to privacy with respect to information sought or received, and materials consulted, borrowed, or acquired.

IV. Librarians must adhere to the principles of due process and equality of opportunity in peer relationships and personnel actions.

V. Librarians must distinguish clearly in their actions and statements between their personal philosophies and attitudes and those of an institution or professional body.

VI. Librarians must avoid situations in which personal interests might be served or financial benefits gained at the expense of library users, colleagues, or the employing institution.

INDEX